Wes Anderson's Symbolic Storyworld

Wes Anderson's Symbolic Storyworld

A Semiotic Analysis

Warren Buckland

BLOOMSBURY ACADEMIC
NEW YORK • LONDON • OXFORD • NEW DELHI • SYDNEY

BLOOMSBURY ACADEMIC
Bloomsbury Publishing Inc
1385 Broadway, New York, NY 10018, USA
50 Bedford Square, London, WC1B 3DP, UK
29 Earlsfort Terrace, Dublin 2, Ireland

BLOOMSBURY, BLOOMSBURY ACADEMIC and the Diana logo are trademarks of
Bloomsbury Publishing Plc

First published in the United States of America 2019
Paperback edition published 2021

Copyright © Warren Buckland, 2019

For legal purposes the Acknowledgements on p. xiii constitute an extension
of this copyright page.

Cover design: Eleanor Rose
Cover image: The Grand Budapest Hotel (USA / Germany, 2014) Directed by Wes
Anderson © Martin Scali / Scott Rudin Productions Collection Christophel / Arenapal

All rights reserved. No part of this publication may be reproduced or
transmitted in any form or by any means, electronic or mechanical,
including photocopying, recording, or any information storage or retrieval
system, without prior permission in writing from the publishers.

Bloomsbury Publishing Inc does not have any control over, or responsibility for, any
third-party websites referred to or in this book. All internet addresses given in this
book were correct at the time of going to press. The author and publisher regret any
inconvenience caused if addresses have changed or sites have ceased to exist, but can
accept no responsibility for any such changes.

Notes69
Library of Congress Cataloging-in-Publication Data
Names: Buckland, Warren, author.
Title: Wes Anderson's symbolic storyworld / Warren Buckland.
Description: New York, NY: Bloomsbury Academic, 2018. |
Includes bibliographical references and index.
Identifiers: LCCN 2018039662 | ISBN 9781501316524 (hardback)
|ISBN 9781501316548 (epdf)
Subjects: LCSH: Anderson, Wes, 1969–Criticism and interpretation. |
Symbolism in motion pictures.
Classification: LCC PN1998.3.A526 B83 2018 |
DDC 791.4302/33092–dc23
LC record available at https://lccn.loc.gov/2018039662

ISBN: HB: 978-1-5013-1652-4
PB: 978-1-5013-7732-7
ePDF: 978-1-5013-1654-8
eBook: 978-1-5013-1653-1

Typeset by Newgen KnowledgeWorks Pvt. Ltd., Chennai, India

To find out more about our authors and books visit www.bloomsbury.com
and sign up for our newsletters.

Contents

List of Figures	vi
List of Tables	vii
Preface	viii
Acknowledgements	xiii

Part One   Theory

1	Symbolic Storyworlds	3
2	Film Theory, Film Analysis	31

Part Two   The Films

3	Unintentional Mediation: *Bottle Rocket*	49
4	Dead Relatives and Intergenerational Relationships: *Rushmore*	71
5	Imperial Kinship: *The Royal Tenenbaums*	87
6	Conflicts of Ambivalence: *The Life Aquatic with Steve Zissou*	105
7	Fraternal Rivalry: *The Darjeeling Limited* and *Hotel Chevalier*	119
8	Human versus Animal Subworld: *Fantastic Mr. Fox*	133
9	The Orphan and the Bachelor: *Moonrise Kingdom*	145
10	Rules of Descent and Laws of Inheritance: *The Grand Budapest Hotel*	157

Part Three   Finale

11	The Symbolic Storyworld of Wes Anderson	169

Works Cited	193
Index	201

Figures

3.1–3.2	Anthony as an object of vision climbing down (*Bottle Rocket*) © Columbia Pictures	63
3.3–3.4	Anthony as a subject of vision moving up (*Bottle Rocket*) © Columbia Pictures	64
5.1	Richie, Margot and Mordecai (*The Royal Tenenbaums*) © Touchstone Pictures	99
6.1	Steve, Ned and Jane (*The Life Aquatic with Steve Zissou*) © Touchstone Pictures	115
9.1	Sam is absent from his tent (*Moonrise Kingdom*) © Focus Features	154
9.2	Sam is present (with Suzy), but the tent is absent (*Moonrise Kingdom*) © Focus Features	154
10.1	Zero standing in the lift by himself (*The Grand Budapest Hotel*) © Fox Searchlight	166
11.1	Tableau shot (*The Darjeeling Limited*) © Fox Searchlight	187
11.2	Close up (*Bottle Rocket*) © Columbia Pictures	187
11.3–11.4	Overhead shots (*Rushmore*) © Columbia Pictures	188
11.5	Centred framing (*Rushmore*) © Columbia Pictures	189

Tables

3.1	The four robberies in *Bottle Rocket*	53
5.1	Status of the Tenenbaum siblings after leaving the family home	93
7.1	Character traits of the three Whitman brothers in *The Darjeeling Limited*	126
10.1	High locations in *The Grand Budapest Hotel*	165
11.1	Strategies for handling death in Wes Anderson's storyworld	184

Preface

Film semiotics, far from being the 'fad' denounced by its critics, actually forms part of the broad drift of contemporary thought.
    Robert Stam, 'Film and Language: From Metz to Bakhtin', 109

Wes Anderson's output should be considered as one continuous thread, each film informing the other, as he builds on his themes and his unique vocabulary.
    Jamie S. Rich, 'Criterion Confessions: The Darjeeling Limited'

An Experiment in Method. Guided by Peter Wollen's provocative reformulation of auteur theory in the revised edition of *Signs and Meaning in the Cinema* (1972), I spent the last few years experimenting: mixing the methods of semiotics and film studies in equal measure to examine the invariant attributes (the symbolic storyworld) running through the films of Wes Anderson. These methods capture the hidden connections, the underlying structures and conflicts at the core of his films. I'm not alone in finding inspiration in Wollen's book. Samuel Wigley reports that 'When, in 2010, *Sight & Sound* magazine polled critics for the best books ever written about the cinema, Peter Wollen's *Signs and Meaning in the Cinema* cropped up repeatedly on ballot sheets, 40 years after it appeared in its first edition' (Wigley 2014). In his response to the *Sight & Sound* poll, UK critic Nick Roddick expressed a general opinion when he claimed that 'if there is one book to rule them all, it is Peter Wollen's *Signs and Meaning in the Cinema*. The revised and enlarged edition of 1972 is the most concise, lucid and inspiring introduction to thinking about film ever written' (Roddick, quoted in Wigley 2014). Wollen's book was instrumental in shaping the nascent discipline of film studies in the late 1960s, especially film aesthetics, film semiotics and auteur theory.

One outcome of Wollen's auteur theory is that its study of auteurs, carried out via semiotics and structuralism, focuses on abstract qualities, which creates a certain analytical distance from the experience of watching films. This is because a film, and the experience of watching it, is the end result of a series of underlying abstract codes and structures. Structuralism and semiotics study this underlying level, not the film's surface or its experience. More generally, like an X-ray, structuralism and semiotics isolate and subtract from tangible surface messages (speech, individual myths, a specific kinship relation, a literary texts, a film, etc.) the abstract codes that produce, organize and confer meaning on those messages. The surface level of experience consists of a vast array of contingent and heterogeneous phenomena; order and unity only exist on the underlying abstract level. Structural and semiotic analysis is conducted at this abstract level in an attempt to discover order and unity.

My experiment does not deny, of course, that Wes Anderson's films consist of many other elements – mise en scène, acting, set design, costumes, music, emotions, affects (many of which have received detailed scholarly analyses: see, for example, Buckland 2012; Kunze 2014; Lee 2016; MacDowell 2010). Rather than repeat these studies, I have instead delimited my research to the analysis of *one aspect* of Wes Anderson's films, the underlying abstract codes that confer order, unity and meaning on them. Chapter 1 outlines the concept of 'the symbolic' developed by Ferdinand de Saussure, Claude Lévi-Strauss, Jacques Lacan and Roland Barthes and conjoins it to the concept of storyworld developed in recent work of narratologists, including David Herman, Marie-Laure Ryan and Mark Wolf – although in the end I adapt Karl Popper's philosophical concept of World 3 to the study of fictional storyworlds. Chapter 2 outlines previous attempts to use structuralism and semiotics to theorize film and conduct textual analyses, focusing especially on auteur structuralism. Chapters 3 to 10 analyse each of Wes Anderson's films in chronological order. These chapters do not present general impressions of the films but instead analyse their internal abstract structures. As this book progresses chapter by chapter, analysis of each Wes Anderson film is complemented with comparisons with his previous films. Chapter 11 reworks these comparative comments and links Wes Anderson's films together under an abstract organizing principle: the symbolic storyworld. This world is not a pre-existing empirical object that simply needs to be observed and described; instead, it has to be painstakingly constructed from the fragments manifest in each film. The key method for constructing this storyworld is 'comparative paradigmatic analysis' (discussed in Chapter 1): the films are compared in order to highlight the structural repetitions and variations among them.

Foregrounding theoretical concepts and methods frequently attracts criticism in film studies, no doubt because it can appear to be mechanical and routine. But such criticism reminds me of what Raymond Queneau said about the process of creative writing: 'the inspiration that consists in blind obedience to every impulse is in reality a sort of slavery. The classical playwright who writes his tragedy observing a certain number of familiar rules is freer than the poet who writes that which comes into his head and who is the slave of other rules of which he is ignorant' (quoted in McNulty 2014, 5). This principle is equally relevant to film analysis: following the rules of a method frees up the analyst because it offers an explicit reference point and defines the boundaries of research, making the research process reflexive. Foregrounding theory and methods also assists the reader in discovering exactly how the film analyses were carried out and how the results were achieved.

Foregrounding apparently 'old' theoretical concepts and methods (structuralism and semiotics) not only attracts criticism, but also outright condemnation. Peter Caws addresses this accusation in the opening pages of his book *Structuralism: The Art of the Intelligible*:

> According to the calendar of cultural trends, structuralism has come and gone […]. But according to the calendar of philosophy, as I read it, structuralism has only just arrived. It has been a serious possibility, as a mode (among others) of understanding some aspects of the world, since the early years of [the twentieth] century, but has begun to achieve focus and formulation only in the last few decades. (1988, xiii)

He adds that structuralism 'managed to pass from novelty to fashion to cliché in a very few years, with hardly any interval of mature reflection' (1988, 2). He dismisses superficial accounts of structuralism and semiotics – accounts that limit their scope and influence to the 1960s and reduce them to fashion and cliché – and instead traces their development back to profound changes in

Western epistemology at the beginning of the twentieth century. Now that the fashion to be a structuralist is over, he argues, it is possible to develop mature reflection on its true scope and influence.

At the end of his book *Twentieth Century Mythologies*, Daniel Dubuisson looks further back in time, and concludes that we must

> reconsider all the problems of the history of European thought within a substantially enlarged scale and frame. The field of contemporary mythological studies is organically tied to that of all Western thought and even at times extends beyond it. Structuralism itself should perhaps no longer be considered merely as a prime event in the history of contemporary thought [...]. Rather, structuralism has been subject to a slow preparation and was made possible by centuries of reflection on substance and form, on idea and category. And it is only because these problems have been turned over a thousand times, indefatigably taken up again and discussed, that it finally has been possible to present them with a new conception – the structural hypothesis – to be added to various earlier ontologies. (2006, 296)

It is worth emphasizing his point that the structural study of myth is 'organically tied to that of all Western thought'; it is not a recent addition to Western thought, for its fundamental premises have been slowly developing for hundreds of years.

Finally, Eleanor Kaufman investigates the structuralism of the late 1960s in its most advanced formulations, especially by Lévi-Strauss and by Gilles Deleuze (in his seminal 1967 essay 'How Do We Recognize Structuralism?' [in Deleuze 2004, 170–92]). Kaufman considers why it was sidelined in 1968 with the advent of post-structuralism. She tentatively suggests that structuralism's ontological mode of abstraction – leading to an extreme form of anti-humanism – was too disquieting and unpalatable (2013, 98–9), as was its discarding of narrative temporality as a mere surface phenomenon in favour of underling logical relations.

Similarly, despite the enormous impact of *Signs and Meaning in the Cinema* in the late 1960s and its historical significance, Wollen's auteur structuralism was quickly superseded by a wave of post-structural film theory in the 1970s, in the form of psychoanalytic theories of subjectivity, ideology and sexual difference. But now it is possible to return to auteur structuralism and develop (to paraphrase Peter Caws) mature reflection on its true scope and influence. The present book studies Wes Anderson's storyworld from the perspective of auteur structuralism, which involves examining core themes and hidden structures, including complex kinship systems and paradigms, supplemented with other symbolic codes such as binary oppositions, mediators, systems of exchange and rules of transformation. Wes Anderson's films are ideal objects for analysis from the perspectives of auteur structuralism and storyworld, for he is renowned for creating a widely recognized, internally coherent fictional universe, one held together by repeated codes and structural principles.

Acknowledgements

The following friends and colleagues have read or listened to various sections of this book, and have offered helpful feedback: Robert Burgoyne, Govind Chandran, Thomas Elsaesser, Ruggero Eugeni, Radomír D. Kokeš, Sunhee Lee, Sian Lincoln, Agnieszka Piotrowska (who offered invaluable feedback on several chapters), Francesco Sticchi, Meryl Suissa, Yannis Tzioumakis and Kim Wilkins. Part of the writing was carried out in Berlin as a Research Fellow at the Freie Universität (Autumn semester, 2016), in the Cinepoetics Seminar run by Hermann Kappelhoff and Michael Wedel (and a special thank you to Michael for giving me a tour of the Babelsberg Film Studio in Potsdam-Babelsberg, just outside Berlin, where parts of *The Grand Budapest Hotel* were filmed).

Part One

Theory

1

Symbolic Storyworlds

Within the framework of a theory of codes it is unnecessary to resort to the notion of extension [reference], nor to that of possible worlds; the codes, insofar as they are accepted by a society, set up a 'cultural' world, which is neither actual nor possible in the ontological sense; its existence is linked to a cultural order, which is the way in which a society thinks [and] speaks.
Umberto Eco, A Theory of Semiotics, 61

Cultural meanings are inherent in the symbolic orders and these meanings are independent of, and prior to, the external world, on the one hand, and human subjects, on the other. Thus, the world only has an objective existence in the symbolic orders that represent it.
Simon Clarke, The Foundations of Structuralism, 2

In his discussion of auteur structuralism in *Signs and Meaning in the Cinema*, Peter Wollen reminds us that it was Jean Renoir who said that directors spend their whole life making one film (1972, 104). Wollen used Renoir's comment to align auteur theory with a fundamental tenet of Claude Lévi-Strauss's structural anthropology: just as the anthropologist collects and studies variations of the same invariant archi-myth (or tale), for Wollen, each film an auteur makes is a variation of his or her archi-film: 'Underlying the different, individual tales was an archi-tale, of which they were all variants' (Wollen 1972, 93).[1] The ultimate goal of auteur structuralism was to construct a model or simulacrum of an auteur's underlying, abstract invariant archi-film. This paralleled the more general goal of continental structuralism and semiotics to construct the complete system of abstract codes or system of intelligibility underlying each symbolic language:

> For every *process* [e.g. manifest messages] there is a corresponding *system*, by which the process can be analyzed and described by means of a limited number of premises. (Hjelmslev 1961, 8)
>
> The goal of all structuralist activity, whether reflexive or poetic, is to reconstruct an 'object' in such a way as to manifest thereby the rules of functioning (the 'functions') of this object. Structure is therefore actually a *simulacrum* of the object, but a directed, *interested* simulacrum, since the imitated object makes something appear which remained invisible, or if one prefers, unintelligible in the natural object. (Barthes 1972, 214–15)
>
> The individual, concrete work will be considered as the manifestation of an abstract structure, merely one of its possible realizations; an understanding of that structure will be the real goal of structural analysis. (Todorov 1969, 70)

Traditional worldviews oppose two realms – an everyday external reality (*res extensa*) and an inner reality (thought, or *res cogitans*), and posit that each is separate and autonomous. The structural and semiotic worldviews introduce the 'symbolic order' as a third realm, existing between the two realities.[2] Lévi-Strauss spelled out the multifaceted nature of the symbolic order: 'Every culture can be considered as an ensemble or a set of symbolic systems, amongst which the most important are: language, marriage-rules, economic relationships, art, science, and religion' (Lévi-Strauss, quoted in Wilden 1981, 255). The symbolic order is not simply an inert system of representation passively reflecting an already meaningful external world to an already structured mind, but is enabling – in the sense that its system of codes constitute and organize both realms, as Umberto Eco's and Simon Clarke's epigraphs opening this chapter attest. The behaviour, experiences, thoughts, beliefs, sexual desires, fantasies and identities of individuals are made possible by the anonymous and impersonal symbolic order. Individuals cannot voluntarily opt in or out of the symbolic, for their identities and worldviews are constructed by and in the symbolic. The various dimensions of the symbolic became the primary object of study for continental structuralists and semioticians, including Barthes, Greimas, Jakobson, Kristeva, Lacan, Lévi-Strauss, Saussure, Todorov and Žižek. (We can follow Herman Parret and refer to the tradition of 'continental structuralism and semiotics' using the more manageable term 'structural semiotics' [see Parret 1983].)[3]

The following study of Wes Anderson aims to construct his 'archi-film' – the invariant themes at the core of all his films – via the concept of the 'symbolic order', supplemented with the narratological concept of 'storyworld'. Storyworld, outlined at the end of this chapter, refers to an abstract totality encompassing everything that fictionally exists across a director's films. To reduce the vagueness of the term 'storyworld', and to avoid discussing each film's storyworld as a distinct entity (see Kunze 2014, 4–5), its system needs to be studied structurally, using the basic methods of structural semiotics. A storyworld emerges from abstract codes and structures – paradigms, kinship structures, binary oppositions, mediators, systems of exchange and rules of transformation. Each film Wes Anderson makes is a partial manifestation of the same abstract symbolic storyworld.

Syntagms and paradigms

> To define [...] messages is to undertake the task of discovering what code enabled them to be produced [...]. Tailoring the [messages] into minimal units, identifying the paradigmatic classes, discovering the rules which obtain in syntagmatic series – all this is daily fare for the semiologist. (Descombes 1980, 100)[4]

The term 'meaning' within structural semiotics is defined narrowly: it is synonymous with 'sense' or 'signification' rather than 'reference'. Signification is an internal value generated from the network of structural relations between codes; a sign is a code that has been manifest in a message in a communicative situation: 'Codes provide the rules which *generate* signs as concrete occurrences in communicative intercourse' (Eco 1976, 49). Codes are fundamental (they constitute the underlying system) whereas signs are transitory effects and partial manifestations of this fundamental system. Structural semiotics replaces the atomistic theory of meaning, which posits a one-to-one direct correspondence or link between a sign and its referent, with a theory in which a sign's meaning is dependent on a series of differential relations to other signs. The structural semiotic method of analysis identifies two permanent axes of relations: the syntagmatic and the paradigmatic. More specifically, the method of analysis aims to segment and classify messages (speech, myths, kinship relations, literary texts, films, etc.) to identify their ultimate constituents – their invariant system of codes (paradigms) and their rules of combination (syntagms). From these analyses, structural semiotics constructs an abstract object, or model.

Analysis is based on several premises: for every message, there is a system of codes that generated it; messages are potentially infinite, codes are finite; messages are continuous observable surface phenomena, codes are discontinuous non-observable latent abstractions; messages are composed of distinguishable parts arranged into linear syntagms, codes are arranged into a system of paradigms. The concept of the paradigm is fundamental to structural semiotics. Paradigms are virtual systems of available options, a network of potential meanings from which one meaning is chosen and realized. A paradigm is therefore a set of latent codes that can occupy the same place in a manifest message.[5] A particular code selected from a paradigm to be manifest in a message gains its meaning in relation to the codes in the paradigm that were not selected to be manifest; although the manifest code appears to be a separate self-contained entity (a sign), it is in fact linked to numerous latent codes. The codes in the paradigm cannot be observed but only inferred, yet they contribute to the meaning of manifest codes by shadowing or 'resonating' with them. Saussure presents the following example of a paradigm (which he calls an associative series):

> Outside discourse [the syntagm], on the other hand, words acquire relations of a different kind. Those that have something in common are associated in the memory, resulting in groups marked by diverse relations. For instance, the French word *enseignement* 'teaching' will unconsciously call to mind a host of other words (*enseigner* 'teach', *renseigner* 'acquaint', etc.; or *armement* 'armament', *changement* 'amendment', etc.; or *éducation* 'education', *apprentissage* 'apprenticeship', etc.). All those words are related in some way. (Saussure 2011, 123)

If some of these words in the paradigm disappeared, the semantic value of the remaining words would change; they would become more diffuse, for the remaining words would need to cover the meaning of the missing words. The opposite happens when new words (such as technical terms) are invented: they divide up the realm of meaning into smaller segments. This is another demonstration of the structural (as opposed to the atomistic) theory of meaning, in which meaning is generated from the network of syntagmatic and paradigmatic relations: the meaning of one sign is dependent on other signs, rather than a fixed relation to a referent. A sign manifest in a message therefore signifies indirectly – in terms of its differential relations to other signs in the message and by invoking the underlying codes not manifest in that position in the message.

The all-or-nothing binary logic constitutes the ultimate type of differential relation between signs. What this means is that a sign or code receives its meaning via its opposition or similarity to other signs. Binary oppositions – such as raw/cooked, male/female, East/West, consonant/vowel – constitute a form of absolute, mutually exclusive relation of difference that symbolic systems impose upon the external world and the human mind. Nonetheless, the mutually exclusive binary opposition is just one type of symbolic difference. Daniel Dubuisson identified no less than fifteen relations of difference in Lévi-Strauss's work, including 'contrary', 'antithetical', 'alternative' and so on, but the mutually exclusive binary opposition remains the dominant relation (Dubuisson 2006, 124–5). Semantics identifies additional oppositions, including 'contrast', 'antonymy' and 'converseness' (see Lyons 1977, chapter 9). In terms of the *similarity* between codes in the same paradigm, Barthes noted that 'the terms of the field (or paradigm) must at the same time be similar and dissimilar, include a common and a variable element' (1984, 133).[6] A. J. Greimas identified three fundamental relations of difference: two based on opposition (contrariety, contradiction), and one based on similarity (implication), which form the foundation of his semiotic square (1987, chapter 3). It is via these specific types of relations that signs signify.

Signs are therefore structurally co-dependent: they reciprocally presuppose each other. A syntagmatic structure is, after all, a combination of paradigmatic codes. Structural semiotics re-conceptualizes all cultural artefacts in terms of reciprocal structural relations, not intrinsic properties. Kinship, one of the most basic symbolic systems governing human societies, is exemplary in this respect, for it creates relations between individuals: an individual's identity is defined by the specific set of symbolic relations he or she enters into with other individuals – who are consequently defined as 'relations', or siblings, people one can/cannot marry, enemies and so on. The kinship categories 'brother', 'sister', 'son', 'daughter' 'father', 'mother' and 'uncle' do not signify by themselves as individual signs. Instead, they only signify in relation to each other, and are distinguished from non-kin. Social relations are based on an individual's identity being defined unequivocally in terms of symbolic kinship categories. Oedipus's crime is not just a biological transgression; his symbolic kinship status is equivocal: 'Oedipus occupies all possible (male) positions (within his own family) but can act appropriately in none' (Jonnes 1990, 226). That is, Oedipus is both husband and son to Jocasta, and brother and father to the children they had together. Such equivocal symbolic identities undermine social relations.

Structural semiotics is based on three additional premises (Descombes 1980, 93–4): the code precedes the message (the system of codes must be in place before it can be manifest); the code is independent of the message (the virtual system of codes is separate from the material message); the code is independent of the emitter (the system of codes determines meaning, not the code user; the code user does not 'express' himself or herself – does not express some authentic experience; instead, his/her intervention simply involves selecting from a pre-existing system of codes).

For both paradigmatic and syntagmatic studies, meaning lies below the immediately perceptible surface content and is generated by an abstract system of differences. Remaining on the perceptible surface gives the false impression that meaning is singular, fixed, natural and self-evident – it simply needs to be experienced. A study based on these assumptions ends up repeating this surface in a description; it does not go beyond the information given.[7] Lévi-Strauss remarks, in relation to these types of studies, 'They demonstrate the obvious and neglect the unknown' (1972, 37). In his analysis of everyday myths, Roland Barthes (1972) followed Lévi-Strauss by deploying structural analysis to expose 'the obvious' (the surface, common sense level of lived experience) as a contingent construction that conceals a prescriptive series of social, political and moral values embedded in the symbolic order.[8] In the early 1960s, Barthes also applied this demystifying approach to the plays of Racine (Barthes 1992), provoking a strong reaction from traditional critics, including Raymond Picard. Serge Doubrovsky identified the conservative premises behind traditional criticism as follows:

> If, as Raymond Picard maintains, the role of criticism is to tell us 'what the work says', then criticism inevitably becomes a *retelling*. It is limiting itself to repeating, less well, what the author has already put better. To confine criticism, by a false epistemology, to the domain of significations explicitly developed by the work itself, in other words to the level of consciousness and communication that the work has *already achieved*, is to condemn it to mere inventorying and reiteration of obvious facts; it is to doom it, where interpretation is concerned, to perpetual *paraphrase*. (Doubrovsky 1973, 101)

Paradigmatic analysis, Lévi-Strauss's preferred method, goes beyond the description of obvious and self-evident surface experiences by generating new knowledge of the underlying codes that constitute those surface experiences.

Paradigm and mediation

In his seminal essay 'The Structural Study of Myth' (in 1972, 206–31) Lévi-Strauss employed structural semiotics to go beyond merely retelling or paraphrasing myths and instead identified their structure and function. To identify *structure*, he carried out a paradigmatic analysis to reorganize a continuous linear mythical narrative into paradigms of comparable elements (using the Oedipus myth as an example). To identify *function*, he focused on the way mediation serves to transform real contradictions outside of myth into symbolically defined oppositions within myth, thereby demonstrating how myth operates as a form of symbolic reasoning that progressively resolves real human puzzles, dilemmas and mysteries on a symbolic level. The essay ends with the enigmatic and controversial 'canonical formula', an algebraic equation that represents the inner dynamics of myth, a dynamics the formula attributes to myth's mediating function (1972, 228). In later work, especially *The Naked Man* (1981), Lévi-Strauss restated his theory of myth by explicitly locating the unresolvable contradictions in the human mind (e.g. abstract unresolvable puzzles concerning life/death, born from one/

born from two), and by defining the origin of myths as the mind's attempt to resolve these contradictions on the levels of the imaginary and the symbolic by translating them into a successive series of binary oppositions, drawn from the everyday external world (earth/sky, water/fire, raw/cooked, day/night, sun/moon, etc.) (1981, 557; 603). Analysis reverses this process, by beginning with the concrete binary oppositions embedded in texts and then working backwards through the binary oppositions towards the unresolvable abstract contradictions.

In contrast to narratologists (such as Propp, Barthes and Todorov) who privileged the syntactic-syntagmatic analysis of structures, premised on temporality and causality, Lévi-Strauss followed Saussure and privileged paradigmatic analysis in order to construct the abstract system of codes underlying myths. Lévi-Strauss disregarded the linear syntagmatic dimension and privileged paradigmatic analysis not only to avoid merely paraphrasing myths as they unfold, but also because the storytelling structure of myth is circular: myths move in a spiral fashion, constantly returning to and repeating with variation the same themes and scenarios in an attempt to resolve contradictions (Lévi-Strauss 1972, 229). A myth's symbolic meanings and function are not therefore located in the continuous, temporal unfolding of concrete narrative events, but in the repetitions and associations embedded in the discontinuous, atemporal abstract organization of those actions and events. Lévi-Strauss's argument is analogous to the conception of space-time in the theory of relativity. Time is experienced as a one-dimensional linear flow of events in three-dimensional space. But in the theory of relativity, spatial events exist together in their totality as a complete four-dimensional block of space-time. Lévi-Strauss's reorganization of myths into paradigms does not repeat the experience of a narrative's linear one-dimensional unfolding, but presents the whole narrative as a block of space-time. Lévi-Strauss used a similar distinction to differentiate anthropology from history: 'Anthropology uses "mechanical" time, reversible and non-cumulative. [...] On the contrary, historical time [...] always appears as an oriented and non-reversible process' (1972, 286). Below we will see that the reversible non-cumulative time of anthropology, together with the space-time analogy of relativity theory, are suitable for understanding abstract storyworlds.

Throughout his work, Lévi-Strauss employed two types of paradigmatic analysis – either a single myth is analysed into paradigms (which he demonstrated in 'The Structural Study of Myth' by analysing the Oedipus myth into four paradigms); or, more commonly, several myths (or versions of the same myth) are superimposed onto each other to identify their similarities and differences. In 'The Structural Study of Myth' Lévi-Strauss demonstrated this comparative type of paradigmatic analysis in a study of several versions of Zuni origin myths (discussed later), in his analysis of two versions of the Asdiwal myth (1967, esp. 33–43), and comprehensively carried it out in his four volume *Mythologiques* – *The Raw and the Cooked* (1970), *From Honey to Ashes* (1973), *The Origin of Table Manners* (1978) and *The Naked Man* (1981). In *The Raw and the Cooked*, he described this comparative paradigmatic analysis in some detail, which is worth quoting in full:

> Considered purely in itself, every syntagmatic sequence must be looked upon as being without meaning: either no meaning is apparent in the first instance; or we think we can perceive a meaning, but without knowing whether it is the right one. In order to overcome this difficulty, we can only resort to two procedures. One consists in dividing the syntagmatic sequence into superposable segments, and in proving that they constitute variations on one and the same theme [...]. The other procedure, which is complementary to the first, consists in superposing a syntagmatic sequence in its totality – in other words, a complete myth – on other myths or segments of myths. It follows, then, that on both occasions we are replacing a syntagmatic sequence by a paradigmatic sequence; the difference is that whereas in the first case the paradigmatic whole is removed from the sequence, in the second it is the sequence that is incorporated into it. (1970, 307)

The first method consists in segmenting one myth into its constituent elements or units (which Lévi-Strauss calls 'mythemes' [1972, 207], the minimal units of mythic meaning) and organizing them into bundles of comparable units – that is, superimposing them onto one another to create paradigms. It is important to stress that myths only acquire meaning or symbolic significance through the discovery of paradigms of comparable units, for these individual units have no independent existence from the paradigms to which they belong. Lévi-Strauss takes the analysis further by establishing the differential logical relations (usually binary oppositions) between these paradigms. The second method, complementary to the first, consists in superimposing entire myths onto one another to discover the comparable units across them. Myths acquire symbolic meaning through the discovery of their comparable units, which demonstrates that each myth is a variation of an archi-myth. This comparative method does not simply involve identifying identical features in different myths. More fundamentally, it also involves the identification of structural relations (or transformations) between myths – the way one myth echoes, reverses, opposes, or inverts another myth or, more generally, the way one myth is a permutation of an earlier telling of a myth (sometimes a stronger version, sometimes a weaker version). The study of transformations, the structural relations between similar myths, therefore constitutes an important part of myth analysis, not only because it reveals that each myth is a variation of an archi-myth, but also because it conceives a mythic system 'not as something inert and stable but in a process of perpetual transformation' (Lévi-Strauss 1973, 354). Both methods are used in this book; in the following chapters, each Wes Anderson film will be subjected to a paradigmatic analysis, and in Chapter 11 key symbolic elements from those films will be compared with one another to establish the attributes of Wes Anderson's symbolic storyworld.

The paradigmatic method of analysis is both conventional and controversial: conventional because it resembles a thematic analysis of film (albeit a structural analysis of themes); controversial because it resembles an allegorical reading strategy, one that not only rejects the experience of surface reality but also challenges causal explanations, leaving the generation of meaning to a series of often unexpected underlying relations and an indirect (indeed oblique) causality. Paradigmatic analysis can thereby be defined in terms of what David Herman calls 'a double coding of what happens in the storyworld' (2002, 48): the surface level of myriad actions and events, on the one hand, and on the other the small underlying core of puzzles, dilemmas and mysteries humans experience regarding nature, kinship relations, birth, life and death.

Lévi-Strauss initially conceived of myth functionally – or, more accurately, in terms of teleological functionalism, which examines phenomena from the perspective of their use and purpose. Myth presents generic fictional solutions to specific real world puzzles, dilemmas and mysteries, and has positive consequences, including the creation of social cohesion. This teleological functionalism is evident in Lévi-Strauss's analysis of individual myths in 'The Structural Study of Myth' when he argued that mythic structure (and structural transformations) provides imaginary (and symbolic) answers to real uncertainties: 'The purpose of myth is to provide a logical model capable of overcoming a contradiction (an impossible achievement if, as it happens, the contradiction is real)' (1972, 229), and 'mythical thought always progresses from the awareness of oppositions toward their resolution' (1972, 224). However, when he analysed hundreds of myths in *Mythologiques*, Lévi-Strauss switched his attention to the structural relations between myths, marginalizing teleological functionalism and focusing instead on formal functionalism, on myth as an internal self-regulating unified system.

In combination with the double coding of myth and the need to read it allegorically, it should be evident that the teleological functionalism of myth is also a form of latent (rather than manifest) functionalism, in which the myth has an ulterior function distinct from its surface function. Lévi-Strauss therefore developed a latent teleological functionalist account of myth. Within this perspective, to overcome real contradictions on an imaginary-symbolic level, myth translates them into analogous terms (contrary oppositions) that can be resolved via mediators. Contradictions are real and absolute, with no real world solutions, no mediation between the opposing terms. 'The Structural Study of Myth' presents three real contradictions: life/death in Zuni and Pueblo myths; the affirmation/denial of the autochthonous origin of mankind in the Oedipus myth (i.e. born from one [the Earth]/born from two ([man/woman]); and undervaluation/overvaluation of blood relations in the Oedipus myth (blood relations are either downplayed, for example when one relative kills another; or the blood relations are more intimate than they should be, for example, when one relative marries another).

Lévi-Strauss's analysis of a series of Zuni and Pueblo myths (1972, 219–24) clearly demonstrates the two types of paradigmatic analysis, the dialectical logic of myth, and the role of mediator. Two fundamental states of being, life/death, emerge as the ultimate real contradiction in these myths. This opposition is absolute and therefore without any mediating term. It is translated in the myths into an analogous opposition between agriculture (life) and warfare (death). Hunting mediates between these two opposed terms because it combines elements from both (the positive value 'life-sustaining food' and the negative value 'killing'). Hunting therefore begins the process of mediation between life and death. Moving in a spiral fashion, Zuni and Pueblo myths return to the agriculture and warfare opposition and replace it with another analogous opposition, between herbivorous animals (agriculture) and beasts of prey (hunting). Carrion-eating animals such as the raven and coyote mediate between these two opposed terms because they combine elements from both: they are 'like beasts of prey (they eat animal food), but they are also like food-plant producers (they do not kill what they eat)' (1972, 224). Because mediators contain elements common to both of the opposing ideas and elements found in neither of them, they progressively neutralize the opposition. Here we see the circular structure of myth combined with its problem-solving function: each act of mediation represents one step in the myth's resolution of a real contradiction; the process is repeated at the next stage with new oppositions and mediators, until the contradiction is resolved on the imaginary-symbolic levels. Mythic thought therefore moves progressively in circles to neutralize (or offer solutions to) contradictions by generating additional sets of oppositions and mediators.[9] The process of mediation and neutralization/resolution is not only circular, but is also a multistage dialectical process, a dynamic process that attempts to unify contradictory elements (thesis, antithesis) into a new synthesis. Lévi-Strauss's main focus is not the actual contradictions that exist in reality, but the mythical contrary terms and their resolution in the symbolic via mediators.

T. K. Seung refined the concept of symbolic resolution (1982, 203–9). He identified three types: resolution by equilibrium, resolution by suppression and resolution by subordination. Lévi-Strauss's model of resolution relies primarily on equilibrium, on keeping the two opposing terms but neutralizing their conflict. Resolution by suppression creates resolution by eliminating one of the two opposing terms, and resolution by subordination keeps the two opposing terms, but creates a hierarchy by relegating one term beneath the other. The term 'symbolic resolution' therefore needs to be qualified and defined in terms of equilibrium, suppression or subordination.

Lévi-Strauss's innovation in the study of myth was therefore to develop a method (paradigmatic analysis) to reveal a myth's paradigms and circular structure, and to explain that structure in terms of its function – to progressively mediate and resolve contradictions within the symbolic order. Jurij Lotman pursued this idea further, arguing that the central function of repetition is to create unity within and across myths. In contrast, narrative is causal, temporal and linear-syntagmatic, for it consists of the organization of historically contingent (rather than cyclical mythological) events. Lotman notes that 'the fixing of unique and chance events, crimes, calamities [...] was the historical kernel of plot-narration' (1979, 163). He then spelled out the historical relation of myth to syntagmatic structure: the repetitive structure of myth is transformed into the linear causal structure of modern storytelling, with its focus on incidental actions and events.

> The destruction of the cyclical-temporal mechanism of texts, (or, at least, the sharp decrease of the sphere of its functioning) led to the mass translation of mythological texts into the language of discrete-linear systems (verbal re-tellings of myth-rituals and myth-mysteries should be considered as translations of this kind) and to the creation of those novelistic pseudo-myths which first come to mind at the mention of mythology. (1979, 164)

Lotman argued that contemporary storytelling embodies both types of structure, in varying degrees: 'The modern plot-text is the fruit of the interaction and reciprocal influence of these two typologically age-old types of text' (1979, 163).

This book foregrounds both types of functionalism (teleological and formal) in Wes Anderson's films. Teleological functionalism demands paradigmatic analysis in order to reveal the human dilemmas latent in stories. Although these dilemmas are wide-ranging, kinship is privileged in this book because it is a core element in Wes Anderson's symbolic storyworld. More specifically, kinship (outlined later) is key to understanding the teleological functionalism of Wes Anderson's films, for they primarily (although not exclusively) attempt to resolve conflicts in kinship. Formal functionalism reveals the complexity of patterning at work in his films. The focus of the following film analyses is therefore dual: to delineate the internal symbolic logic of Wes Anderson's storyworld, and to focus on the way kinship problems are resolved. Before discussing kinship systems, we first need to address the question: How exactly is a paradigmatic analysis carried out?

Paradigmatic analysis

J. Patrick Gray (1978) identifies five stages in Lévi-Strauss's method of structural myth analysis:

1. Identify binary oppositions and mediators
2. Identify a myth's ultimate constituents (gross constituent units, or mythemes)
3. Find an individual myth message (by organizing the mythemes paradigmatically, into bundles of mythemes)
4. List links to other myths (comparative analysis that specifies repetitions and transformational relationships between myths)
5. General comments

The idea behind stage (1) is that the symbolic manages the continuous flux of everyday experience by organizing and reducing it to simple structures – primarily binary oppositions. In more technical terms, continuous analogue experiences are digitized into discrete discontinuous binary codes. Lévi-Strauss also argued that myths establish a symbiotic relation between human societies and nature, whereby human societies can draw upon nature (the environment, changes in seasons, etc.) in order to survive. This is why fundamental elements (fire, water, sky etc.) are significant to myth and storytelling more generally, as are directions (up/down, and other forms of navigation). Binary oppositions and the tensions between them constitute the virtual values of a particular set of myths, which add up to create a symbolic storyworld.

In terms of mediators, Gray identifies two types: 'One type of mediating element is an object or a person that brings two opposites into contact, without itself partaking of the nature of either' (1978, 86). The second type of mediator, discussed in the previous section, is dialectical: 'This type of mediator actually partakes of the nature of both of the opposite elements. Therefore it reconciles the contradiction' (1978, 86). Both types of mediator operate in Wes Anderson's storyworld.

The idea behind (2) and (3) is to analyse a story or myth into short sentences (mythemes) and reorganize them into paradigms of repeated or similar units in order to identify the myth's latent or underlying meanings, the internal symbolic values between the mythemes that hold the paradigms together. We have already encountered Lévi-Strauss's justification of this method. Gray presents a straightforward explanation:

> The question is what the myth means. We cannot tell from the syntagmatic sequence alone, which is just the order of episodes in the myth [...]. But if we take each episode as a separate element, compare it with the other elements of the myth regardless of the positions in the story development, and look for common features we can uncover a meaning. (1978, 80)

Analysis of paradigmatic meaning focuses on two types of relation: relations between mythemes *within* each paradigm, and relations *between* paradigms.

In practice, when implementing Lévi-Strauss's method, one generally begins with stage (2), identifying the basic narrative units of a film, before moving on to stage (3), organizing similar actions into paradigms. Binary oppositions (stage 1) – and other types of relation – are generally identified while carrying out stages 2 and 3. The organization of paradigms in myths or films is not as systematic and as integrated as linguistic paradigms in the language system (*la langue*). Christian Metz spelled this out in relation to film: 'Cinematic codes do exist, but they do not have the constancy and stability of natural languages. The student of film, like the speaker of a natural language, is faced with pre-existent forms which are anterior to his own activity, but not to the same degree, nor in the same way' (1974b, 17). Cinematic (and mythic) paradigms are more contingent and open-ended.

Stage 4 involves carrying out activities 1 to 3 over several myths. The results of each individual analysis are compared in order to find either structural repetitions/similarities among the group of texts (their invariant traits), or transformational differences (addition, subtraction, inversion, substitution, transposition) among the texts. Because the analysis was not carried out by a group of researchers, then need to make notes for others stage (5) is unnecessary.

Yet, Gray does not distinguish between Lévi-Strauss's analysis of tangible qualities and formal-structural qualities of myth.[10] Lévi-Strauss began with tangible qualities but gradually worked his way towards structural qualities. He began his analysis of myth by organizing tangible qualities into oppositions: raw/cooked, fresh/rotten, dry/wet, and so forth. 'But now', he continued, 'the second stage of my analysis reveals terms which are still contrasted in pairs but whose nature is different in that they refer less to a logic of qualities than to a logic of forms: empty and full, hollow and solid, container and contents, internal and external, included and excluded, etc.' (1973, 472). This second stage of analysis is more abstract, for it isolates the formal dimension of myth from its tangible qualities. The following analysis of Wes Anderson's films maintains a balance between form and tangible qualities.

Fredric Jameson sees in Lévi-Strauss's method of analysis the perfect balance between the formal-structural and social analysis of texts. For Jameson, Lévi-Strauss does not abandon the formal for social content, but construes

> purely formal patterns as a symbolic enactment of the social within the formal and the aesthetic. Such symbolic functions are, however, rarely found by an aimless enumeration of random formal and stylistic features; our discovery of a text's symbolic efficacity must be oriented by a formal description which seeks to grasp it as a determinate structure of still properly formal contradictions. (Jameson 1981, 77)

Jameson can only integrate Lévi-Strauss's work into his Marxist framework by foregrounding myth's teleological functionalism. But the advantage of Lévi-Strauss's teleological functionalism is that it is tied to the form of a text, an emphasis rarely found in traditional Marxist analyses, which focus on social and material realities extrinsic to texts.

Elementary and complex structures of kinship

Kinship relations constitute a significant dimension of the symbolic order and a fundamental object of structural analysis and study. Lévi-Strauss's *The Elementary Structures of Kinship* (1969), first published in 1949, was a pioneering work of structuralism that reduced a heterogeneous array of specific kinship bonds, particularly marriage practices across numerous societies, down to a small abstract underlying system of general rules that constitute all the logical possibilities of kinship relations. In the final pages Lévi-Strauss summarized his findings:

> We have thus established that superficially complicated and arbitrary rules may be reduced to a small number. There are only three possible elementary kinship structures [bilateral, matrilateral, and patrilateral cross-cousin marriage]; these three structures are constructed by means of two forms of exchange [restricted and generalized]; and these two forms of exchange themselves depend upon a single differential characteristic, namely the harmonic or disharmonic character of the regime considered. (1969, 493)

The Elementary Structures of Kinship is invaluable as an early demonstration of the significance of structural analysis as applied to kinship. However, rather than engage with the specialized technical kinship terms Lévi-Strauss employs in the earlier mentioned quotation and throughout his book, we should note that these specialized terms have a limited value in the analysis of Wes Anderson's films, because they name elementary kinship structures found in non-Western and in indigenous societies, whereas Western societies are based on complex kinship structures. For Lévi-Strauss, kinship rules are universally founded on a negative determination – the prohibition of incest. But, in addition, elementary structures are founded on positive determinations, a set of kin preferences that stipulate specific partners (and the specialized terminology names those preferences). Complex structures do not specify a set of kin preferences, but are instead based on an expansive network of sociological factors, such as a partner's religion, or class, or are based on choice governed by desire and sentiment (the 'romantic love complex'), rather than rules stipulating specific partners. To outline these complex structures, we first need to identify the foundational concepts of Lévi-Strauss's theory of kinship – including alliance (or exchange), woman as sign, incest prohibition, nature/culture – and address their problems, particularly their totalizing, universal status.

Lévi-Strauss's reduction of the heterogeneous array of kinship rules to a general system was made possible by replacing descent theories of kinship (a diachronic model that defines kinship in terms of consanguine relations between generations) with kinship governed by alliance (a synchronic model that defines kinship in terms of co-operation and especially exchange between social groups). Lévi-Strauss argued that the universal prohibition against incest necessitates exchange, because the women that the men of a kinship group are forbidden to marry are exchanged with women of another kinship group whom they can marry: 'The relationship of reciprocity which is the basis of marriage is not established between men and women, but between men by means of women, who are merely the occasion of this relationship' (1969, 116). Exchange therefore avoids incest and creates affinal bonds of alliance between the different groups, thereby creating social links between those groups.

The kinship system's response to the incest taboo generates three logical possibilities of exchange: (1) men exchange women, (2) women exchange men, or (3) both male and female members of a family leave to join or create new families. Lévi-Strauss privileged (1), woman as a sign exchanged between men, because of the patriarchal and patrilineal bias of the majority of societies. Judith Butler (1990, chapter 2) also finds this bias to be an unacknowledged assumption operating within Lévi-Strauss's theory of kinship. By defining culture, language and the exchange of women in terms of a universal prohibition (incest), Lévi-Strauss tended to reify patriarchy and heterosexuality. That is, he defined the existence of kinship relations only in terms of men's domination over women within a heterosexual society founded on sexual difference. This is a normative, totalizing definition that leaves no possibility of transforming women's social status and gender identity. Maurice Godelier developed a similar critique, arguing that 'what is constituent [in kinship systems], owing to the incest taboo, is the obligation to exchange. But exchanging women is not the universal condition for alliance and kinship' (Godelier 2011, 125). Instead, Godelier defines exchange more broadly, with men's exchange of women reduced to one socially contingent form (in indigenous societies), part of a more variable and expansive matrix of sexual and social relationships. He argues that, in the West, the third option prevails: 'As for the third possibility, it occurs every day in European and Euro-American cognatic societies, where sons and daughters leave their family to live with the one they have chosen' (2011, 125). In other words, he identifies (along with Judith Butler, David Schneider, Clifford Geertz, Marilyn Strathern, among others) complex (in the sense of open) structures of kinship in contemporary Western societies, which mix rules of descent and alliance (rather than favouring one over the other).[11] Rules of descent are therefore still relevant to understanding kinship. In Western societies, descent relations are bilineal or cognatic – they are traced through both the father and mother. Those relations are also both consanguine and social, which means that biological and social descent coincide. Traditionally, in the West a child's descent relation is based on two biological parents and on two social roles (mother and father) embedded in those biological parents. In contrast, in a patrilineal descent relation, while it is also traced biologically through both a father and a mother, socially it is related only through the male line. And a matrilineal descent relation is traced both biologically and socially through the female line.

In contemporary Western societies based on the nuclear family, traditional kinship bonds have been loosened with the development of divorce laws, cohabitation without marriage, and the legalization of gay marriage. One major outcome is the decline of the symbolic order – conceived as the universal Other that upholds patriarchal law, meaning and kinship relations. The decline of the symbolic is most forcefully registered in the symbolic function of the father as figure of authority, as defender of patriarchal law and order regulating desire and socialization: 'the symbolic father function itself has become questionable', argues Paul Verhaeghe. 'As a result', he continues, 'the number of hysterical subjects who are on the run, looking for a new master, is on the increase' (Verhaeghe 2000, 137–8). He adds that:

> Contemporary sons have great difficulties in regarding their fathers as representatives of ancient patriarchal authority. As a consequence, the security and protection associated with that authority has disappeared, resulting in ever-increasing levels of anxiety and thus aggression in the sons. The absence of the possibility of identifying with the symbolic function itself condemns the contemporary male to staying at the level of the immature boy and son, afraid of the threatening female figure, which once more assumes its atavistic characteristics. These sons are just wandering around, staying forever in the same position, owing to the lack of an identificatory figure; thirty-year-old kids and adolescents of forty are no longer the exception. (2000, 138)

Father figures no longer embody symbolic authority, the pacifying ego-ideal, but become rivals. That is, with the demise of the symbolic, the realm of the imaginary, including narcissism and individual competitiveness, takes its place. Symbolic father figures and sons also compete with one another over the same woman – a scenario Wes Anderson stages in a number of films (especially *Rushmore* and *Life Aquatic with Steve Zissou*). At the same time, women are no longer assigned a submissive position: 'The absence of the security-enhancing symbolic law regulating desire and enjoyment invests woman with all the ancient masculine fears, which results in a turnaround: today, we have woman-the hunter and man-the-hunted' (2000, 139). Another consequence of the decline of the symbolic order is its replacement with a network of multiple, autonomous, incompatible ethical committees defending the interests of different social groups.

The following analyses of Wes Anderson's films focus on the complex mix of descent and alliance in the symbolic orders of contemporary Western societies, on the general activity of exchange between social and sexual groups (not exclusively heterosexual marriage) that aim to create social cohesion and group identity, and the creation of small autonomous groups of like-minded individuals. The openness of Western kinship systems (and their decline) also means that kinship analysis of films should not be limited to the Oedipal complex. Other anthropological concepts of kinship such as marital residence (patrilocal, matrilocal, neolocal), and extended family units need to be taken into account.

Stories and kinship

Denis Jonnes (1990) presents a compelling case for studying stories by way of kinship: 'storytelling cannot be conceptualized independently of a system defined by a particular order of interpersonal relation; specifically, that subsumed by the term "family" (and ancillary processes "courtship", "engagement", "marriage", etc.)' (1990, 6). And: 'At the moment we refer to a "character" [. . .] we do so with respect to his/her role as "father", "mother", "son", "daughter", "suitor", "lover", "mistress", or as "helper" or "obstacle" to those positioned within kinship structures' (1990, 234). Rather than conceiving characters merely in terms of the actions they perform (actants), Jonnes fills in these categories with their kinship attributes – not with the biological referent (atomistic theory of meaning) but with signs defined structurally. For example, he speaks of the 'paternal function' rather than the biological father. Also, abstract narrative concepts such as 'conflict', 'transformation', and 'resolution' are similarly filled in: conflict/transformation/resolution are conceived in terms of kinship relations between characters, while character transformations are defined in terms of new kinship role (the son becomes a husband and/or father). These kinship relations are supplemented with relations of friendship, and official relations to authority figures (head teacher, judge). Within the complex kinship systems in the West, traditional family roles are supplanted by friendship bonds, a group identity rather than strictly kinship identity (Jonnes 1990, 266). This group identity is fundamental to several Wes Anderson's films.

Storyworlds and world logic

> More and more, storytelling has become the art of world building, as artists create compelling environments that cannot be fully explored or exhausted within a single work or even a single medium. The world is bigger than the film, bigger even than the franchise – since fan speculations and elaborations also expand the worlds in a variety of directions. (Jenkins 2006, 114)

> While narrative is constructed from causal, spatial, and temporal linkages, a world is constructed from various infrastructures, including maps (spatial links), timelines (temporal links), histories and mythologies (causal links), genealogies (character linkages and relationships), and other systems including natural, cultural, and social structures. When a large enough number of elements from these systems are combined in a consistent fashion, a kind of 'world logic' starts to form, by which one can see how a world works and how its various systems are interrelated. (Wolf 2012, 128–9)

In his Introduction to Matt Zoller Seitz's *The Wes Anderson Collection* (2013), Michael Chabon presents a summary of the commonly received view of

Anderson: 'In their set design and camerawork, their use of stop-motion, maps, and models, Wes Anderson's films readily, even eagerly, concede the "miniature" quality of the worlds he builds. And yet these worlds span continents and decades. They comprise crime, adultery, brutality, suicide, the death of a parent, the drowning of a child, moments of profound joy and transcendence' (2013, 22). And in the *LA Times*, Mark Olsen reiterates these points by noting that 'Wes Anderson doesn't so much make movies as create worlds', worlds that are viewed through 'meticulously constructed visuals' (2014). The films of well-established auteurs such as Wes Anderson create a self-contained homogeneous fictional storyworld. The attribution of a storyworld to a director can only be established if, collectively, elements from these films can be combined in a consistent manner, leading to the formation of a self-sufficient internally coherent fictional reality (but, as with all fictional worlds, they are incomplete – only parts are described or inferred). The coherence and consistency of this fictional world is not to be assumed, but needs to be established via analysis. This conception of an auteur's work sharing a fictional world rejects the naïve realist view of cinema (cinema simply reflects reality), together with the romantic view of the director as an individual expressing personal experiences. This is because storyworld is not some ineffable or unique vision, it is not the expression of some personal meaning or experience, but is simply an effect of the specific selection and combination of pre-existing codes and structures. Lévi-Strauss noted that: '[Humans] never create absolutely: all they can do is to choose certain combinations from a repertory of ideas which it should be possible to reconstitute' (quoted in Miriam Glucksmann 1974, 89). The code user (speaker, writer, filmmaker) therefore submits to the code, to its meanings and limits (or submits to the law of the signifier, in Lacan's terms).[12] The storyworld of a different auteur would have a different modality, based on their own distinct selection and combination of pre-existing codes and structures.

The observations of Chabon and Olsen highlight a basic truth about narrative fiction films: they create worlds, not just a linear sequence of events. Each narrative text implies a fictional world beyond the boundaries of (or distinct from) the text. Many terms designate the represented level of fiction films: 'diegesis', 'fabula', 'small world', 'fictional world', 'imaginary world', 'possible world', 'storyworld'. The structuralists bracketed off issues of representation and reference to focus instead on identifying the constituents of the linear unfolding plot/syuzhet. The recent use of the word 'world' in narratology (Doležel 1998; Eco 1994, chapter 4; Herman 2002, 2009; Pavel 1986; Ronen 1994; Ryan and Thon 2014; Wolf 2012) indicates a shift back towards reference – but conceived as non-actual other worlds, or fictional storyworlds generated by plots (Herman even defines plot as the mere blueprint for constructing a storyworld [2009, 105]). 'Storyworld' describes a totality shared by a group of films. Storyworld is independent of a particular text: it is not tied to a specific manifestation in a film, but transcends each manifestation, giving the impression that it is an internally coherent pre-existing world. As Mark Wolf points out (2012, 132), while casual viewers primarily follow a film's narrative, fans focus on how a film contributes to the more expansive storyworld. In addition, auteur critics focus on a director's storyworld, while fans and film critics also discuss the storyworld of a franchise (e.g. *Star Wars*).

The concept of the storyworld therefore goes beyond the manifest content of a group of texts, for it designates the more expansive abstract, non-manifest realm of co-existing possibilities or immaterial alternatives, a virtual system of values and a preferential ordering of those values. Storyworld is atemporal and paradigmatic; it is equivalent to a block of space-time, which can only be partly manifest in texts. Yet, it is often discussed in mimetic terms, focused only on the possibilities that are realized or represented. This is evident in popular accounts (Chabon and Olsen, among many others), while theoretical accounts emphasize the reader's or spectator's cognitive modelling of the represented storyworld. To explore the full potential of the storyworld's abstract, virtual system of values and possibilities, we need to return to the foundations of semiotics.

The non-mimetic, abstract concept of storyworld is implicit in the semiotic activity of constructing an underlying, abstract invariant 'object'. In 'The Structural Study of Myth' Lévi-Strauss noted that 'By systematically using this kind of structural analysis it becomes possible to organize all the known variants of a myth into a set forming a kind of *permutation group* [...]' (1972, 223; emphasis added). Each permutation represents just one variant or possible combination of elements; collectively, this group represents all the possible permutations of the abstract underlying storyworld. Translated into auteur studies, this means that each Wes Anderson film is a variant or permutation of the Wes Anderson archi-film. The study of storyworld privileges repetition of elements across myths (or a director's films) because repetition indicates their significance (a standard trait of auteur theory).

Similarly, A. J. Greimas did not simply call the underlying system a set of codes, but instead used the more expansive term 'semantic universe', or the totality of virtual significations, which cannot be conceived in its entirety. A text or group of texts presupposes a semantic universe that it can only manifest in part (the semantic micro universe). In other words, the semantic universe names the non-manifest system of codes (the totality of signification prior to articulation), whereas the semantic micro universe is a partial manifestation of the semantic universe in a text or group of texts. In *Structural Semantics* (1983, 257–95), Greimas analysed the fictional micro universe of novelist Georges Bernanos (which I briefly summarize in Chapter 11).

Semantic universes and abstract storyworlds are similar to Karl Popper's philosophical concept of World 3 (Popper 1972, chapters 3 and 4). World 1 refers to physical reality (existing independently of the human mind), and World 2 to cognitive psychological reality (mental states and thoughts), while World 3 refers to abstract objects that emerge from the human mind (including mathematics, language, theories, storytelling – the realm of the symbolic). World 3 mental objects are more general and impersonal than World 2 mental objects: they transcend individual human minds. For example, a language exists in its totality in World 3, whereas an individual language speaker may only know or understand part of that language (World 2). When language is manifest in speech or written sentences, it becomes part of World 1, but language is not reducible to World 1 (or World 2). Popper's concept of World 3 is less mimetic than narratological theories of storyworld, and is therefore invaluable because it focuses attention on the abstract structures that constitute the storyworld's symbolic dimension.

In the terms of auteur theory, World 1 refers to an individual film – either on the filmographic level (the film as physical object), or the filmophanic level (the film as projected on a screen), to use Etienne Souriau's terms (outlined in more detail in Chapter 2). World 2 refers to the diegetic level of an individual film. World 3 refers to a director's storyworld, their own particular semantic micro-universe. For example, Wes Anderson's storyworld is an abstract totality encompassing everything that is fictionally possible in his films, but which is only partially represented in the diegesis of each film. The analysis of each individual Wes Anderson film carried out in Chapters 3 to 10 aims to construct the director's invariant archi-film – his abstract storyworld, or semantic micro-universe. Wes Anderson is particularly apt for this type of study because, collectively, his films are renowned for their consistency and internal coherence.

One theory and the principle of pertinence

> To undertake this research, it is necessary frankly to accept from the beginning (and especially at the beginning) a limiting principle.... . [I]t is decided to describe the facts which have been gathered *from one point of view only*, and consequently to keep, from the heterogeneous mass of these facts, only the features associated with this point of view, to the exclusion of any others. (Barthes 1984, 154; emphasis in the original)

This book does not aim to analyse and explain everything in Wes Anderson's films. Instead, it follows the principle of pertinence in order to isolate and analyse a singular – although central – dimension in his films, the abstract, symbolic dimension, occasionally supplemented with comments on how the symbolic is visually and aurally manifest in specific shots and scenes. The principle of pertinence constrains the researcher to focus only on the relevant (pertinent, essential) traits of an object while filtering out all other traits. What is relevant is dependent on or defined by the goal of the research and the theoretical perspective adopted to achieve that goal. Structural semiotics, for example, focuses on the underlying system of signification while ignoring the surface aesthetic traits of phenomena. In other words, the principle of pertinence enables the researcher to abstract and isolate from the phenomena the relevant aspects of the object of study. Barthes called this a limiting principle, which his student Christian Metz put into practice in his film semiotics: 'It is because the analysis searches for a system that it must select from among the elements of the filmic text, retaining some as relevant and temporarily ignoring others' (Metz

1974b, 73). The following analyses are limited to the perspective of structural semiotics (paradigms, kinship, transformations, binary oppositions, mediation, exchange, symbolic storyworld); they only focus on the features associated with this point of view. Yet, this perspective is not applied mechanically. Not all these concepts from structural semiotics are equally relevant to each film. For example, kinship is key to *The Royal Tenenbaums* but marginal to *Bottle Rocket*; the film itself dictates whether kinship structures are foregrounded or negligible. This adherence to one perspective helps to maintain focus, precision and rigor, thereby avoiding a broad, eclectic approach informed by multiple theories and perspectives. Asking if the structural semiotic approach is the 'correct' perspective to view Wes Anderson's films (or to analyse films in general) is like asking if the rules of chess are correct or not: such a question misses the point of analysing cultural artefacts, which surely is to generate new insights into what appears to be known and familiar, to reveal something previously overlooked or hidden. These insights are generated from and can be checked against an explicitly defined methodology whose results can be unexpected and counter-intuitive.

* * *

In *Mythologiques*, Lévi-Strauss embedded the mythic tales into his chapters (and reproduced them indented), before analysing and comparing them to other myths. He also generated a number of tables and charts, which enabled him to compare sections of the same myth, or compare myths to one another. I follow the same practice in the following pages. Each chapter begins with a plot summary that identifies (and numbers) the main sequence of actions in each film. The summaries are not formally rigorous in identifying these sequences, but are informal. There is only a general (not a strict) correlation between scenes in a film and the numbered sequence of actions.

Notes

1 'Archi' names the kernel of features that remain constant across two or more entities. In structural linguistics, the concept was developed within phonology: 'the archiphoneme is the sum of *the relevant features common to two*

or more phonemes which alone present them all' (Martinet 1964, 69; emphasis added). Hjelmslev preferred the term 'syncretism', the overlapping or merging of features (1961, 88).

2 Without suggesting complete assimilation, these three levels of reality can be mapped onto Karl Popper's concept of Worlds: World 1 refers to physical reality, World 2 to inner reality, while the symbolic is similar to World 3. I discuss this further at the end of the chapter.

3 In general, structuralism is broader and more fundamental than semiotics. Semiotics involves the application of structuralism to sign systems. Linguistics is a small component of semiotics (it is just one sign system among many), despite Roland Barthes' reversal (1984, 79). Continental theorists used the term semiology, Saussure's preferred term in his *Course in General Linguistics* (2011, 15–16). Linguistics only plays a small role in semiology (and in this study), even though continental semioticians in the twentieth century learnt about semiotics through linguistics. But this does not mean that semiotics is reducible to or dependent on linguistics.

4 Like Roman Jakobson, Descombes employs the more general terms 'message' and 'code' rather than '*la parole*' and '*la langue*'. The latter pair belongs to the structural analysis of natural (verbal) language, whereas 'message' and 'code' derive from cybernetic theory and apply more generally to systems of signification. See Roman Jakobson, 'Pattern in Linguistics' (1971, esp. 224). Christian Metz also adopted the message/code opposition in *Language and Cinema* (Metz 1974b).

5 Poetic language deviates from this rule, as Jakobson argued in his famous definition of the poetic function: '*The poetic function projects the principle of equivalence from the axis of selection* [paradigms] *in to the axis of combination* [syntagms]' (1981, 27; emphasis in the original). Codes in the paradigm that are normally substituted for one another appear sequentially ordered in the syntagm/message, creating a rhythm that draws attention to the message.

6 Roman Jakobson added: 'The selection [from the paradigms] is produced on the basis of equivalence, similarity, dissimilarity, synonymy and antonymy, while the combination, the build-up of the sequence, is based on contiguity' (1981, 27).

7 Jerome Bruner's constructivist theory of psychology also proposes the need to go beyond the information given: 'We propose that when one goes beyond the information given, one does so by virtue of being able to place the present given in a more generic coding system and that one essentially reads off from the coding system additional information either on the basis of learned contingent probabilities or learned principles of relating material' (Bruner 2010, 224).

8 The logic of the symbolic is not neutral, but is a form of organization skewed to the values of one social group. This is how Anthony Wilden distinguishes myth from ideology: ' "A myth which is the property of a class" is in effect a definition of ideology. The myth then ceases to serve the neutral function of organization pure and simple; it serves as the *rationalization* of a given form of social organization' (Wilden 1980, 10). Political resistance to normative symbolic orders such as patriarchy does not necessarily involve the destruction of the symbolic (the anarchist agenda), but involves the formation of more egalitarian types of symbolic order.

9 In providing imaginary and symbolic solutions to real contradictions, myth becomes ideology: 'ideology is not something which informs or invests symbolic production; rather the aesthetic act is itself ideological, and the production of aesthetic or narrative form is to be seen as an ideological act in its own right, with the function of inventing imaginary or formal "solutions" to unresolvable social contradictions' (Jameson 1981, 79). Lévi-Strauss's formulation (the imaginary resolution of real contradictions) constitutes the conceptual foundation of Fredric Jameson's important book *The Political Unconscious* (from where this quotation is taken).

10 In 'Structure and Form' (1976), his review and critique of Propp's *Morphology of the Folktale* (1968), Lévi-Strauss distinguished structure from form and criticized Propp for his formalism. However, we see in the following quotations that Lévi-Strauss continues to use the word 'form', as does Fredric Jameson. I return to this structure/form distinction in the final chapter.

11 'Today claims to the hegemony of one thesis over the other, to the primacy of alliance over descent or vice versa, of one school over the other, are a thing of the past' (Godelier 2011, 127).

12 Following Chomsky (1964), Umberto Eco (1976, 161; 1979, chapter 2) distinguishes between 'rule-governed' and 'rule-changing' creativity, in which the latter involves the invention of new codes and new rules of combination. He analyses metaphor as a form of 'rule-changing' creativity.

2

Film Theory, Film Analysis

The goal toward which all descriptive work strives is not the film as a real discourse (a series of images, sounds, and words arranged in a certain order, an object that may be attested), for the latter is already an achieved object before the analysis even begins. What a description hopes to establish is, rather, the system which organizes this realization: the structure of this text, and not the text itself. The system is nowhere clearly visible in the actual unwinding of the film: a system, as such, is never directly attested.

Christian Metz *Language and Cinema*, 73

Abstraction and analysis

'A film is difficult to explain because it is easy to understand', wrote Christian Metz in his first essay on film semiotics (1974a, 69). Analysis of narrative film is cursed for the reason Metz indicates: it is easy to understand because it appears to be self-evidently meaningful; comprehension is apparently immediate and spontaneous. What is there to explain when a phenomenon is instantly understood? Film analysis is in danger of remaining too close to this literal, experiential level of understanding, the basic level of narrative unfolding. The danger is that such analyses end up summarizing the direct content that preoccupies the analyst's attention: that which is pregiven or self-evident. We have already seen in Chapter 1 in regards to myth and kinship analysis that, for Lévi-Strauss, such analyses 'demonstrate the obvious and neglect the unknown' (1972, 37), the obvious being what Metz called 'the film as a real discourse', 'an achieved object before the analysis even begins'. Similarly, Fredric Jameson calls this type of analysis a 'basic error', for it simply 'rewrites the primary narratives *in terms of another narrative*, rather than in terms of a synchronic system' (1981, 122; emphasis in the original). By synchronic system, Jameson means the underlying system of codes that constitute the experience (the impression or illusion) that film is self-evidently meaningful. Going beyond simply understanding films to explaining them involves abstraction and analysis, the reduction of actual films to syntagmatic structures and paradigmatic systems. Abstraction filters out all but the essential elements of a phenomenon, its underlying invariant properties and laws. Analysis then takes apart those properties and laws, breaks them down into their constituent units.

This chapter provides a brief overview of previous film theories and methods based on structural semiotics, to determine their value in going beyond the film's linear surface level to analyse its virtual, abstract realm of codes, the underlying invariant properties and laws that govern the surface level. This chapter focuses on auteur structuralism, with passing reference to structuralist theories of genre, film semiotics, textual analysis, second wave feminist film theory and the concept of the film's diegesis.

But before the brief overview of these areas of film theory and analysis, it is worthwhile pointing out that the type of film analysis carried out using linguistics, semiotics and structural anthropology fundamentally reconceives a film from a theoretical viewpoint. However, this theoretical way of thinking does not involve a direct comparison between film to language and/or myth. Instead, it involves a more fundamental understanding of their relation to storytelling. What myth and contemporary storytelling share are 'elements [that] can be taken as universal forms of thought, experience, and imagination, of which mythic figures, like realistic images, are only a partial variation. It is not a direct influence or a return to archaic origins that updates and modernizes myth but a wide-ranging study of poetic perception' (Meletinsky 1998, 264–5). Myths are one early variant of the many genres of storytelling (legends, folktales, drama, narrative film etc.), each of which is formally, socially and historically specific; nonetheless, they all share the central core of story logic. 'Myths, folktales, fairytales', Robert Scholes argues, 'are the prototypes of all narrative, the ancestors and the models of later fictional developments. In studying the history of narrative, we find that in modern times forms have developed which elaborate and transform the basic constituents of primitive fiction almost beyond recognition' (Scholes 1974, 60–1). Nonetheless, despite these transformations (in which mythic time is replaced with calendar time, conflict between gods and humans is replaced with social and family conflicts, etc.) he goes on to argue that 'modern fictional forms have never lost touch with the primitive entirely and have frequently returned to their sources to draw upon the almost magical power they possess' (Scholes 1974, 61). And we saw in Chapter 1 that Jurij Lotman mapped the historical transformation of cyclical myth into linear plot.

Symbolic systems, including language, kinship, myth, narrative, literature and film, emerged as dominant objects of study in the twentieth century, especially in Russian formalism, Prague structuralism, French structuralism, narratology and semiotics. These disciplines attracted widespread attention in the 1960s, initially in Europe and later globally. As I mentioned in the Preface, rather than view these disciplines as intellectual fads that emerged in the 1960s and died out in the 1970s, this book instead places them within a substantially longer time frame of (predominately) Western intellectual history. Terence Hawkes traces structuralism back three hundred years, specifically to Giambattista Vico's *The New Science*, first published in 1725 (Hawkes 1977, chapter 1). Critics of semiotics and structuralism miss the significance of the place of these two disciplines within this enlarged time frame. Semiotics does not constitute a recent addition to Western thought, but has been progressively refined and transformed over hundreds of years, and continues to develop and deepen its insights (although now out of the spotlight).

Structural semiotics fundamentally challenged common assumptions about film authorship and filmic realism. Traditional auteur critics borrow from Romanticism the notion that the auteur is an individual whose free will, desires, beliefs and intentions consciously create a film's fictional storyworld. Auteur theory confers upon the individual primary status by focusing on direct expression, first-hand lived experience and aesthetic taste. Structural semiotics opposes Romanticism, particularly its solipsistic philosophy of the subject. A film's meaning is not the product of an individual's private consciousness freely creating. Nor is filmic meaning determined by film's recording capacity, its 'direct', 'naturalistic' referential relation to reality.

Instead, meaning was relocated within the filmic text itself, the result of taking a small system of pre-existing signs and following pre-existing rules of combination and transformation to manifest a new permutation of signs. Structural semiotics privileges the autonomous symbolic realm of language and signs, the level of signification, while downplaying individual subjectivity (expression) and reality as sources of meaning. Auteur structuralism redefines the status of director as auteur, by reducing the auteur to a specific structure that underlies and gives shape to their films.

Auteur structuralism

Auteur structuralism does not create a simulacrum of film's underlying codes in general (this is the task of film semiotics [Christian Metz 1974a; 1974b]), nor does it analyse films in isolation. Auteur structuralism begins with the group of films made by the same director and then attempts to reconstruct the specific system of codes they share. Identification of a consistent system confirms the status of the director as an auteur, whereas the lack of a consistent system demotes them to the status of a *metteur en scène*. Whereas 'director' is a pregiven industry category, 'auteur' is an abstract critical category that organizes and unifies a group of films around a single centre. Auteur structuralism defines this unity as abstract, not material or pregiven, and identifies it via rigorous methods of structural semiotics, especially paradigmatic analysis. Analysing the system of codes underlying an auteur's films is a controversial endeavour because such an abstract 'object' of analysis (the archi-film) is initially unknown or latent, and therefore sometimes requires considerable analytical work to model it, the results of which usually conflict with obvious, self-evident surface meanings. But this system of codes underlying an auteur's films is just one small fragment of the symbolic order, which consists of multiple systems of codes underlying culture. The specificity of a director's underlying system is a matter of the specific combination of codes.

The following overview of auteur structuralism examines the various theories in terms of the way they implement steps (1) to (5) of Lévi-Strauss's structural myth analysis (as discussed by J. Patrick Gray [1978] and outlined here in Chapter 1). The initial formation of auteur structuralism's object of study, the abstract archi-film, emerged in a short statement by Geoffrey Nowell-Smith in his book on Visconti, first published in 1967. Nowell-Smith focused on the identification of ultimate thematic constituents, stage (2) of myth analysis as outlined by Gray:

> The purpose of criticism becomes therefore to uncover behind the superficial contrasts of subject and treatment a structural hard core of basic and often recondite motifs. The pattern formed by these motifs, which may be stylistic or thematic, is what gives an author's work its particular structure, both defining it internally and distinguishing one body of work from another. (Nowell-Smith 1967, 10)

Nowell-Smith adopted the structural semiotic perspective by going beyond the superficial surface level of a film to examine the underlying structure of themes. Although he mentions that these structures can be either stylistic or thematic, in practice his book employs abstraction and analysis to extract a few thematic structures in Visconti's films, via stage (2) of myth analysis (identification of ultimate thematic constituents), plus stage (1), identification of a system of oppositions within those constituents – opera/real life, opera/pop music, decadence/progress, idealism/realism. The remainder of the book reads like a traditional auteur study. For example, this comment on *La Terra Trema* (1948) is typical: 'It is in the choice of concrete and immediate determinations that Visconti reveals most clearly his own artistic personality' (1967, 48). Nowell-Smith doubted the feasibility of carrying out a completely structural analysis of a director's work (1967, 12), ruling out stage (4), comparative analysis, which translates in auteur structuralism into the structural comparison of a director's films to discover the values embedded in their symbolic storyworld.

Alan Lovell's chapter-length thematic reading of Don Siegel followed in 1968. Like Nowell-Smith, Lovell also implemented stage (2), identification of ultimate thematic constituents, and stage (1), identification of a system of oppositions within those constituents, but was more optimistic than Nowell-Smith in implementing stage 4, comparative analysis, ending up with a list of Don Siegel's binary oppositions, comprising of: adventurer/society, crime/law, passion/control, anarchy/organization and violence/tranquillity (1975, 27).

For Lovell, structuralism offers a precise description of the films, in opposition to an evaluation. What stands out today in Lovell's reading is his clear-cut delineation of themes, rather than the structuralist methodology, which (as with Nowell-Smith) is used with a light touch.

Structuralism is more evident in Jim Kitses' *Horizons West*, a study of three directors of the Western – Anthony Mann, Budd Boetticher and Sam Peckinpah (Kitses 1969). In this book-length study Kitses has space to delineate the structural themes and binary oppositions (stages 1 and 2) of the Western genre and a director's manipulation of those themes and oppositions across their oeuvre (stage 4): 'The form [of the Western] can provide a director with a range of possible connections and the space in which to experiment, to shape and refine the kind of effects and meaning he is working towards' (1969, 26). Here we see Kitses adopting the structuralist focus on the possible messages (the 'range of possible connections') that can be generated from the complete system of the Western's genre codes. He also defined the Western in terms of a series of oppositions operating at different levels: firstly, the master opposition wilderness/civilization, under which are listed the secondary oppositions individual/community, nature/culture and the West/East, which in turn are supplemented with a third level of more local oppositions (1969, 11). Kitses employed the structural framework to demonstrate that a director must constantly work with and against pre-existing genre conventions, themes and structures. In Anthony Mann's Westerns *The Naked Spur* (1952), *The Last Frontier* (1955) and *Man of the West* (1958), for example, Kitses identified a dynamic interplay between individual and community – a rather general trait of the Western, which nonetheless enabled Mann 'to return time and again to the strange neo-classic conflict of passion and duty that was always to preoccupy him'. Furthermore, 'Mann was never to resolve the tension' (1969, 33). In addition, the landscape of the Western, another general trait, offered Mann 'an unparalleled opportunity to explore through the dialectic of landscape and hero the interior and finally *metaphysical* conflict of his characters' (1969, 33; emphasis in the original). The chapter on Mann investigates in some detail the hero, the villain, the community and the landscape. Kitses's aim of listing the genre's binary oppositions in the book's opening chapter is not simply to spot them in a director's films, but to employ them to investigate how each director works and experiments with those oppositions, to see what opposition he or she combines in their films, to determine what side of the opposition is emphasized, and to determine whether the tension within the oppositions are resolved. Kitses demonstrated how detailed and complex a binary analysis can become, and how such an analysis can be used to delineate in precise terms a director's specific manipulation of themes, structures and genre conventions.

From 1967 to 1969 Nowell-Smith, Lovell and Kitses represented a transitional period for auteur structuralism, where structuralism was tentatively introduced into film studies. Auteur structuralism achieved a fuller statement in Peter Wollen's chapter on auteur theory in *Signs and Meaning in the Cinema* (1969; 1972), a canonical work that shaped film studies, as I pointed out in the Preface. Wollen's book begins with a chapter discussing the work of Eisenstein, followed by the chapter on auteur structuralism and ends on a chapter on film semiology (although it primarily applies the semiotics of C. S. Peirce to the film image). In the Postscript to the 1972 edition, Wollen argued that

> by a process of comparison with other films, it is possible to decipher, not a coherent message or world-view, but a structure which underlies the film and shapes it, gives it a certain pattern of energy cathexis. *It is this structure which auteur analysis disengages from the film.* (1972, 167; emphasis added)

Wollen's auteur chapter is programmatic: it only applied structural analysis informally and schematically to the comedies and dramas of Howard Hawks, but more rigorously to the Westerns of John Ford.

Wollen's structural analysis of Ford's Westerns implements stages (1), (2) and (4). In terms of (1) and (2), the identification of thematic units and their organization into binary oppositions, Wollen notes that 'The most relevant are garden versus wilderness, ploughshare versus sabre, settler versus nomad, European versus Indian, civilised versus savage, book versus gun, married versus unmarried, East versus West' (1972, 94). 'Wilderness versus garden' is, according to Wollen, the 'master antinomy in Ford's films' (1972, 96) – and, in fact, one of the master antinomies of American culture, structuring its founding myth. A second related antinomy is between nomad (living in the wilderness) and settler (in the cultivated garden) (1972, 97). Both pairs feed into the quest for the Promised Land, a major theme in Ford's films. In terms of heroes who rule in his new land, Wollen divides them into another binary opposition: rational legal authority versus charismatic authority. Wollen therefore identified three binary oppositions dominant in Ford: wilderness/garden, nomad/settler and rational legal authority/charismatic authority. He gave three examples, focusing on the heroes in *The Searchers* (1956), *The Man Who Shot Liberty Valence* (1962) and *My Darling Clementine* (1946). Like Nowell-Smith, Lovell and Kitses, Wollen's method is dominated by stages (1), (2) and (4), although his chapter is distinctive in the level of clarity and detail he achieves in elucidating John Ford's symbolic storyworld from a structuralist perspective.

Stage 3 of myth analysis, paradigmatic organization of constituent units, is rarely implemented in film studies. But a few examples exist. In 'Paradigmatic Structures in *Young Mr Lincoln*', Richard Abel employed stages 1, 2 and 3 of myth analysis. He engaged with two previous analyses of John Ford's *Young Mr. Lincoln* (1939) – by the editors of *Cahiers du cinéma* (1972) and by Bill Nichols (1975) – in order to isolate paradigmatic structures in the film, in particular 'the recurrence in the narrative of specific paired sequences and the position/movement of the Lincoln figure within the frame in these and related sequences' (1978, 20). Abel argued that the recurrence of these paired sequences 'acts as a structural paradigm for the moralizing discourse of the film' (1978, 20).

The film's opening scene depicts the young Lincoln delivering an election speech. But the outcome of the election is not shown; instead, it is followed by a scene where Lincoln takes law books from the Clay family as payment for farm supplies. Abel notes that, in their famous analysis of the film, the editors of *Cahiers du cinéma* argue that the two scenes mark the film's main theme, the repression of politics by morality. For Abel, this particular juxtaposition is repeated twice (with variation) at significant moments in the film: when Lincoln addresses the lynch mob outside the jail (after the arrest of the two Clay brothers), followed by a scene where he talks to the Clay family; and towards the end of the film, after he wins the court case defending the Clay brothers, he stands outside the courthouse in front of a crowd, which is followed by a final visit to the Clay family.

Abel not only focuses on the repetition of juxtaposed narrative events (Lincoln standing on a porch addressing a crowd/talking to the Clay family), but also the repetition of film style: for example, in the three porch scenes, Lincoln is filmed with a low camera angle and in high contrast light (1978, 20–1). But there is also progression within these paradigmatic repetitions: Lincoln's lame political speech in scene 1 is transformed into a powerful speech outside the jail; and outside the courtroom he does not need to speak at all, for he has already attained mythical status (1978, 22–3). Although limited to one film, Abel's analysis is notable for presenting a paradigmatic analysis together with the structural study stylistic repetitions.

Beverle Houston and Marsha Kinder carried out a detailed comparative paradigmatic analysis of director Nicholas Roeg in chapter 6 of *Self and Cinema: A Transformalist Perspective* (1980). In the first half of the chapter (1980, 345–74) they analysed four films (*Performance* [1970], *Walkabout* [1971], *Don't Look Now* [1973] and *The Man Who Fell to Earth* [1976]) by identifying the ultimate constituents or units of meaning they all share (stage 2) and organizing them into paradigms across the four films (stage 4). For example, one of the many units of meaning they identify in all four films is: 'the visitor's main goal is to save self or family' (1980, 350):

Unit of meaning:

Visitor's main goal is to save self or family

Performance:

Self (Chas tries to save himself)

Walkabout:

Themselves (the two children abandoned in the desert attempt to save themselves)

Don't Look Now:

Family, including themselves

The Man Who Fell to Earth:

Tommy Newton tries to save his family, his planet, and himself.

Houston and Kinder also organize the units of meaning into binary oppositions (stage 1). They identify: confrontation between insiders/outsiders, life/death and advanced culture/primitive culture, oppositions that map onto each other:

> Insiders-Life-Advanced culture / Outsiders-Death-Primitive culture

In Roeg's films, Houston and Kinder argue, 'advanced culture' represents 'life' and 'insiders'. Yet, although advanced culture dominates and survives, it nonetheless wastes its resources: for example, the criminal world of *Performance*, the city in *Walkabout*, England in *Don't Look Now* and Earth in *The Man Who Fell to Earth* (1980, 366). In contrast, 'primitive culture' represents 'death' and 'outsiders'. Primitive culture is arid and declining, but has a greater potential for life: for example, the Chelsea underworld in *Performance*, the outback in *Walkabout*, the underworld in *Don't Look Now* and Newton's home planet in *The Man Who Fell to Earth* (1980, 366).

Finally, Houston and Kinder call these four films variations of the same Nicholas Roeg myth, and begin to map the transformational relations between the films: 'In several ways, *Walkabout* is a complete inversion of *Performance*, offering the most pessimistic version of the myth, where failure occurs in both worlds and in all aspects of the encounter for both visitors and hosts' (1980, 370). The failure occurring in both worlds refers to the inability of the children (the visitors) in *Walkabout* from the so-called advanced world to adapt to the desert, and the failure of the Aborigine boy's walkabout. In addition, '*The Man Who Fell to Earth* offers a complex inversion of both *Performance* (the visitor [Tommy Newton] declines rather than grows, rejects and is rejected by the extended group in the new world, and longs for his family back home) and of *Walkabout* (reversing the role of visitors and hosts while retaining the pessimism and political focus)' (1980, 371). Houston and Kinder developed one of the most detailed paradigmatic analyses of an auteur's work to date.

Structural theories of genre

Structuralism not only transformed auteur theory. It also changed the nature of genre study:

> Following Lévi-Strauss, a growing number of critics throughout the seventies dwelled on the mythical qualities of Hollywood genres and thus

on the audience's ritual relationship to genre film. [...] Far from being limited to mere entertainment, filmgoing offers a satisfaction more akin to that associated with established religion. Most openly championed by John Cawelti, this ritual approach appears as well in books by Leo Braudy, Frank McConnell, Michael Wood, Will Wright, and Tom Schatz. (Altman 1984, 8–9)

Altman distinguishes between a semantic and a syntactic approach to genre: whereas the semantic approach 'stresses the genre's building blocks', the syntactic view 'privileges the structures into which they are arranged' (1984, 10). Both approaches complement each other in the same way that auteur structuralism combines thematic (semantic) and structural (syntactic) analysis. Furthermore, like the auteur's films, genre films are conceived as social forms that address and resolve real contradictions on imaginary and symbolic levels.

From the perspective of structural semiotics, 'auteur' and 'genre' are not opposed to each other but are systems of codes operating at different textual levels: 'genre-structure and author-structure were seen as concepts of a different order existing side by side' (Willemen 1980, 2). We have already seen that Kitses developed a hybrid auteur-genre study (auteurs of the Western) via structuralism (1969). Will Wright's *Six Guns and Society* (1975) presented a more rigorous structural analysis of the Western genre. Inspired by Lévi-Strauss, Wright identified four basic binary oppositions at work in Westerns: inside society/outside society; good/bad; strong/weak; and wilderness/civilization (1975, 49). But Wright also followed Vladimir Propp (1968) and privileged plot functions, or narrative sequences (the syntagmatic axis), rather than the paradigmatic axis. He identified four plot types: the classical plot, the revenge variation, the transition theme and the professional plot. His method of analysis combines the study of binary oppositions and plot functions, and he criticized Lévi-Strauss for ignoring the syntagmatic dimension of myths and storytelling.

Textual semiotics

Textual analysis is premised on semiotic theory, although it is applied to shots and scenes, not to the structure of themes. As such, this type of work is marginal to this study of Wes Anderson. We will just note in passing that, in 'Problems of Denotation in the Fiction Film' (1974a, 108–46), Metz employed the structural linguistic method of segmentation and classification to identify a paradigm of syntagmas from which a filmmaker can choose to represent profilmic events in a particular sequence. Each syntagma is identifiable by the specific way it structures the spatio-temporal relations between the profilmic events it depicts. Metz detected eight different spatio-temporal relationships in total, which constitute eight different forms of image ordering (*syntagmas*). Metz called the resulting 'paradigm of syntagmas' the *grande syntagmatique* of the image track. These image syntagmas form a paradigm to the extent that they offer eight different ways of constructing an image sequence. 'Problems of Denotation in the Fiction Film' successfully identified an autonomous level of meaning in the cinema (syntagmas) and constructs a paradigm.

Raymond Bellour's textual analyses are more nuanced than Metz's *grande syntagmatique* because he worked at the level of the shot – or, more accurately, the structural relations between shots. Just as the structuralist analyses oppositions and differences in various symbolic systems, so Bellour analysed the oppositions and differences between shots (rather than focus on the shots themselves). Shots signify via their structural differences to other shots, rather than in terms of their intrinsic qualities. In his analysis of the Bodega Bay sequence from *The Birds* (Hitchcock 1963), Bellour analysed the way successive shots differ in relation to three binary oppositions: close/distant framing; seer/seen; and male/female (2000, 28–67). The progression from shot to shot in this sequence is not random or haphazard, but is systematically structured around these oppositions. Bellour analysed the systematic structure of oppositions (plus repetition and alternation) in other key films and sequences, including *The Lonedale Operator* (D. W. Griffith 1911), *The Big Sleep* (Hawks 1946) and *North by Northwest* (Hitchcock 1959) (Bellour 2000).

Second wave feminist film theory

Structuralism and semiotics opened up the possibility of understanding the way images work as signs and symptoms, patterns of rhetoric, narrative and narration. A previously invisible world whose images, sensations and inklings had previously evaded one's grasp materialised with the language that could name its objects, like the appearance of invisible ink in front of a flame. (Laura Mulvey 1989, xiii)

The sociological 'image-of-women' approach to film analysis is based on the naïve reflectionist theory, which states that reality can be fully present in the photographic image, and that the depiction of reality is often distorted, leading to biased images. But this theory is based on the false assumption that abstract categories such as gender identity are fixed entities simply waiting to be represented, and that representation can potentially offer a full, accurate image of gender. The second wave feminist film theorists – including Laura Mulvey and Elizabeth Cowie, among others – challenged these false assumptions:

> The work of film is not […] the simple representation of an already constituted meaning or content. As a consequence, therefore, it must be involved in producing meanings, and hence in producing specific definitions of women. […] 'Woman' is not given, biologically or psychologically, but is a category produced by signifying practices. (Cowie 1997, 19; 25)

The sociological 'images' approach is empirical in its rejection of abstract levels of meaning. It valorizes immediately observable content and meaning as external, pregiven and stable. It ignores film's underlying abstract system of codes, and fails to analyse in depth abstract elements such as the film's overall patriarchal narrative structure – which, like all structures, is not immediately given in experience, and cannot be reduced to experience.

Building upon structuralism, semiotics and psychoanalysis, second wave feminists developed a critique of the image and the reflectionist approach to representation by conceptualizing the film as text or specific signifying practice, which examines film's production of meaning rather than simple reproduction of it. They took from semiotics the notion that meaning emerges out of non-meaning, from the selection and combination of codes on the level of the filmic text. Like Metz and other film semioticians, they advocated the need to identify and analyse those meanings generated specifically in the filmic text: 'Playing on the tension between film as controlling the dimension of time (editing, narrative) and film as controlling the dimension of space (changes in distance, editing), cinematic codes create a gaze, a world, and an object, thereby producing an illusion cut to the measure of desire' (Mulvey 1989, 25). Here we are far from the images approach to film, for Mulvey is theorizing cinema's specific *creation* of a gaze, a world and an object, not its simple reproduction.

Diegesis and film worlds

The term 'diegesis' is traditionally used in film studies to designate the film world/universe – the spatio-temporal parameters within which a story (actions, events and characters) unfolds. Diegesis is broader than story; the diegesis is the place where a story develops. Étienne Souriau introduced 'diegesis' into film studies in his article 'La structure de l'univers filmique et le vocabulaire de la filmologie' ('The Structure of the Filmic Universe and the Vocabulary of Filmology') (1951).[1] The diegesis forms just one of seven levels of the filmic universe:

1. Afilmic reality (the reality that exists independently of filmic reality)
2. Profilmic reality (the reality photographed by the camera)
3. Filmographic reality (the film as physical object, structured by techniques such as editing)
4. Screenic (or filmophanic) reality (the film as projected on a screen)
5. Diegetic reality (the film's fictional storyworld)
6. Spectatorial reality (the spectator's perception and comprehension of a film)
7. Creational reality (the filmmaker's intentions)

The afilmic exists outside the realm of the cinema, whereas the profilmic exists inside the realm of the cinema. However, both these levels are then defined as existing outside the filmic text. Whereas the afilmic and profilmic are extra textual, the following three types of filmic reality are textual: the filmographic contains the screenic, and the screenic contains the diegesis. The final two levels of filmic reality are cognitive, referring to the spectator's comprehension of film, and the film as conceived by the filmmaker. For Souriau, the diegetic is inferred from the filmophanic; only part of the diegesis is seen on screen, for the rest is presupposed. Anne Souriau significantly developed this idea further, as Eleftheria Thanouli points out: for Anne Souriau, 'the diegesis […] is a potential existence (*existence en puissance*) compared to the actual work (*existence en acte*)' (2014, 134). Anne Souriau concluded that multiple films can embody the same diegesis, demonstrating that she was working towards a concept of shared storyworld (with an emphasis on 'world', rather than the unfolding 'story').

In *Film Worlds* (2015), Dan Yacavone developed the philosophical significance of the storyworld for film studies. Yacavone distinguishes artistic worlds from fictional storyworlds: 'It is vital and necessary to distinguish between the more or less skillfully constructed fictional storyworlds present within narrative films and the larger, multi-dimensional, and aesthetically realized worlds of films as artworks' (2015, 4). By fictional storyworlds, Yacavone means the spatial and temporal dimensions of a film's narrative and, beyond narrative, to the semantic domain of represented objects as abstracted from a film or group of films. By films as artworks, he means that these fictional storyworlds are placed within a larger context that takes into account film 'form, style, and creativity' (86) together with 'a film's perceptual and affective experience' (186). In other words, Yacavone's notion of film as artwork focuses on the phenomenological surface level of film as well as its underlying storyworld.

Film style

In his book on Visconti, Nowell-Smith had already highlighted the danger of ignoring style in the structural approach to auteurism: 'The structural approach […] brings with it, however, problems of its own [such as the neglect of] the importance of the non-thematic subject-matter and of sub-stylistic features of the visual treatment' (1967, 10–12). In his review of Wollen's book, Sam Rohdie also mentioned that film style should be incorporated into a deep thematic study, otherwise one ignores film's specificity: 'There is nothing in Wollen's argument specific to the medium of the movies or the way in which Ford and Hawks handle that medium. […] If structuralism is the key to cinematic understanding it needs to be used on various levels specific to the medium' (1969, 68–9). In the above survey, we saw that Metz, Bellour and especially Mulvey privileged the structural analysis of film style. Wollen also acknowledged that a structural analysis limited to underlying themes risks reductionism: reducing myths, fairy tales and American movies down to the same basic elements. He therefore recognized that films need to be studied 'not only in their universality (what they all have in common), but also in their singularity (what differentiates them from each other)' (1972, 93). The analysis of a film's singularity must incorporate a film's style. In the final ten pages of his chapter on the auteur theory (which are usually excised when the essay is anthologized), Wollen reflects on his methods by charting the distinction between composition and performance in music, painting and theatre. Whereas composition is coded or digital communication, consisting of discrete units, performance is graded on a continuous, analogue scale. I return to Wollen's discussion of film style at the end of this book, where I briefly enumerate the characteristic stylistic traits of Wes Anderson's films.

Note

1 Eleftheria Thanouli points out that the use of the term 'diegesis' in film studies is attributable to Anne Souriau, Etienne Souriau's daughter, a member of his research group in aesthetics at the Institute of Filmology at the University of Paris: 'Etienne Souriau acknowledges the contribution of his students to his vocabulary of filmology, without specifying his daughter's input (Souriau 1951, 231). However, when Anne Souriau wrote the "diegesis" entry for the *Vocabulaire d'esthétique*, a collective volume initially edited by Etienne Souriau and completed posthumously by herself, she claims full rights for the coinage of the term' (Thanouli 2014, 134).

Part Two

The Films

3

Unintentional Mediation: *Bottle Rocket*

The main aim of the following analyses is to reduce a film, conceived as a syntagmatic message, down to an underlying system of paradigms. Analysis of a paradigmatic bundle gradually works towards the abstraction and isolation of symbolic meanings within the bundle. The major paradigms in *Bottle Rocket* (1996) include the planning, the enactment and the celebration of the robberies. Additional significant structures in the film include a circuit of exchange and gift-giving, mediation and binary oppositions.

Plot synopsis

(1) Anthony Adams (Luke Wilson) leaves a voluntary sanitarium in Arizona. His friend Dignan (Owen Wilson) helps him 'escape'. Anthony indulges Dignan by pretending to escape (he climbs out of his hospital window using knotted sheets). (2) On the bus, Dignan presents Anthony with a 75-year plan of their future, including practice and real robberies. He briefly mentions Mr Henry (a professional thief). (3) Anthony and Dignan, now outside, continue to talk about their future. (4) Practice robbery at Anthony's home. (5) In a drug store, Anthony and Dignan celebrate their practice robbery. Dignan reveals he stole some earrings with the intention of selling them. Anthony storms out. (6) Outside, Anthony says he bought the earrings for his mother's birthday (indirectly revealing that, for practice, they robbed the house of Anthony's parents). (7) Anthony meets his much younger sister Grace at school. Anthony asks her to return the earrings. She perceives Anthony as a failure and expresses her dislike for Dignan. Bob Mapplethorpe (Robert Musgrave) is introduced as another friend of Dignan's. (8) Anthony, Dignan and Bob in Bob's car. Anthony is upset with his sister, and Bob mentions his problematic relation with his brother, Jonathan/

Future Man (Andrew Wilson). (9) At Bob's house. Bob and his brother fight; Anthony and Dignan sit by the pool. Anthony talks of his former girlfriend Elizabeth (they broke up during an argument over water sports; Anthony then went to the sanitarium in the desert). (10) Gun practice. The 'team' (Anthony, Dignan and Bob) tries out and then buys some guns. (11) Dignan explains to Anthony and Bob his plan to rob a bookstore. His mania to be in control and plan every detail creates tensions within the team. (12) Bookstore robbery. (13) The team celebrates the robbery. Anthony discovers that Mr Henry runs a landscaping company. (14) Road trip: Anthony then finds out that Mr Henry fired Dignan. (15) The team buys fireworks and pulls into a motel. (16) At the motel, Anthony dives into the pool. When he emerges, he sees housekeeper Inez (Lumi Cavazos). (17) Bob and Dignan go to the barbershop. Bob discovers his brother, Future Man, has been arrested. (18) At the same time, Anthony follows Inez around the hotel. Inez allows Anthony to keep a photo of his sister. (19) The team discusses what to do about Future Man. (20) Inez and Anthony meet in the swimming pool. (21) Inez and Anthony depart (but a false departure, since they meet again the next day). Anthony gives his watch to Inez. (22) Bob leaves with the car, leaving Dignan and Anthony stranded at the motel. (23) Inez and Anthony make love. (24) Inez and Anthony invite Dignan to a bar, because he looks forlorn and is firing fireworks into the ground. However, in the bar Dignan is beaten up. (25) Anthony asks Inez to leave with him, but she refuses because she is unable to be so spontaneous. Another hotel worker, Rocky (Donny Caicedo), translates, but creates a misunderstanding, by suggesting that Inez does not love Anthony. (26) Dignan and Anthony leave the motel. Anthony gives Inez a letter from Anthony. Translating for Inez, Rocky says to Dignan 'Tell Anthony I love him.' Dignan misunderstands, thinking that Rocky loves Anthony. (27) Dignan steals a car and drives back home with Anthony. But the car breaks down, and Dignan punches Anthony after realizing he gave all of their money to Inez. They go their separate ways. (28) Anthony and Bob are seen working various small time jobs. Anthony writes a letter to his sister Grace. (29) After several months, Dignan and Anthony meet up again. (30) Anthony meets Mr Henry (James Caan), his business partner Bowboat (Takayuki Kubota) and Applejack (Jim Ponds). (31) Anthony eventually joins Dignan's team (out of pity). (32) Dignan and Bob meet up again, and Bob joins Dignan's team (but only after Bob punches

Dignan). (33) Dignan's team meets up with Mr Henry's team at the country club, including safecracker Kumar (Kumar Pallana). Future Man sees the group and makes fun of his brother. Mr Henry, in turn, insults Future Man. (34) Anthony and Dignan stakeout Hinckley Cold Storage. Dignan finally passes on Inez's message of love to Anthony. (35) Anthony phones Inez and rekindles their relationship. (36) The robbery of Hinckley ice storage quickly disintegrates and Dignan is arrested. (37) Mr Henry robs Bob's house and takes all the valuables. (38) Anthony and Bob visit Dignan in prison. They exchange gifts. When they depart, Dignan pretends to escape.

The opening scene of *Bottle Rocket* manifests a distinct hierarchal structure. It begins by quickly establishing a strong bond of friendship between the two characters, Anthony and Dignan. However, it is not a friendship between equals, because there is a clear hierarchy between them. Dignan is positioned as the subordinate: he is incompetent, insensitive and continually misunderstands the situations he finds himself in, but Anthony is benevolent and protective towards him. Dignan is dependent on Anthony, which means Anthony is dominant and holds the power in their relationship, but he disavowals his power and pretends to delegate it to Dignan. Dignan is a fictional character whose personality traits – excessive planning, hyperactivity and nervous behaviour – closely follow the textbook case of someone suffering from manic disorder. We see this in the opening scene: Anthony's 'escape' from the sanitarium is unnecessary. But because Dignan planned it, Anthony decides to carry it out. This opening scene sets a pattern for the remainder of the film, in which Dignan plans a series of robberies, prefaced with scenes of excessive planning and are followed by scenes of celebration.

Paradigms

Planning paradigm

(2) Dignan presents Anthony with a 75-year plan, including a series of robberies.

(11) Dignan explains to Anthony and Bob his plan to rob a bookstore.
(34) Anthony and Dignan stakeout Hinckley Cold Storage.

In line with his manic disorder, Dignan devotes a disproportionate amount of time preparing the robberies. The practice one (4) forms part of his 75-year plan that he spells out to Anthony on the bus (2). Only Dignan and Anthony take part in the robbery; direct reciprocation therefore exists between them: Dignan is in charge because he planned it and Anthony followed the plan. However, we soon realize that Anthony was really in charge, since it is his house, and he instructed Dignan not to steal valuables. Dignan then violated the law of reciprocation between the two of them by stealing the earrings, which explains why Anthony becomes angry with him. In the second robbery (12), three members take part. At the planning stage (11), Dignan is required to negotiate with the two other members. Anthony again hands over power to Dignan, although Bob is more reluctant. Dignan exaggerates the risks involved in robbing a bookshop, and overreacts to the inattention Bob (and Anthony) pays to his plans. He is only able to maintain group dynamics through an appeal to emotions rather than through the soundness of his plans. The Hinckley robbery (36) is also planned excessively; it involves a prolonged stakeout, although we only witness the final stage (34). This robbery also involves two additional members, Applejack and Kumar (both of whom are associates of Mr Henry). The third robbery therefore involves five members, a group too large for Dignan to manage. Despite the excessive planning, this group quickly falls apart and the robbery is unsuccessful. The result of this third robbery is that Dignan is caught and jailed. In prison, he pretends to enact an escape plan (discussed below).

Robberies paradigm

(4) Practice robbery at Anthony's home.
(12) Bookstore robbery.
(36) The robbery of Hinckley ice storage.
(37) Mr Henry robs Bob's house.

Table 3.1 The four robberies in *Bottle Rocket*

	Actual (+)/Practice (−)	Successful (+)/Unsuccessful (−)	External (+)/Internal(−)
1	−	+	−
2	+	+	+
3	+	−	+
4	+	+	−

The main repeated action, the kernel of the film, consists of four robberies, which can be explored by bundling them together into a paradigm. The four units in this paradigm are structured according to a series of values organized into binary oppositions: practice/real; successful/unsuccessful; external (to Dignan's team)/internal (see Table 3.1).

The first one, of Anthony's parents (4), is a practice robbery, is successful (with one flaw), and is internal. The second, the bookshop (12), is actual, successful, and external. The third and fourth take place at the same time: the third (Hinckley cold storage, 36) is actual, unsuccessful, and external, while the fourth (Bob's house, 37) is actual, successful, and internal (it is carried out by Mr Henry, who embodies some characteristics of the trickster).

Multiple permutations and relations exist among these four robberies. Robberies 1 and 4 are similar to the extent that they are successful and internal – committed against the team. But 1 is a practice robbery, while 4 is actual; in 1 none of the valuables are (or should) be taken; in 4 all the valuables are taken. Robberies 2 and 3 are two actual robberies Dignan plans. One is successful, the other unsuccessful. Robberies 2 and 4 are actual and successful robberies, although 2 is external (and is planned by Dignan) while 4 is internal (and is planned by Mr Henry). Robberies 1 and 2 are contrasted the most: although both are successful, 1 is only a practice while 2 is actual, and 1 is internal while 2 is external. Other permutations are not manifest in the film. For example, there is no unsuccessful practice robbery (whether internal or external), and no actual robbery that is both unsuccessful and internal.

Celebration of robberies paradigm

(5) In a drug store, Anthony and Dignan celebrate their practice robbery.

(13) The team celebrates the bookstore robbery.
(38) Anthony and Bob visit Dignan in prison.

The first celebration, in the drug store (5), is excessively positive, as indicated in Dignan's dialogue with Anthony: 'Real fast, man. And good intensity. […] By the way, great job in there. It was nice working with you.' These positive statements give Dignan an air of self-importance for what was a menial job, revealing a mismatch between his actions and his grandiose assessment of those actions. However, this positivity comes to an end with a sudden negative note: Anthony gets angry with Dignan for stealing his mother's earrings with the intention of selling them. The second celebration (13) repeats this pattern: it is also excessively positive and also ends on a sudden negative note: Anthony discovers that Mr Henry merely runs a gardening company. The third 'celebration' is the inverse: there is no celebration because Dignan is arrested and jailed. However, this negativity is reversed when Anthony and Bob visit him in jail (38). Dignan still feels pleased ('We did it though, didn't we?'). The celebrations of Dignan's team are structured identically, with a value inverted towards the end. In the first and second celebrations, positivity is inverted into negativity. In the third, these values are themselves inverted, from negativity to positivity. The fourth robbery is planned and carried out by Mr Henry, not Dignan's team. (We do not see Mr Henry plan the robbery, and his celebration is muted: he stands by the roadside smoking a cigar while a removal truck is loaded up with the contents of Bob's house.)

Even when jailed, Dignan continues to misunderstand the situations he finds himself in. He still judges the Hinckley robbery to be a success and, when he discovers that his idol, Mr Henry, robbed Bob's house, he says (to Anthony and Bob) that he thought about robbing the place himself, thereby aligning himself with Mr Henry. Soon afterwards, he feels no anger against Mr Henry, even though Mr Henry simply saw Dignan's robbery of Hinckley as an opportunity to rob Bob's house. Nonetheless, Dignan shows some awareness of his own situation in the film's final moments. He suddenly springs upon Anthony and Bob a plan to escape from jail. They look confused and bewildered as Dignan explains the plan, until his smile suggests he is simply joking. This final scene is the opposite of the opening: Anthony pretending to escape from the sanitarium

(1) is answered by Dignan's pretence in planning an escape from jail (38). More specifically, the relation between (1) and (38) is coded via two binary oppositions:

Voluntary/involuntary

Real/pretend.

Anthony voluntarily entered the sanitarium, but really carried out a pretend escape, while Dignan is jailed involuntarily and pretends to carry out a real escape. The real/pretend opposition is therefore used twice, in that Anthony's pretend escape is really carried out, while Dignan's real escape is only pretence. In other words, Dignan is now 'in' on the pretence – he understands the need for pretence and humour to maintain team dynamics.

Gifts and exchange

Dignan steals the earrings of Dignan's mother during their practice robbery (4). In doing so, he stepped outside the practice (he violated a rule that Anthony had established). But, more fundamentally, he violated the act of gift-giving. The earrings were a gift (a symbol of exchange) between Anthony and his mother. Dignan undermines that relationship. However, this negative form of exchange has a positive counterpart. Although Anthony indulges Dignan selflessly, suffering his mania and transgressions, Anthony does indirectly receive something (or someone) from him in return: Inez. The solidarity between Anthony and Dignan is secured through Dignan providing a partner for Anthony. (The network of symbolic exchanges between Dignan, Anthony and Inez is outlined in more detail in the next section.)

Exchange and gift-giving dominate the developing relationship between Anthony and Inez. Soon after meeting Inez, Anthony looks at and then appropriates a photograph from her locket (18); Inez reluctantly agrees to give it to him – reluctant because it is a photo of her younger sister, not her. Anthony decides to keep it anyway – which confers upon his action the barest hint of sororal polygyny.[1] On their first departure, Anthony reciprocates the gift-giving, by giving Inez his watch. This symbolic exchange becomes 'real' the next day when Anthony and Inez have sex in one of the hotel rooms. In their second departure, Anthony gives Inez (via Dignan) an envelope of cash (a form of bridewealth). In the final scene (38), Dignan receives a food package from Anthony and Bob and, in return, he gives them belt buckles, gifts he made in jail. Although Inez is not present in this final scene, Anthony implies that he and Inez are now a couple, and mentions that Inez will bring a gift package for Dignan on the next visit.

Dignan as (unintentional) mediator

In Oedipal terms, the narrative of *Bottle Rocket* moves from Anthony's pre-Oedipal relation with his mother to a mediation of his desire through the Symbolic/the Oedipus complex, signified via a replacement of his mother for a 'substitute', Inez. Dignan is the mediator: he disrupts Anthony's over-attachment to his mother and guides him towards Inez. More specifically, Dignan's role as mediator involves several stages:

(i) *Anthony's mother (earrings)–Dignan–Anthony.* As we saw earlier, Dignan steals the earrings of Anthony's mother. This upsets Anthony to such an extent that he walks away from Dignan and momentarily stops 'indulging' him (stops pretending). Anthony mentions that he bought the earrings as a birthday present (a gift) for his mother. The earrings symbolize Anthony's connection to his (absent) mother (she is never seen in the film). Dignan has disrupted this link.

(ii) *Anthony–Dignan–Grace.* Because of Dignan's violation of the rules of the practice robbery, Anthony visits his sister Grace at school and asks her to return the earrings to their mother's jewellery box. Although they have not met for months, this seems to be the only reason Anthony goes to meet his sister. Grace expresses her dislike for Anthony's friends, especially Dignan.

(iii) *Anthony–Dignan–Inez.* Dignan chooses the motel where his team will hang out after the bookshop robbery. It is at this motel that Anthony meets Inez. When leaving the motel, Dignan passes Anthony's envelope of money to Inez but does not immediately pass on the message of love from Inez to Anthony (due to his misunderstanding of Rocky's role as translator – Dignan misunderstands his own role as mediator). When Dignan finds out that Anthony gave Inez all of their money – after the car breaks down (27) – Dignan reacts to Anthony the same way that Anthony reacted to Dignan when he stole the earrings (6) – Dignan steps out of his role as team leader and becomes upset and angry. Actions (6) and (27) therefore repeat the same emotional reaction between the same two characters, but it is inverted in (27) because it is now Dignan who is angry (and ends up punching Anthony). They then go their separate ways and do not meet up again for several months. When Anthony and Dignan reignite their friendship, Dignan finally (and unintentionally) passes on Inez's message of love to Anthony (by remarking that Rocky said he loved Anthony).

Anthony's recognition that Inez loves him generates the opposite response to Dignan stealing the earrings: Anthony becomes excessively happy (35). Symbolically, this message is the direct reply to the stealing of the earrings:

(6) Stealing of earrings / (34) Message of love from Inez

(+Anthony's reaction [7]) (+Anthony's reaction [35])

However, it is significant that Inez initially uttered the message to Dignan when he gave her the envelope of money. This exchange of money therefore creates a three-way indirect circuit of reciprocity:

(6) Stealing of earrings / (26) Exchange of money / (34) Message of love from Inez

(+Anthony's reaction [7]) (+Dignan's reaction [27]) (+Anthony's reaction [35])

The first two actions, (6) and (26), are symbolically equivalent and elicit a similar reaction: Anthony regards Dignan's stealing of his mother's earrings to be a transgression and reacts negatively; Dignan regards Anthony's gift of money to Inez to be a transgression and reacts negatively. Dignan's stealing of the earrings angers Anthony because it disrupts his relation to his mother. Anthony's gift to Inez angers Dignan because he sees it as a threat to his and Anthony's friendship. The symbolic meaning of the actions and the emotional reactions to those actions are therefore the same, but the source of the reaction is inverted: Anthony/Dignan. The third action (34) is the opposite to the first (6): while the stealing of his mother's earrings angers Anthony because it disrupts the filial bond between him and his mother, Inez's message of love obviously delights Anthony because it creates an alliance between him and Inez. Anthony's negative reaction to the first action is balanced out by his positive reaction to the third action. As pointed out above, the opposition between (6) and (34) can be read as an Oedipal transformation.

Dignan's role is instrumental in each of the three actions: he steals the earrings from Anthony's mother; he gives to Inez the envelope of money from Anthony; he passes on Inez's message of love to Anthony. Dignan therefore acts as the mediator between Anthony and women – Anthony's mother, his sister and his new girlfriend, Inez. But Dignan's mediation is unintentional, or based on misunderstanding: he takes the earrings in the robbery, which were forbidden (which Grace has to return); he gives Inez the envelope of cash from Anthony, not knowing it contains all of their money; he passes on Inez's message of love to Anthony (several months late, and by saying that it is Rocky who loves him). Anthony (but not Dignan) realizes that Rocky was mediating (translating) for Inez. Yet, in the film's final scenes, in prison, Inez is absent. Only Anthony and Bob visit Dignan in jail. The three men are united, and the previous tensions within the group have gone, or are repressed. Even Bob mentions he has to some extent reconciled his differences with his brother. Inez's absence from this scene of three men united evokes Lévi-Strauss's contention that social bonds are created via men's exchange of women. (In chapter 1 we established this as one contingent form of exchange rather than the only form of exchange between social groups.) In *Bottle Rocket*, Inez has not so much established bonds but has helped to stabilize the bonds in Dignan's team. Dignan's function as (unintentional) mediator has paid off.

Binary oppositions

An important binary opposition at work in *Bottle Rocket* and other Wes Anderson films is individual/collective. The individual is coded negatively, as the outsider is unable to integrate into society, while the collective is a social group linked by shared values and co-operation. Anderson's films consist of outsiders trying to form their own collective, a group of dysfunctional individuals who have trouble working co-operatively as a team. *Bottle Rocket* consists of two teams of petty criminals:

Dignan–Anthony–Bob, and

Mr Henry–Applejack–Kumar–Rowboat–Dignan

Dignan's team is precarious and quickly disintegrates, before reforming and disintegrating a second time. Dignan's mania makes him unsuitable for a leadership role, although Anthony tries to support him. Bob's relation to the group is the most tenuous, evident when he leaves Dignan and Anthony stranded at the motel to take care of his jailed brother – jailed because Bob is growing marijuana in their garden. (Bob therefore leaves due to guilt rather than fraternal love.) During the Hinckley job, Bob complains to Anthony that he does not want to be part of the robbery. He breaks his walkie-talkie and then takes the lift up to the second floor, initiating the collapse of Dignan's plan. As suggested earlier, it is only when Anthony's relationship with Inez is secured that the team becomes stable.

Dignan initially forms his erratic team for the bookstore robbery, but it soon disintegrates at the motel. After the robbery, the team purchase fireworks and celebrate with them. This is clearly the highpoint for the team (reflected in the film's title), and Dignan's elation is manifest in his reckless behaviour of lighting and throwing fireworks. One of his low points is when Bob disappears with the car and Anthony spends time with Inez. Dignan spends his time alone, and his isolation and dejection is again signified via fireworks, by lighting them and pointing them wastefully at the ground. Within a matter of days, he has transitioned from the head of a team to a solitary individual.

The team totally disintegrates when Dignan punches Anthony in the face (27) and then walks away. In their reunion (29), Anthony's response is to shake hands with Dignan. The handshake is structurally opposed to the punch (closed fist/open hand) and is the beginning of Dignan's reforming of the team for the Hinckley job. But, when Anthony and Dignan go to see Bob (32), they end up fighting – Bob punches Dignan. In symbolic terms, Bob punching Dignan in (32) is an indirect response to Dignan punching Anthony in (27), with Antony offering a handshake. This expresses the indirect reciprocity within Dignan's team. Furthermore, in (24), Dignan is also punched in the face in a bar, after he accuses one of the locals of cheating. And Mr Henry practices martial arts and is seen on one occasion hitting Rowboat in the face. By itself, throwing a punch simply constitutes part of the surface action in a film. But it is an action repeated regularly within *Bottle Rocket*.

Mr Henry's team consists of gardeners and petty criminals. Although he is American, members of his team are ethnically coded: Rowboat is Japanese, Kumar is Indian and Applejack is Caribbean. Dignan (American) is only a member temporarily, and he establishes his own team as a way to gain recognition (especially from Mr Henry) and solidarity (with his friends). Dignan is at different times a member of both teams, and again takes on the role of mediator. He 'borrows' Kumar and Applejack on the Hinckley job, while Mr Henry and Rowboat sneak away to rob Bob's house. Kumar and Applejack are false helpers on Dignan's team: Kumar cannot crack the safe at Hinckley, and Applejack has a heart attack during the robbery. (However, Dignan's team members are also incompetent: Bob breaks his walkie-talkie and also decides not to remain in place on the ground and Anthony expresses doubt in carrying out the robbery and does not remain in his place as lookout on the rooftop.)

These two teams come together for the purposes of exchange and security. Yet, the relation is not equal, but asymmetric, and is organized according to the following binary oppositions, with the first term of each pair applying to Mr Henry's team:

Superior/inferior

Older/younger

Strong/weak

In the end, the co-operation between the two teams of petty criminals in *Bottle Rocket* is really just a smoke screen that allows Mr Henry to rob Dignan's team while it is away carrying out its own robbery.

Above/below, sky/water

We can go deeper into the abstract symbolic meanings underlying *Bottle Rocket* by drawing together a number of fragments of the above analysis into a coherent system. What emerges is the film's emphasis on movement along the vertical dimension. At this point, I am reminded of Krystyna Pomorska's analysis of *War and Peace* in terms of rotation. Rather than write about the content of the novel, Pomorska isolated its various uses of circular movement:

> In *War and Peace*, an entire network of [rotation] symbols is in play. The novel begins with a simile of a spindle, paralleled by the image of a lathe with its turning wheel, and then with a clock paralleled by a turning screw that does not fit its proper path. Another set of imagery involves a more abstract idea of rotation, such as the changing seasons, the famous symbol of the oak, or the succession of generations who experience exactly the same phenomena of life, and so on. Moreover, the symbols so conceived are in opposition to one another within the author's artistic system: idle rotation, the 'vicious circle', is opposed to 'natural' rotation, the circle of life itself. (Pomorska 1992, 7)[2]

Pomorska abstracts from a novel that overwhelms its reader (in terms of content – characters, actions, events) an underlying system of rotation symbols, and then characterizes those symbols in terms of parallel actions and binary oppositions. This system of rotation at once structures the novel and conveys an implicit series of meanings.

Similarly, movement along the vertical axis structures *Bottle Rocket*. In (1), Anthony climbs down from the hospital window from the second floor (in the US; the first floor in the UK) using bed sheets tied together. This image of climbing down from sky to earth is a fundamental feature of mythology. Lévi-Strauss's key myth in *The Raw and the Cooked* (1970), the Bororo myth called the 'bird-nester' (which he labels M_1), involves the bird-nester being helped down from a high ledge (as does variations of the myth); climbing down to the ground is a key feature of several myths about the origin of women (M_{29}–M_{33}); and a number of myths about the origin of cultivated plants involve a star-woman coming to earth – M_{87}, and so forth. However, this structural feature of climbing down takes on a different meaning in each of the myths Lévi-Strauss analyses and in Wes Anderson's film. In *Bottle Rocket*, it signifies the relation between Anthony and Dignan, Anthony's willingness to indulge Dignan, and also his status over him. Later in (16), Anthony emerges up from the water in the swimming pool at the hotel and sees Inez for the first time. Water plays a key role in mythology, although again its meaning changes according to the position it occupies in a structure. Lévi-Strauss emphasizes that water is structurally positioned in relation to death in the Bororo myth of the bird-nester: 'Water and death are therefore always connected in native thought. In order to procure the one, it is necessary to undergo the other. This is exactly what the Bororo myth about the bird-nester is, in its peculiar way, trying to convey' (1970, 192). He goes on to point out that the Bororo do not see death procured by water as final, for they emphasize resurrection (1970, 195), a rebirth from water, a meaning also prevalent of course in Christianity – the cleansing and rebirth enacted in baptism, in the flood, and so forth. Anthony's emergence from the pool and seeing Inez completely transforms his life, as he tries to explain to her the night before he leaves the motel. Anthony: 'All right, this is how I see it. Beautiful, intelligent girl from Paraguay. By chance happens to be working at a roadside motel in the middle of nowhere. Lost and confused, totally lost, incredibly unhappy person accidentally wanders in off the highway, and they meet, and they fall in love, and it's perfect.' Meeting Inez is a form of rebirth for Anthony, visually symbolized in his emergence out of the pool and seeing Inez for the first time, and later confirmed in his conversation with her. His conversation also emphasizes that their bonding is based on a chance encounter and on physical attraction, rather than prescribed by elementary structures of kinship (I address kinship later).

Anthony's emergence up from the pool and seeing Inez is structurally related to his climb down to Dignan – his movement in these two scenes constitutes a directional opposition. The vertical axis (organized around two binary oppositions: above/below, sky/water) is therefore key to positioning the relation between Anthony, Dignan and Inez. Moreover, this directional opposition is manifest in the film via point of view shots. In the film's opening scene, we see from Dignan's point of view Anthony climbing down to ground level. When Anthony sees Inez for the first time, it is via his point of view as he emerges up from the water to Inez at ground level. When he climbs down, Anthony is the object seen in the point of view, but when he swims up and sees Inez, he is the subject seeing (See Figures 3.1 to 3.4). Furthermore, as in the myths Lévi-Strauss analyses, 'above' is mapped onto 'sky', and 'below' is mapped onto 'water'.

Figures 3.1–3.2 Anthony as an object of vision climbing down (*Bottle Rocket*) © Columbia Pictures

These binary codes undergo a transformation when Dignan finally takes Anthony to see Mr Henry (30). Mr Henry is located high up on his office building, and sprinkles water onto Dignan at ground level. Here we see an inversion of the binary oppositions: with Mr Henry, 'above' is mapped on to 'water' (more specifically, water becomes rain – not only is he a trickster, but also a rainmaker). In addition, Mr Henry takes the same spatial position to Dignan that Anthony takes – both are initially seen to be spatially above Dignan.

Figures 3.3–3.4 Anthony as a subject of vision moving up (*Bottle Rocket*) © Columbia Pictures

Verticality is also key to the Hinckley robbery, especially movement up and down the lift/elevator (and, more generally, each character's spatial position) in the building. The robbery takes place on the second floor (US). Earlier in the film, Anthony's hospital room (where he recovers) is located on the second floor, and the team's motel room was located on the second floor (room 212), while Inez and Anthony make love in a nearby room on the same floor (room 215). In the Hinckley robbery, Anthony is initially on the roof before moving down to the second floor, and then down to ground level to escape. Only

Dignan goes below ground level, into the basement when the police chase and capture him. He is arrested in a cold storage room with ice on the floor (the police tell him to freeze, and then they manhandle him as he rolls around in the ice). With Anthony, 'below' is associated with 'water', but for Dignan 'below' is associated with 'ice'. With Mr Henry, water is associated with 'above' (rain).[3]

In *Bottle Rocket* water goes through a series of transformations, from water in a pool (that is, cultivated water, rather than natural) to rain (in this instance it is cultivated, not natural) to ice (manufactured to create an artificially cold environment). Anthony is linked to the pool and with below, Mr Henry with rain and above, and Dignan with ice and below. But Dignan is also tangentially related to both rain and pool: the 'rain' is poured onto his head and, when Inez and Anthony are in the motel swimming pool (20), Dignan turns up but sits by the pool and does not go in because he says he did not bring his swimming trunks. Although he does not go into the pool, Dignan still disrupts an intimate moment between Anthony and Inez. This three-way dynamics is reversed when they go to the bar (24). After making love (23), Anthony and Inez approach Dignan, who is aimlessly lighting fireworks. They invite him to join them, which he does so reluctantly.

Kinship

Filial relationships in *Bottle Rocket* are minimal because parents are absent (one scene is set in Anthony's house and several in Bob's house, yet the parents are never seen). Mr Henry plays the role of a false father figure, especially for Dignan – false because he is initially presented as Dignan's ego-ideal, but in fact, only considers how he can exploit Dignan. Dignan appears to be an only child and lives with his mother and stepfather. He is the typical Wes Anderson character: a dysfunctional solitary male who tries to establish a community of like-minded individuals, to fill in the absence of filial (and, in this instance, sexual) relationships. Dignan, Anthony and Bob are diverse in terms of class relations: working class/middle class/rich respectively. They are also marginal to society, collectively signified through their role as petty criminals committing robberies (stealing breaks social bonds) and also through their individual flaws – Dignan's mania and incompetence, Anthony's 'exhaustion' (the official reason for his hospitalization), Bob's lack of direction and maturity – separate them out from prescriptive, normal identities. Within this team, only Anthony attempts to establish a sexual relationship (the issue does not arise with Dignan or Bob).

The bond between Anthony and Inez is an interethnic relationship (North/South America), which is complicated by a language barrier (English/Spanish). The film is not, therefore, restricted to reproducing whiteness. Instead, in this early Wes Anderson film, we see a positive interethnic relationship develop, one that decreases social distance by increasing integration. However, Jonah Weiner identifies in the film what Judith Butler calls white culture saturated with anxiety. Weiner argues that the Anthony-Inez relationship is strongly asymmetrical, with Inez in the subordinate position: 'In *Bottle Rocket*, the Paraguayan housekeeper Ines [sic] is [...] a service-industry hottie with whom a depressed Anderson hero (in this case, Luke Wilson's Anthony) becomes obsessed. Helping this obsession along is the fact that Ines can barely speak English, making her a convenient projecting screen for Anthony's fantasies about purity and true love.' He ends his discussion of *Bottle Rocket* by noting that 'So it's barefoot, towel-folding Ines to the emotional rescue' (Weiner 2007). Although this asymmetry exists, especially since Inez is an immigrant working in a low-paid job and is unable to (initially) speak English, she is not simply depicted as a blank canvas for male fantasies. Instead, she is portrayed as independently minded, studious (she is learning English), and level-headed woman with a plan, especially evident when she refuses to spontaneously leave her job and elope with Anthony, who initially has no plan for a secure future (and has never worked a day in his life, as his sister Grace reminds him). It is clear that Anthony has to transform, and adopt some of Inez's work ethic, if the relationship is to work.

Anthony has a problematic relation to his much younger sister Grace, while Bob has a problematic relation to his older brother Future Man. The relation between Anthony and Grace is intergenerational: she is a 'caboose baby', significantly younger than her brother, to the extent that their relationship is coded as a parent-child relationship. However, Anthony appears to be estranged from his sister, and in an unusual reversal, it is Grace (who is eight or nine, while Anthony is in his mid-twenties) who sounds more like the adult. As well as disapproving of his friends, she asks the adult-sounding question: 'What's going to happen to you, Anthony?' Grace does not recognize her much older brother as an adult (symbolizing, perhaps, his immaturity, or pre-Oedipal attachment to his mother), but talks to him as if she is an adult. The letter Anthony writes to her (after he has met Inez) tries to redress that imbalance (28).

Lévi-Strauss mentions in passing that intergenerational kinship bonds are fairly common in indigenous societies: 'many societies practise the confusion of generations, the mingling of ages, the reversal of rôles, and the identification of what we regard as incompatible relationships' (1969, 487). These 'incompatible' relationships are important because they ensure that the process of exchange continues between clans and families, thereby ensuring the continuation of society. It is only when individuals stop interacting entirely that society's continuation is threatened.

A note on variations

One tenet of Lévi-Strauss's myth analysis is that no one true version of a myth exists. Instead, a myth consists of a large number of variations and retellings, all of which are incomplete. In film analysis, this tenet can be applied on at least two levels: to a single film or to a director's oeuvre. In terms of a single film, there is no one true version, but several versions, especially early films (where exhibitors regularly recut films), but also director's cuts of films, or films subsequently remade (e.g. short films remade into feature-length films, or the same director remaking his or her own feature film – as with Hitchcock's *The Man Who Knew Too Much* [1934; 1956] and Heneke's *Funny Games* [1997; 2007]). As I pointed out in chapter 1, the fundamental premise of this book is that a director's entire output can be read as variations of their invariant 'archi-film'.

Bottle Rocket exists not only as a feature-length film, but also a 14-minute black and white short, made four years earlier in 1992 and available on the

Criterion DVD. In addition, deleted scenes from the feature-length film also appear on the Criterion DVD, and the shooting script (significantly different to the final feature film) is available online.

The short version of *Bottle Rocket* (1992) focuses on the three main characters – Anthony, Dignan and Bob (played by the same three actors) – and contains earlier versions of the following actions, interspersed with new actions:

(3) (Anthony and Dignan walking)

(4) (robbery of house)

(5) (talking in the drug store, ending on the moment Dignan says he stole the earrings)

(6) (Anthony and Dignan walking, with Anthony talking about the earrings)

*New action: Anthony steals a wallet from car and splits the money ($8) with Dignan

*New action: Anthony and Dignan meet up in a café with Bob; they talk about growing marijuana

*New action: Temple Nash talks to Anthony, Dignan, and Bob about weapons

(10) (Gun practice. Anthony, Dignan and Bob try out and then buy some guns from Temple Nash)

(11) (Dignan explains to Anthony and Bob his plan to rob a bookstore); this repeated scene is intercut in the 1992 short with shots of the bookstore

(12) (Bookstore robbery); only the beginning is shown; the actual robbery is not filmed.

(13) (Anthony, Dignan and Bob celebrate the robbery); Anthony and Dignan re-enact the robbery for Bob (who remained in the getaway car);

*New action: Bob departs; Anthony and Dignan race one another as the credits begin.

The dialogue in some of the repeated scenes (3, 5 and 13) is significantly different, the delivery of lines is flat and the camerawork is informal. The film begins and ends with Anthony and Dignan, while Bob is introduced in the middle. Robberies constitute the two main actions, although only the first

(4) is enacted (and then celebrated [5]); the second one is planned (11) and then celebrated (13), but is not seen. The kernel of the feature film is therefore already formed in the short version. The feature film version involves a series of additions, expansions and transformations: it works backwards to offer backstory on both Anthony and Dignan; it introduces a love interest (Inez); a father figure (Mr Henry); problematic sibling relations (Grace; Future Man), and includes two additional robberies (Hinckley, and Bob's house).

Notes

1 Sororal polygyny is a kinship rule permitting a man to marry two sisters. In *Bottle Rocket*, Anthony marrying Inez and her younger sister is, of course, an unrealized, prohibited paradigmatic option, which is nonetheless indirectly conveyed in the film's syntagmatic structure – it does have a tenuous presence in the film. After all, if Anthony had returned the photo and instead asked for a photo of Inez, this faint echo of sororal polygyny would not exist at all in the film.
2 In this quotation, Pomorska is summarizing her paper 'Tolstoi's Rotary System (On Symbolism in *War and Peace*)', (with Mark Drazen), in Pomorska (1992, 70–9).
3 Bob is, in one instance, also related to water via the pool. In (9), Bob and his brother Future Man fight over the state of the swimming pool, which Bob was meant to clean. The fight is over the presence of one leaf Future Man found floating in the pool, signifying Future Man's overaggressive behaviour towards his brother, but also his distaste in seeing an element of nature (a leaf) in the cultivated water (swimming pool).

4

Dead Relatives and Intergenerational Relationships: *Rushmore*

Rushmore (1998) is structured by a series of binary oppositions and an intergenerational conflict between the main characters. The film consists of a large number of short scenes – it jumps to a new place, time and action frequently, which partly accounts for the large number of events (64) in what is a comparatively short film (90 minutes). This is exacerbated by the use of five episodic sequences.

Plot synopsis

(1) Blue curtain opens onto Rushmore High School. (2) In class, Max Fischer (Jason Schwartzman) solves a complex geometry equation. (3) In chapel, Herman Blume (Bill Murray) gives a speech. Max is present but initially asleep (the previous scene is retrospectively defined as a dream/fantasy). He wakes up and listens attentively to Blume's suggestion to 'take dead aim at the rich boys'. (4) Outside, Max introduces himself and his chapel partner Dirk Calloway (Mason Gamble) to Blume. The school principal, Dr. Guggenheim (Brian Cox), informs Blume that Max is one of the worst students at the school. (5) Montage sequence showing Max's many extra-curricular activities. (6) Red curtain with 'September' imposed over it. The curtain opens, revealing (7) Max talking to Guggenheim. Max is close to being expelled due to low grades. (8) He later discovers that Latin is to be taken off the school's curriculum (a decision he supports). (9) Via a library book, *Diving for Sunken Treasure* by Jacques-Yves Cousteau, he meets Miss Cross (Olivia Williams), by spying on her in her class. (10) Max directs a rehearsal of his play *Serpico*. (11) Max outside, talking to Mrs Calloway, and

directing school traffic. A classmate accuses him of trying to gain sexual favours from Mrs Calloway. (12) Max talks to his father, Bert Fischer (Seymour Cassel), a barber, about low grades and lack of a girlfriend. (13) Max meets Miss Cross and talks to her about his ambitious (unrealistic) academic plans. He discovers she is not in favour of the school's plan to drop Latin. (14) Episodic sequence in which Max saves Latin. The sequence ends with Max's nemesis, Magnus Buchan (Stephen McCole), insulting him for making Latin a requirement. (15) Max meets Mr Blume again, who invites Max to work for him. Max lies about his father's profession (neurosurgeon). (16) Birthday party for Blume's twin sons. Blume, dejected and unhappy because his wife is flirting with another man, dives into the swimming pool. (17) Max meets Miss Cross in her classroom. They feed the fish. He discovers she was married, but that her husband (Edward Appleby) died. Max tells her that his mother is dead. (18) Max visits Mr Blume in his office and asks him to fund an aquarium. (19) Episodic sequence showing Max planning the aquarium. (20) Max and Miss Cross in the library. They discuss 'friendship'. (21) First night of *Serpico*. (22) Max ensures his father leaves after the performance, and then meets up with Blume, Miss Cross and Miss Cross's friend, Peter (Luke Wilson). At dinner, celebrating the opening night of the play, Max belittles Peter and declares his love for Miss Cross. (23) Blume meets up with Miss Cross to pass on a letter from Max, in which he apologizes and invites her to the unveiling event (the start of the aquarium), to be built on the Rushmore baseball field. (24) At the event, Miss Cross fails to show. But Guggenheim turns up, and expels Max from Rushmore. (25) Green curtain with October projected on it opens. (26) Max introduces himself to the class at Grover Cleveland High School. Margaret Yang (Sara Tanaka), a fellow pupil, introduces herself to Max. He cuts her off in mid-sentence and leaves. (27) After practicing fencing on his own, he phones Blume to discuss Miss Cross. Blume, at Rushmore spying on Miss Cross, tries to discourage Max from seeing her. (28) But Max visits her at Rushmore (after a brief confrontation with Magnus), and shows her the library book by Cousteau, which used to belong to her husband Appleby. Miss Cross reveals that Max reminds her of Appleby. (29) Montage sequence showing Max pursuing several school and leisure activities. (30) He passes Margaret in the school corridor and signs her up to his play, without asking her if she wants to be in it. (31) Blume meets Miss Cross, and they go for a walk. Dirk sees them, and demands that Blume break off the relationship. (32) Magnus meets Dirk and tells him about the lies Max is spreading about his mother. (33) Max rehearses a new play, and receives a letter from Dirk, informing him of Blume and Miss Cross. (34) Blume leaves Miss Cross's house and confronts Max, who is waiting outside. (35) Max briefly confronts Miss Cross (and Guggenheim) at Rushmore. (36) Max meets Mrs Blume, and informs her of her husband's relation to Miss Cross. (37) Blume checks into a hotel. In his hotel room, he is attacked by a swarm of bees. Max is shown leaving a hotel elevator with a box labelled 'Rushmore Beekeepers'. (38) This initiates an episodic sequence in which Blume destroys Max's bicycle, Max tampers with the brakes of Blume's car, Blume almost crashes his car, Blume describes Max to the police, Max is arrested at school, and his father collects him from jail. (39) At Rushmore, Dirk and his friends attack Max, before he visits Guggenheim to try to get Miss Cross fired. But Guggenheim informs him she has already resigned. (40) In Miss Cross's classroom, Max and Miss Cross directly confront each other. Her direct language in part challenges his fantasy image of her. (41) Leaving Rushmore, he confronts Magnus, who punches Max, giving him a black eye. (42) Max and Blume meet at the cemetery, at his mother's grave. Max admits defeat. (43) Blue curtain: November. (44) Max works at his father's barbershop. (45) Margaret visits Max at home, but he refuses to see her. (46) Episodic sequence of Max and his father, Miss Cross, and Blume eating thanksgiving dinner by themselves. (47) Dirk watches Max working at the barbershop. (48) Red curtain: December. (49) Dirk meets Max at the shop. They reconcile (Dirk gives Max a gift, and he cuts Dirk's hair), and he informs Max that Guggenheim is ill in hospital. (50) Max visits Guggenheim in hospital. (51) When leaving, he meets Blume (who has a black eye), who informs Max he has not seen Miss Cross for several weeks. (52) Max pretends he has been hit by a car outside Miss Cross's house, in order to gain entry. Miss Cross (sleeping in her dead husband's childhood bedroom) tells him her husband drowned, and he tells her that his mother died of cancer. Miss Cross soon figures out (from the fake blood) that Max is lying about the car crash, and sends him away. (53) Max and Dirk flying a kite. Margaret turns up with a model airplane. Max apologizes to both of them. He develops an interest in Margaret. Max begins to form a new club devoted to kite-flying. (54) Max meets Blume outside his father's barbershop. He introduces Blume to his father, and persuades Blume to invest in the aquarium. (55) Episodic sequence of Max and Blume designing the aquarium. (56) A card announcing the aquarium groundbreaking event. At the event, Blume realizes Miss Cross is not planning to turn up. (57) Max visits Miss Cross, and praises Blume. (58) Max buys dynamite. (59) He goes to Rushmore, shoots Buchan with a pellet gun (in response to the punch he received earlier), and then offers him a part in his next play, *Heaven and Hell*, which Buchan accepts. (60) Orange curtain: January. (61) Opening night: Max dedicates his play to his mother and to Appleby. At the intermission, Blume and Miss Cross drink coffee together. (62) The play ends with Max's character and Margaret's character declaring their love for each other. (63) In the celebrations after, Max introduces his father to his friends, confirms that Margaret is his girlfriend, while Blume and Miss Cross are back together. In this final scene, every character enters the shot. (64) Blue curtain closes.

Oppositions and paradigms

Scenes (2) and (3) introduce five fundamental oppositions that dominate the whole film:

Reality/fantasy
Clever/naïve
Popular/unpopular
Rich/poor
Insider/outsider

They are arranged principally around Max Fischer. In scene (15) Max is associated with another binary opposition:

Lie/truth

in which he lies to Blume about his father's profession. And in (52) Max lies to Miss Cross about being hit by a car. Like Dignan in *Bottle Rocket*, Max is the typical Wes Anderson character: a dysfunctional solitary male attempting to establish (via his many clubs) a community of like-minded individuals, to fill in the absence of filial (his dead mother) and sexual relationships. Max fantasizes about being clever and popular, which compensates for his actual standing in the school as an unpopular and naïve outsider, and he is the only student to applaud Blume's comment about taking 'dead aim at the rich boys'.[1] Max is therefore coded in terms of the negative values in these oppositions – he lives in a fantasy world, he is unpopular, naïve, poor, an outsider and he lies. Max's naivety is coded in several ways throughout the film – academic failure, sexual inexperience and foolish behaviour. Scene (7) confirms Max's academic failure when Guggenheim warns him about his low grades, and Max raises the issue of his scholarship, confirming that he is poor (in relation to the other pupils at this private school). His sexual naivety is conveyed in his fantasmatic relation to older women – Mrs Calloway and Miss Cross. (I will refer to Olivia Williams's character as 'Miss Cross' because this is the way she is addressed throughout most of the film. Herman Blume does occasionally use her first name [Rosemary] when developing a relationship with her.) Nonetheless, Max is successful at extracurricular activities, especially writing plays and staging them – he even received a scholarship to Rushmore by writing a play. He is a successful playwright because he is able to stage his fantasies and desires in the plays (although he has a tendency to plagiarize films in his writing). He is also motivated by his dead mother, who encouraged his writing when he was young. She suggested he submit a play to get a scholarship at Rushmore, and we see a message from his mother imprinted on his typewriter cover: 'Bravo Max, Love Mom.'

The narrative moves gradually towards the mediation and resolution of (most of) these six oppositions. Initially, Max is unable to accept the reality of his situation. The key terms the film privileges concern his naïve, fantasmatic relation to older women, particularly Miss Cross, a relation ambiguously coded as a replacement for his dead mother (a parental figure) but also as an Oedipal substitute for his mother (a love interest). I pointed out in Chapter 1 that ambiguous kinship relations are transgressive and create conflict, not least because the relation is intergenerational (Max is 15 while Miss Cross is 28, to be addressed in the kinship section later).

Max first 'meets' Miss Cross by spying on her in class (9), an action Blume repeats later in the film – at the beginning of (23), and in (27). Max and Miss

Cross are properly introduced in (13) where Max talks about his unrealistic academic plans to study mathematics and pre-med at a major university ('My top schools where I want to apply to are Oxford and the Sorbonne. My safety is Harvard'). Their additional meetings constitute one of the film's key paradigms:

Max and Miss Cross paradigm

(9) Max spies on Miss Cross in her classroom

(13) Max meets Miss Cross and talks to her about his unrealistic academic plans

(17) Max meets Miss Cross in her classroom. They feed the fish and talk about their dead relatives (his mother; her husband Edward Appleby)

(20) Max and Miss Cross in the library discussing 'friendship'

(22) Max declares his love for Miss Cross at dinner

(28) A brief reconciliation as they talk about the Cousteau library book/Appleby

(40) Max and Miss Cross directly confront each other in her classroom

(52) Max (apparently injured) and Miss Cross in her/Appleby's bedroom. She tells him her husband drowned, and he tells her that his mother died of cancer

(57) Max visits Miss Cross at her new school, and praises Blume

(61) Reconciliation at the opening night of *Heaven and Hell* (dedicated to Appleby and Max's mother)

The values in this paradigm are polarized around the reality/fantasy opposition: Max's fantasmatic overinvestment in Miss Cross/the reality that the relationship is impossible. Overshadowing this relationship are two dead relatives, Max's mother and Miss Cross's dead husband, Appleby:

Max's mother and Edward Appleby sub-paradigm

(17) Max and Miss Cross talk about their dead relatives (Appleby, mother)

(52) Max and Miss Cross tell each other how their relatives died

(61) *Heaven and Hell* is dedicated to Appleby and Max's mother

Max and Miss Cross go through a similar experience of loss: both are in mourning; both idealize the person they loved and lost; and both need to accept the loss of the dead person and connect to a new person (to avoid the pathology of melancholia). But they handle their loss differently: Max tries to deal with the gradual loss of his mother to cancer (when he was only seven) by attracting attention to himself, building up his self-esteem by writing plays (an activity his mother encouraged), and by pursuing Miss Cross, while Miss Cross copes with suddenly losing her husband at a young age by maintaining a sense of her husband's continuing presence, by working in the school where he studied, and by living in his room in his parents' house.[2] In other words, Max is driven to fill the gap created by his absent mother by reaching out (largely unsuccessfully) to others, while Miss Cross tries to fill the gap by maintaining contact with her lost husband's possessions and surroundings. They therefore have different strategies for coping with their respective losses. By courting Miss Cross, Max thinks their two absences will cancel each other out. This is a simple but naïve solution, for it ignores their different approaches to mourning. The dedication of his play in scene (61) is a significant symbolic gesture in Max's mourning process: it signifies his ability to come to terms with his mother's death, and it indirectly acknowledges the impossibility to form a relationship with Miss Cross, thereby paving the way to establishing a relationship to an alternative love interest, Margaret Yang.

Margaret Yang is introduced in scene (26). Max initially ignores her. In scene (30) he signs her up to his play but does not seek her willingness in doing so – she is just another character in his play. His lack of interest in her is confirmed in scene (45) when he refuses to see her. Nonetheless, he prizes her gift of a potted plant (a detail not in the script), and goes to the cemetery with it, presumably to put it on his mother's grave. This suggests he has mixed feelings about Margaret: taking the potted plant to the cemetery/to his mother is a symbolic acknowledgement of Margaret's possible role as a love interest. In scene (53) Max not only apologizes to Margaret, but also develops an interest in her – especially when he sees her rather elaborate flight plan for her model plane, and when he discovers she faked some of her school work: he realizes they are kindred spirits. But Max only expresses his love for Margaret openly in the fantasmatic context of his play. Furthermore, the dialogue Max writes for his female lead still betrays his naivety towards women: while pointing guns at each other on the battlefield, Max (Esposito) says: 'Will you marry me, Le-Chahn?' to which she responds 'You bet I will.' Outside the play, he is more modest in acknowledging Margaret as his girlfriend, and the film ends with him dancing with Miss Cross (while Margaret dances with Blume). The resolution of Max's conflicts is complete and absolute in the play, much more tenuous outside it. By the end of the film Max is able to maintain a balance between fantasy and reality. He no longer tries to impress Miss Cross or make advances towards her; instead, he maintains a formal distance from her. In terms of T. K. Seung's three types of resolution (1982), *Rushmore* achieves resolution via equilibrium.

However, before this tenuous reconciliation is achieved, Max is desperate to get Miss Cross's attention and to please her. He saves Latin classes at Rushmore and tries to build an aquarium for her, even though she did not ask for either, and she did not seek his attention. In contrast, Margaret Yang does seek his attention. She speaks to him after class, visits him at home, decides to perform in his play and turns up (by chance?) in the kite-flying scene.[3] Max's initial reaction to Miss Cross and Margaret is opposite: attraction/aversion. The film moves towards the repression of Max's attraction to Miss Cross and to the reversal of his aversion to Margaret. In fact, it is Max's eventual attraction to Margaret that replaces/represses his attraction to Miss Cross.

The rich/poor opposition is hardly acknowledged in the film's dialogue; except for the moments when he mentions his scholarship, Max only talks about being poor once, to Blume in scene (15), although even then it is in the context of a lie ('my father may only be a doctor, but we manage'). Max's poverty is evident when he leaves school and works in his father's barbershop. Fantasy/reality is a more dominant opposition in the storyworld: as well as the dream/fantasy (2), Max articulates his fantasies in his plays. We see two rehearsals and two opening nights:

Max's plays paradigm

(10) Max directs a rehearsal of his play *Serpico*

(21) First night of *Serpico*

(33) Max rehearses a new play

(61) and (62) Opening night of *Heaven and Hell*

Max appears to have adapted Sidney Lumet's film *Serpico* (1973) to the stage, although it is billed at the beginning of scene (21) as 'a new play by Max Fischer'. Scene (21) is taken directly from the film (in a tense meeting with prosecutors, Serpico is reluctant to testify to the grand jury about police corruption and tries to leave, with the excuse he needs to put a dime in the parking meter), although scene (10) is Max's addition. Scene (10) is a fragment of a narrative, consisting of a conversation between Frank Serpico and 'Willie', in which Frank appears to have solved a major plot point. He also informs Willie that 'You were wrong about Enrique Sanchez. He died in his sleep.' These elements do not appear in Lumet's film. Scene (33), showing Max and Margaret on stage, is an anomaly; it seems to belong to another made-up scene in *Serpico*, although it appears after the opening night. And it does not fit into *Heaven and Hell*, which is based on *Apocalypse Now* (Francis Ford Coppola, 1979).

The plays make Max more popular (even with his nemesis, Magnus), although he remains an outsider throughout the film: he distances himself from others by playing the role of temperamental successful writer, in which he thinks he can act differently, as his behaviour in scenes (20) to (22) demonstrates. Even in his own fantasy (2), he is distinct from the other students: he is not paying attention to the class, but is reading a broadsheet newspaper (which, because of its size, isolates him in his own space); he is dressed differently (in a blazer – although this is true outside his fantasy as well); and he presents himself as intellectually superior because he is the only one who can solve the complex geometrical equation.

Max's lies are directed towards the two adults, Blume and Miss Cross. They are worked through and negated towards the end of the film, in two successive scenes: when Max begins to date Margaret (53) and when he takes Blume to his father's barbershop (54).

Paradigms and mediation

The Max-Miss Cross paradigm can be explored further via the concept of mediation. Blume initially acts as mediator between Max and Miss Cross, when he goes to Rushmore to deliver Max's letter to her in scene (23). But his act of mediation quickly leads to him taking Max's place, initiating a conflict between them lasting from scene (34) to (42), when Max concedes to Blume at his mother's gravestone. In *Bottle Rocket*, by contrast, Dignan acts as mediator between Anthony and Inez, but he never threatens to take Anthony's place. Blume as mediator does not so much resolve the opposition between Miss Cross and Max, but instead displaces Max by taking his position. Within the film's logic, this is a legitimate move, for whereas the Max/Miss Cross opposition cannot be resolved (due to age difference, their different ways of mourning, and Miss Cross's lack of desire for Max), the Blume/Miss Cross opposition can be resolved, for they take an interest in each other (we can see this when they exchange first names at the end of the scene). Max's displacement leaves his desire free-floating/repressed. He only reignites it for Miss Cross one more time when he realizes that she has lost interest in Blume. This final act (52), involving deception, ends once and for all Max's attempt to form a relation with Miss Cross. In scene (21), the opening night of *Serpico*, the lead actor punches Max, making his nose bleed. Miss Cross sees this and expresses concern. Max tries to replicate this concern by faking a car accident and using fake blood. In other words, his only modus operandi is fantasmatic, using fakery. As he leaves Miss Cross's home, he finally realizes that he cannot break out of his fantasmatic relation with her. It is significant, therefore, that in the next scene (53) Max reconciles with Margaret and takes an interest in her. The kite-flying scene (53) is pivotal in initiating Max's sexual maturity and to his attempts to keep reality and fantasy in balance.

This is confirmed in scene (57), when Max visits Miss Cross at the Webster Smalley School for Girls to defend and praise Blume. Scene (57) is therefore the 'answer' to scene (23). In (23), Blume acts as mediator:

(23)
Miss Cross
    Blume (mediator)
Max

Rather than mediating between Miss Cross and Max, Blume takes Max's place. The friendship between Blume and Max is transformed into a rivalry. In (57):

(57)
Miss Cross
    Max (mediator)
Blume

Max and Blume reverse roles. Furthermore, Max is able to mediate between Miss Cross and Blume, and also reverses the rivalry between himself and Blume back into friendship. To say that the later scene is the 'answer' to the earlier one means that a transformation has taken place between them: the later one (57) is an inversion of the earlier one (23). Three terms are in play: mediation, friendship and rivalry. In scene (23), Blume acts as mediator between Miss Cross and Max. He calls Max his friend, but by the end of the scene he becomes Max's rival. In scene (57), Max acts as mediator between Miss Cross and Blume. He began as Blume's rival, but at the end of the scene he calls Blume his friend. Miss Cross remains the constant, while Max and Blume swap roles as mediator, swap roles as Miss Cross's love interest and, because of the latter, they also transform in relation to each other: from friends to rivals and back again. Max continues his role as mediator on the opening night of his play *Heaven and Hell* (61): he ensures Miss Cross and Blume sit together on the opening night (the title of the play is in itself an opposition in need of mediation). Max's mediation works, for they begin to reconcile during the intermission. We could argue that they reconcile only because Max acts as mediator (a role he carries out because he has come to terms with his mother's death and with the impossibility of forming a relationship which Miss Cross, both of which he signifies via the play's dedication). In contrast, the reconciliation of Max and Margaret does not require a (direct) mediator – although it does require Max's prior act of mediation between Blume and Miss Cross. (The script gives Dirk a role as mediator between Max and Margaret – see note 3 – but this has been changed in the final version of the film.)

Before Max reconciles Blume and Miss Cross, she lived alone after rejecting both men. Yet, the film's narrative logic does not see this to be a satisfactory state for her to occupy. She can only pursue her career by resigning from Rushmore (an all-male school) to work at an all-girl school. And the narrative logic requires her to find a replacement for her dead husband in order to come to terms with her loss.

The pairing off of Max and Margaret and Blume and Miss Cross by the end of the film is suggested indirectly much earlier, in scenes (30) and (31). Max signs up Margaret to his play, and Blume visits Miss Cross and they go for a walk. The very juxtaposition of the two scenes, their syntagmatic relation, in itself foreshadows the final permutation of relations between these four characters. In addition, Max signing up Margaret to his play gives him the scope to eventually declare his love for her – at least within the context of the play. Furthermore, Margaret is more active than Miss Cross and Max – she actively pursues Max (and this is why no mediation is required). However, at this stage in the film, Max is still fixated on Miss Cross. In the anomalous scene from a play (33), Margaret reads out a line in which Max is meant to kiss her. But Max verbalizes this action rather than enacting it: 'Then he kisses her and we're out'. Immediately afterwards, he receives the note from Dirk informing him of Blume and Miss Cross's liaison. It is as if the 'threat' of Margaret's kiss brings forth Dirk's note about Max's love interest, Miss Cross.

Another paradigm dominates the film:

Water paradigm

- (9) Max meets Miss Cross via the library book, *Diving for Sunken Treasure* by Jacques-Yves Cousteau
- (16) Blume dives into the swimming pool
- (17) Max and Miss Cross feed the fish in her classroom
- (18) Max asks Blume to fund an aquarium
- (28) Max talks to Miss Cross about *Diving for Sunken Treasure*
- (52) Miss Cross tells Max her husband drowned (and Max is wet because it is raining outside)
- (55) and (56) – the aquarium project is re-initiated (the card announcing the groundbreaking has a seahorse on the front)
- (66) During the intermission of Max's play, Blume and Miss Cross drink coffee outside, where it is raining

First, some comparative paradigmatic analysis between films. Scene (16) in *Rushmore* is the opposite of scene (16) in *Bottle Rocket*. They contain the same two elements (pool, relationship), but are used in opposite ways and appear in reverse order: swimming *up* from/diving *down* into water, and *beginning/ending* of relation with a partner. In *Bottle Rocket*, Anthony emerges from the pool and sees Inez for the first time, initiating a relationship with her. In *Rushmore*, Blume sees his wife flirting with another man, so he dives into the pool and remains at the bottom. Is he thinking of ending his relationship while he is under water? Soon afterwards, he begins pursuing Miss Cross. When Blume leaves home, after his wife discovers (from Max) about the relationship, he checks into a hotel (37). He mentions to the desk clerk that he is getting divorced, and then he asks where the pool is. The pool therefore seems to be an important location for him in regards to his relationship to/breakup with his wife.

Blume's decision to remain under water at the end of scene (16) creates a weak link between himself and Appleby, for we discover later that Appleby drowned, leaving Miss Cross a widow. Scene (17) shows Max and Miss Cross feeding fish. Max is pursuing her and also discovers that Appleby died (but only later does he discover it was via drowning). But Appleby has indirectly led Max to be Cross via the book *Diving for Sunken Treasure*. And, of course, the relationship among Miss Cross, Blume and Max is worked out via attempts to build an aquarium.

Rushmore is structured around a number of other (weak) paradigms. One involves an exchange of letters: Max writes to Miss Cross (23) to apologize for his behaviour at dinner in the previous scene; Dirk writes to Max about Miss Cross and Blume (33); in the script (but not in the film), Dirk pretends to be Max and writes to Margaret, to encourage them to meet up; and Miss Cross receives a card inviting her to the groundbreaking event (56). Two of these letters generate undesired results for the sender: Blume delivers Max's letter in (23) and falls in love with Miss Cross, displacing Max; and Miss Cross does not turn up to the groundbreaking event (56). But Dirk's letters have a positive effect for the recipient: Max discovers that Blume and Miss Cross are having a relationship, which eventually persuades Max to abandon his futile pursuit of her, and (in the script) Dirk assists Max in establishing a relationship with Margaret.

Two types of curtain (diegetic and non-diegetic) also punctuate the film. Differently coloured non-diegetic curtains simply demarcate the months, plus the film's opening and closing: (1) Blue; (6) Red; (25) Green; (43) Blue; (48) Red; (60) Orange-Beige; (65) Blue. Curtains also appear in the film – when rehearsing, or in the final play, but also when Max ignores Margaret (he sees her but then draws the curtain to block her view).

Kinship

Consanguine relationships in *Rushmore* are more prominent than in *Bottle Rocket*. Max's father and Blume's family (wife, twin sons) are evident in several scenes. For most of the film, Max feels embarrassed about his real father and looks up to the rich and successful businessman Blume as a symbolic father figure (in the same way that Dignan looks up to Mr Henry). Max's embarrassment regarding his father and his obsession with status defines him as an hysteric, in Žižek's sense of the term: 'There lies the problem of the hysteric: the central figure of his universe is the "humiliated father", that is, he is obsessed with the signs of the real father's weakness and failure, and criticizes him incessantly for not living up to his symbolic mandate' (1999, 334). This precisely defines Max's relation to his real father. 'Beneath the hysteric's rebellion and challenge to paternal authority', Žižek continues, 'there is thus a hidden call for a renewed paternal authority, for a father who would really be a "true father" and adequately embody his symbolic mandate' (1999, 334). This defines Max's relation to Blume. But, Blume (like Mr Henry) is the typical *post*-Oedipal father figure – in which the 'post' signifies what Žižek calls 'the disintegration of paternal authority' (1999, 368), for the father figure in itself no longer upholds symbolic authority. (The post-Oedipal father is not about the efficacy of individual fathers, but signifies the demise of the paternal authority as such, which is then manifest in the films via weak father figures.) What this means is that the son no longer perceives father figures as his ego ideal, representing symbolic authority, but as his ideal ego, an imaginary competitor (Žižek 1999, 334). Max initially perceives Blume as his ego ideal, embodying the symbolic paternal function. But Max and Blume soon become rivals for the same woman, Miss Cross, and try to eliminate each other in the episodic sequence (38) – where they destroy each other's mode of transport – and in (42) (the tree Max had planned to fall on Blume at the graveyard does fall at the end of the scene). Max also uses the Rushmore bees to attack Blume. This is where *Rushmore* differs from *Bottle Rocket*: there is no sexual rivalry between Dignan and Mr Henry, simply an issue of and ego ideal who turns out to be a fraud (but which does not devastate Dignan).

Equally significant to what Max perceives as his 'ineffectual' father is his dead mother. We have already seen how Max's mourning for his dead mother structures his world, a death paralleled in the death of Miss Cross's husband, Appleby. However, in kinship terms, these deaths are not identical: the mother–son relation is filial and (naturally) intergenerational, whereas Cross–Appleby is affinal and presumably generational (we do not discover his age). The film's narrative is resolved via potential affinal relationships. Max substitutes an intergenerational (non-)relationship with Miss Cross with an interethnic relationship with the Asian American Margaret Yang,[4] a relationship that echoes Anthony's relation to the Paraguayan Inez in *Bottle Rocket*.

Notes

1. The film's script (dated 12 May 97) has Max disagreeing with Blume about 'rich kids' when they meet outside the chapel. But this line has been removed from the final version of the film. http://www.pages.drexel.edu/~ina22/splaylib/Screenplay-Rushmore.pdf.
2. Miss Cross lives in the house of her dead husband's family. In terms of marital residence, we see the wife moving to her husband's family (patrilocal residence). The unusual issue here is that she is living in the home after the death of her husband.
3. In the script, the scene takes place at a frozen pond. Margaret skates towards Max and Dirk. She received a note (written in crayon) to meet Max at this location. Max realizes that Dirk arranged for Margaret to meet him. This means that Dirk plays the same mediating role in *Rushmore* that Dignan plays in *Bottle Rocket*.
4. A line of dialogue in the script identifies Margaret as Korean, but this line has been cut from the film.

5

Imperial Kinship: *The Royal Tenenbaums*

The film's title, *The Royal Tenenbaums* (2001), appears in the storyworld: it is on the cover of a book that is part of the film's diegesis, rather than where it is conventionally found, on what Etienne Souriau (1951) called the filmophanic level (that is, on the surface of the image). Like *Rushmore*, the main sections of *The Royal Tenenbaums* are strongly marked: *Rushmore*'s theatrical curtains are replaced with book chapter headings (plus a narrator's voiceover): more specifically, the film is demarcated into eight chapters plus a prologue and an epilogue. But these merely constitute surface features of the film. This chapter focuses on three kinship relations at the centre of the film's underlying structure.

Plot synopsis

(1) Title sequence: library book, book covers, dinner placement card. (2) Prologue: An extended expositional scene, complete with voiceover narration, introducing the Tenenbaum house, three Tenenbaum children (Margot, Richie, Chas), their best friend Eli Cash, and the accomplishments of the Tenenbaum children: (i) Margot is a playwright (her adopted status is emphasized); (ii) Richie is a tennis pro (and owns a falcon called Mordecai); and (iii) Chas is in finance (and also made money breeding Dalmatian mice). (iv) The Tenenbaum parents, Royal and Etheline, are planning to separate. (3) Title card insert: 'Cast of Characters (22 years later).' (4) Credit sequence: static tableau shots introducing the characters. (5) Title card insert: 'Chapter One'. (6) Another extended expositional scene, complete with voiceover narration, detailing the current problems of the Tenenbaums: (i) Royal Tenenbaum (Gene Hackman) is asked

to vacate his hotel room due to non-payment (and he has not seen his family for three years); (ii) Richie Tenenbaum (Luke Wilson) gave up professional tennis and is sailing on an ocean liner; he sends a letter to Eli Cash (Owen Wilson), acknowledging that he is in love with his adopted sister Margot Tenenbaum (Gwyneth Paltrow); (iii) Margot, married to neurologist Raleigh St. Clair (Bill Murray), is depressed and secretive, and has not written a play in seven years; (iv) Chas (Ben Stiller) has two sons, Ari and Uzi, and a dog Buckley; Chas is traumatized by his wife's death in a plane crash; (v) Etheline (Anjelica Huston) is an archaeologist, and receives a marriage proposal from friend and business adviser Henry Sherman (Danny Glover); (vi) Eli Cash has become a celebrated novelist. This extended sequence ends with (vii) Pagoda (Kumar Pallana), personal assistant to Royal, informing Royal of the marriage proposal. (7) Title card insert: 'Chapter Two'. (8) Chas, Ari and Uzi move into Chas' old room in the Tenenbaum house. (9) Royal has a medical check-up. (10) Etheline visits Margot. Margot decides to return to the Tenenbaum family home, where Eli is waiting for her in her bedroom. (11) Royal meets Etheline and tells her he is ill. (12) Montage sequence of Margot, Richie, Chas, Eli and Henry responding to the news of Royal's illness. Margot's response is that 'We're not actually related', and Richie decides to return to the family home. (13) Margot greets him at the pier in New York. (14) At the family home, Richie sets free his falcon Mordecai and reads Margot's published plays. (15) Title card insert: 'Chapter Three'. (16) (i) Royal visits the family home to talk to his children; he raises the issue of Margot's adoption; and (ii) He meets Henry for the first time. (17) Eli tells Margot about the letter he received from Richie. (18) Henry talks to Etheline about his proposal, and they kiss. (19) Royal meets Ari and Uzi. (20) Title card: 'Maddox Hill Cemetery'. (21) (i) Visit to the graves of Royal's mother and of Chas' wife; (ii) Margot reveals to Ari and Uzi that she is adopted and explains how she lost part of her finger (on a visit to her biological family); (iii) tells Richie she knows about the letter he sent to Eli; and (iv) There is also a brief flashback to Richie's last tennis game. (22) Richie visits Eli and realizes Eli has a drug problem. They talk about Richie's feelings for Margot. (23) Title card insert: 'Chapter Four'. (24) Royal is thrown out of his hotel. (25) He takes up residence in the family home, pretending to be ill. (26) Richie in his yellow tent on the landing. He talks to Chas. (27) Royal realizes that Eli is having an affair with Margot. (28) Raleigh visits the Tenenbaum house. He talks to Margot, and then to Richie about Margot. (29) Royal takes Ari and Uzi on a 'reckless' outing in the city. (30) Chas confronts Royal about taking his children on the outing; Royal tells Chas that he must be having a mental breakdown due to the death of his wife. (31) Title card insert: 'Chapter Five'. (32) Royal and Etheline go for a walk in the park and talk affectingly about the past. (33) (i) Etheline decides not to go out with Henry; (ii) Royal and Henry confront one another. (34) Henry investigates Royal's 'illness', and discovers he is not ill; Royal leaves the house. (35) Title card insert: 'Chapter Six'. (36) Royal and Pagoda stay in a small room in the 375th Street Y. (37) Margot meets Eli; they tell each other they are not in love with one another. (38) Raleigh and Richie read a file on Margot compiled by a private detective: montage sequence showing her smoking habits and many love affairs. (39) Royal applies for a job at the hotel he used to live in. (40) Reaction to private detective's file on Margot: Raleigh falls into a stupor, and Richie attempts suicide, but is rushed to hospital in time. (41) Episodic sequence showing Etheline, Chas and Margot separately rushing to the hospital. (42) The family surround Richie's hospital bed. (43) Royal, working as an elevator attendant at the hotel, hears of Richie's attempted suicide and rushes to the hospital. (44) In the hospital, Raleigh confronts Margot about her extra-marital affairs; Henry turns up. (45) Royal and Pagoda turn up at the hospital in the evening, but are not admitted. Outside, they see Richie boarding a bus. (46) Richie returns home, and talks to Margot in his yellow tent. They declare their love for one another, and kiss. (47) Title card insert: 'Chapter Seven'. (48) On the roof of the Palace Hotel. Richie tells his father that he loves Margot. Royal apologizes for not being a good father. Mordecai returns. (49) Richie, Royal, and Pagoda visit Eli to help him with him drug problem. But Eli escapes. (50) Royal tries to discuss Richie with Margot, without success. (51) Royal tries to take out Ari and Uzi to the cemetery, but Chas stops him. Royal goes alone. (52) Royal hands over divorce papers to Etheline, and compliments Henry ('he's everything I'm not'). (53) Title card insert: 'Chapter Eight'. (54) Wedding day of Etheline and Henry: Chas mentions to Henry that they are both widowers; Eli crashes his car in front of the house killing the dog Buckley, but Royal saves Ari and Uzi; Chas confronts Eli, and hits Richie in the eye; Chas and Eli realize they need help; Chas and Royal begin to reconcile – Royal presents him with a Dalmatian dog. (55) Richie, Margot and Mordecai on the roof of the Tenenbaum house. Richie and Margot share a cigarette. (56) Montage sequence, complete with voiceover: (i) Buckley is buried; (ii) Etheline and Henry finally marry; (iii) Margot's new play is staged; (iv) Raleigh and his patient Dudley on a lecture tour; (v) Eli in a rehabilitation hospital; (vi) Richie teaches tennis to children; (vii) Royal, Ari, Uzi, and Chas on a 'reckless' outing in the city; and (viii) Royal and Chas in an ambulance, after Royal has a heart attack. (57) Title card insert: 'Epilogue'. (58) Royal's funeral.

Three kinship relations dominate *The Royal Tenenbaums*:

(a) Royal–Etheline–Henry
(b) Royal–Margot
(c) Richie–Margot–Raleigh–Eli

These kinship relations are structured around conflicts articulated in oppositions. The first relation sets up a clear binary opposition: Royal/Henry, in which the focus of the opposition is Etheline. The second relation is based on a binary opposition Royal/Margot, defined in terms of Royal's kinship definition of Margot. The third relation sets up a three-way opposition between Richie/Eli/Raleigh, in which the focus of the opposition is Margot. Outside these three relations is the opposition Chas/Richie, in which the focus of the opposition is Royal, their father.

The three kinship relations (a)–(c) and the first three oppositions constitute the core of the film's symbolic logic. Two central characters unite them – Royal Tenenbaum and Richie Tenenbaum. Royal is central to two kinship structures, (a) and (b), and his symbolic role is key to (c). In terms of oppositions, he is of course directly involved in the Royal/Henry and Royal/Margot conflicts; and his symbolic role of father is indirectly the cause of the Richie/Margot/Eli/Raleigh conflict. He is also the cause of the Chas/Richie conflict. Yet, the film's logical trajectory aims to degrade Royal Tenenbaum's symbolic function as head of the family and as paternal ideal. It is the role of the father function as guarantor of the symbolic that is at stake, not simply the inability of the character (Royal) to fulfil the father function, although the significant gap between Royal and his father function draws attention to the purely symbolic and therefore precarious status of this function.

Within (c), Richie's relation to Margot presents a conflict that the film's logic only resolves in part, due to Margot's ambiguous kinship status:[1] while the ambiguity is addressed in relation to Royal (she is his 'adopted' daughter), the ambiguity is not addressed in relation to Richie: the meaning of 'sister' is discussed but remains unresolved. Additionally, this kinship relation parallels kinship structure (a), as I will illustrate later in this chapter. Moreover, this parallel structure is established by Richie indirectly functioning as mediator between his father and Henry–Etheline, which has the effect of resolving or neutralizing the binary opposition between Royal and Henry.

Kinship conflicts

The Royal Tenenbaums begins with 14 minutes of exposition, and the narrative (a narrative conflict) gets underway when Royal announces his separation from Etheline and leaves the family home in scene (2) (iv). When Henry proposes to Etheline, Royal perceives this as a conflict in kinship. Royal, the patriarch alienated from his own family for 22 years, tries to return and restore family unity and take his dominant place within it. But his position is a sham: he is homeless and broke, and deceives his way back into his family by pretending to be ill. His return to the position of paternal authority is based on a lie. Royal is the typical post-Oedipal father, a familiar figure in Wes Anderson's films (beginning with Mr Henry in *Bottle Rocket* and then Blume in *Rushmore*). These post-Oedipal fathers become more complex from film to film. As Chris Robé (2013, 115–17) points out, Royal's return to the family home is not only motivated by poverty and his sense of male privilege, but also by what Royal sees as a racial threat to his family, from the African American Henry Sherman. But the film has a happy ending, the mixed race marriage of Etheline and Henry (compare to the successful relationship between Anthony and Inez in *Bottle Rocket*, and Max and Margaret in *Rushmore*).

The film's second kinship relation, Royal–Margot, is structured around the conflict involving Royal's kinship naming of Margot. Royal always presents Margot as his adopted daughter, which highlights that Royal is her father only on a symbolic level, that she is not related by blood to the rest of the family. Instead, she is a stranger introduced but never fully integrated into the Tenenbaum family. In this instance, the gap between the biological and the symbolic is exaggerated, leading to Margot's neurosis.

The film's third kinship relation, Richie–Margot–Raleigh–Eli, is structured around the conflict involving the breakdown of Margot's marriage to Raleigh, which brings to the fore Eli's sexual relationship with and Richie's love for Margot. The latter instigates a potential case of sibling incest – potential because their sibling relationship is not consanguine, but is only coded as brother-sister on the symbolic level. Again, the biological and social do not coincide, which creates more friction.

The film's second and third conflicts are inversely related: the second conflict over-states Margot's distance from the Tenenbaum family,[2] while the third conflict under-states her distance from the Tenenbaum family, especially in regards to Richie. To echo Lévi-Strauss's analysis of the Oedipus myth (1972, 213–18), these conflicts in the film undervalue/overvalue blood relations. Royal overemphasizes Margot's non-consanguine status, while Richie underemphasizes it, by thinking of Margot as a blood relative with whom he cannot have a relationship. As we shall see, the opposition is not absolute, but is more complicated, because Margot internalizes Royal's evaluation of her, and Richie feels ambivalent about Margot's kinship status (in opposition to Eli, who unequivocally sees her as Richie's blood relative). Margot's adopted status creates confusion within the film's storyworld in regards to the kinship category she belongs to; because her relation to the Tenenbaums is not consanguine, an internal distance is created between her and the rest of the family.

Kinship and marital residence

When they become adults, the Tenenbaum siblings leave home to set up their own living arrangements (see Table 5.1): Margot marries Raleigh and Chas marries Rachel (and are the only couple to have children). Anthropologists identify three types of marital residence: patrilocal, matrilocal and neolocal (the married couple reside in or near the residence of the husband's family, the wife's

Table 5.1 Status of the Tenenbaum siblings after leaving the family home

	Chas	Margot	Richie
Married	+	+	−
Own Home	+	+	−
Children	+	−	−

family or they set up their own residence, respectively). Margot and Chas each set up a neolocal residence. Margot is rejected by her blood relatives (an event never explained in the film) and is adopted by the Tenenbaums. In the brief flashback where Margot seeks out her blood relatives (21) (ii), her alienation from them is conveyed visually (she stands awkwardly in a rural setting wearing her mink coat), and physically (her father accidently cuts off part of her finger). Yet, she does not feel stability in the Tenenbaum family either. In particular, Royal's separation from the Tenenbaum family leaves Margot feeling rejected by a father figure for a second time (she questions him about the reasons, and asks 'Is it our fault?'). Her response to this instability is to seek love from many different people and to marry an older man (a father figure). Richie does not marry and has no home, but is instead shown travelling the globe on an ocean liner. His love for Margot creates the film's main narrative tension: not only does Margot have to contend with rejection from her biological father and then from her symbolic father, but she also has to deal with her (symbolic) brother's love for her.

In the second extended expositional scene after the credits (6), all three Tenenbaum children are shown to be unhappy. They decide to return to their family home, leading to the creation of what anthropologists call a joint or extended family. An extended family consists of two or more generations of adults, plus their children, living in the same home. From scenes (14) to (25) the family unit consists of Etheline, her children Margot, Chas and Richie, and Chas's children. This set up resembles or simulates a matrilineal family system, with the mother in charge and the father on the periphery. This, in fact, is the family structure under which the Tenenbaum children grew up after their parents separated. From (25) to (34) Royal rejoins the family unit. The partners of the married children are not, however, present in the house: Margot is separated from Raleigh, and Chas' wife is dead. But Henry and Eli do visit the Tenenbaum house, as does Raleigh.[3] The Tenenbaum home contains multiple kinship conflicts and rivalries: Henry is a suitor for Etheline and is in conflict with Royal, while both Raleigh and Eli are competing for Margot's attention (while Richie's love for Margot is gradually revealed as the film progresses). Henry succeeds in eliminating his rival from the family home by exposing his fake illness (34), while Margot ends up rejecting both Raleigh and Eli, but only after she has declared her love for Richie (and he has declared his love for her). This mutual declaration of love and Margot's rejection of Eli and Raleigh resolves all but the quasi-incest issue structuring their relationship, leading to a deadlock of desire. The kinship tensions within the Tenenbaum family can be delineated more clearly via a series of paradigmatic analyses.

Paradigms and mediation

How are the film's three kinship conflicts mediated and resolved? Royal's conflict with his wife (and towards Henry) is suddenly resolved soon after hearing about Richie's love for Margot. Richie plays the role of mediator in resolving this conflict.

Paradigm (a): Royal–Etheline–Henry

- (2) (iv) Royal announces his separation from Etheline
- (6) (v) Etheline receives a marriage proposal from Henry
- (6) (vii) Pagoda informs Royal of the marriage proposal
- (16) (ii) Royal meets Henry for the first time
- (18) Henry talks to Etheline about his proposal, and they kiss
- (33) (i) Etheline decides not to go out with Henry; (ii) Royal and Henry confront one another
- (34) Henry discovers that Royal is not ill; Royal leaves the house
- (52) Royal hands over divorce papers to Etheline, and compliments Henry
- (54) Wedding day of Etheline and Henry (postponed)
- (56) (ii) Etheline and Henry finally marry
- (58) Royal's funeral

Within this paradigm, (52) is pivotal; all the sequences above it (except (2) (iv), which initiates the paradigm) share the same value – Royal's hostility to Henry. From (52) onwards, the value of the sequences reverses, and Royal demonstrates kindness towards Henry. The paradigmatic structure cannot by itself explain this sudden reversal; it can only be explained in terms of mediation. In (34), Royal undergoes a reversal of fortune (he loses his place in his own family home) and experiences a moment of self-recognition (he recognizes he has lost his status as father figure). He stops pretending to be ill and announces to the whole family that he has genuinely enjoyed their company. We next see him applying for the job of lift/elevator operator (39), an unskilled low-paid job that reinforces his reversal of fortune and the demise of his symbolic status as a powerful father figure. In (43), he rushes to Richie's bedside, and in (48) Richie informs him that he is in love with Margot. Scene (52), Royal handing over divorce papers to Etheline and complimenting Henry, is Royal's response to scenes (43) and (48). We need to go back much further to discover Richie's special status in relation to his father. In (2), the narrator informs us that Royal invited Richie on outings to the city and that the other children were never invited. In (21) (i), at the cemetery, Royal asks Richie about Henry:

ROYAL
Henry Sherman. You know him?
RICHIE
Yeah.
ROYAL
Is he worth a damn?
RICHIE
I believe so.
Royal nods.

Later, in (24), when thrown out of his hotel room, Royal phones Richie and asks if he can stay in his room. Royal turns Richie's bedroom into a fake hospital bed, while Richie camps out in the ballroom in his tent. The image of

Royal's fake hospital bed contrasts with Richie's real hospital bed as he recovers from his suicide attempt. This sets up a symbolic opposition between Royal and Richie: false hospital bed (Royal)/real hospital bed (Richie).

Royal always looks to Richie for advice and assistance. Scene (21) (i) – especially Richie's reply to this father – initiates the resolution of the conflict between Royal/Henry. Nonetheless, it takes Richie's suicide attempt (his response to Margot's many love affairs) and his declaration of love for Margot to mediate and resolve the conflict between Royal and Henry. As symbolic father, Royal prohibits the union of Richie and Margot, for it signifies incest, at least on a symbolic level. But Royal's reversal of fortune (leading to the demotion of his symbolic status) leads to his recognition that he is unable to re-establish his place in the Tenenbaum family. Richie's suicide attempt is indirectly caused by the prohibition of incest, of which Royal is the enforcer. This is why Richie visits him to confess his love for Margot. Royal's response is initially equivocal but soon concedes that he has no authority over the matter. This recognition of his loss of symbolic status also leads him to accept the marriage of Etheline to Henry.

But Royal's reversal is not so clear-cut. Although he acts as the symbolic father prohibiting incest between consaguines, he stresses that Margot is not a blood relation.

Paradigm (b): Royal–Margot

How is Margot's kinship status resolved in the film? We shall initially investigate it in relation to Royal, before considering her relation to Richie.

- (2) (iv) Royal emphasizes Margot's adopted status
- (12) Margot emphasizes her adopted status when reacting to the news of Royal's illness ('We're not actually related')
- (16) (i) Royal visits the family home to talk to his children (and mentions Margot's adoption)
- (21) (ii) Margot reveals to Ari and Uzi that she is adopted
- (48) On the roof of the Palace Hotel. Richie tells his father that he loves Margot
- (56) (iii) Margot's new play; on stage scene (2) (iv) is acted out

In (2) (iv), part of the film's long opening expositional scene, Royal emphasizes Margot's adopted status, and in (12) and (21) (ii), we see that Margot has internalized Royal's view of her. Royal's characterization of Margot's adopted status eventually backfires when Henry exposes Royal's illness as fake (34). As he is waiting for a taxi to take him from the family home, Royal sees Henry and Margot standing side by side, watching him. Royal points to Henry and says to Margot 'He's not your father', to which Margot responds 'Neither are you'.[4] In (56) (iii), part of the final montage sequence, a short extract from Margot's new play is shown: in an autobiographical moment, we see actors playing Royal and Margot on stage, with Royal introducing Margot as his adopted daughter. This creates a rhyme within the paradigm, for (56) (iii) repeats (2) (iv). The Tenenbaums are in the audience, but only Royal reacts to this scene by laughing at it. (Margot is similar to Max in *Rushmore*, in that both express their childhood emotional conflicts via theatrical staging.) The staging of the conflict holding paradigm (b) together does not resolve the conflict, but it does articulate it in symbolic terms, bringing a moment of recognition in Royal as he laughs at the staged scene. Sequence (56) (iii) is not the first staging of Margot's plays: in (2) Royal attends Margot's eleventh birthday party, in which her first play is staged (with animals as the main characters). Royal is dismissive of it ('It was just a bunch of little kids dressed in animal costumes'), another rejection she receives from a father figure. Margot's kinship status comes into focus in the third paradigm.

Paradigm (c): Richie–Margot–Raleigh–Eli

The complexity of the Richie–Margot–Raleigh–Eli kinship relationships covers most of the film. At its core is the relationship and conflict between Margot and Richie, which is articulated in the following scenes:

Paradigm (c) (i): Richie–Margot

(2) (i) Richie and Margot camp out in the natural history museum (Eli left out)

(2) (ii) On the roof of the Tenenbaum house: Young Richie with Mordecai

(6) Richie sends a letter to Eli acknowledging that he is in love with Margot
(13) Margot meets Richie at the pier
(14) On the roof of the Tenenbaum house: Richie sets free Mordecai and reads Margot's published plays
(21) (iv) Flashback to Richie's final tennis game (with Margot and Raleigh, newly married, in the audience)
(26) Richie reads Margot's published plays in his yellow tent
(28) On the roof of the Tenenbaum house: Raleigh talks to Richie about Margot
(38) Flashback. On the roof of the Tenenbaum house: Young Margot smoking
(40) Richie attempts suicide after finding out about Margot's many affairs and relationships
(46) Resolution in the yellow tent
(48) On the roof of the Palace Hotel. Richie tells his father that he loves Margot
(55) Richie, Margot and Mordecai on the roof of the Tenenbaum house. Richie and Margot share a cigarette

The Margot–Richie relationship is held together by two secrets: Richie and Margot are secretly in love with each other, and Margot secretly smokes. The two secrets are bound together syntagmatically: in the graveyard scene (21), Margot tells Richie she knows about the letter he sent to Eli. At the same moment, she drops her cigarettes. Margot immediately denies they are her cigarettes, and Richie does not discuss the content of the letter, but simply asks why Eli would reveal its contents to Margot. At this stage in the narrative, both characters disavowal their secrets: they are unable to communicate their desire to each other. The two secrets are again linked in scene (42), Richie's recovery in hospital after his attempted suicide. Raleigh says that Margot almost killed her brother (because Richie is in love with her), and then immediately asks Margot for a cigarette. Yet, it is Richie's suicide attempt that unblocks his ability to communicate his desire: he confesses to Margot that he loves her (46), and he informs his father (48). Both secrets are revealed and acknowledged by scene (55) and is signified spatially in an emblematic shot of Margot and Richie sitting together sharing a cigarette (Figure 5.1).

Figure 5.1 Richie, Margot and Mordecai (*The Royal Tenenbaums*) © Touchstone Pictures

The Margot–Richie relationship is also marked spatially: the main location where this relationship is articulated is up on the roof of the Tenenbaum house. The following scenes take place there:

Paradigm (c) (ii): Tenenbaum roof

- (2) (ii) Young Richie with Mordecai
- (14) Richie sets free Mordecai and reads Margot's published plays
- (28) Raleigh talks to Richie about Margot
- (38) Young Margot smoking
- (55) Richie, Margot, and Mordecai. Richie and Margot share a cigarette

Although scene (2) (ii) does not directly involve Margot, it introduces the rooftop location, codes it as Richie's space, and introduces us to his falcon, Mordecai. The significance of this scene in terms of Margot becomes evident retrospectively. Scene (14) sets up a link between Mordecai and Margot – a metaphorical link of substitution: Richie consoles himself with the loss of Mordecai by reading Margot's plays. Mordecai and Margot are similar to Richie in that they are equally objects of affection for him. In setting Mordecai free, Richie leans instead towards Margot, or at least Margot's plays. The plays are in themselves a stand in for Margot, although a metonymic stand in: a contiguous detail that indirectly signifies her. (Richie is again seen reading Margot's plays in his yellow tent [26]). Roman Jakobson explains how metonymy (and its near equivalent, synecdoche) works in fiction: 'In the scene of Anna Karenina's suicide Tolstoj's artistic attention is focused on the heroine's handbag; and in *War and Peace* the synecdoches "hair on the upper lip" or "bare shoulders" are used by the same writer to stand for the female characters to whom these features belong' (Jakobson and Halle 1971, 92). Margot is caught up in a web of metaphorical substitutions (Mordecai) and metonymic contiguities (plays). Even the biblical meaning of the falcon's name is indirectly relevant in respect to Margot's status in the Tenenbaum family, for Mordecai raises the orphan Esther.[5] We next see Richie on the roof in scene (28), when Raleigh talks to him about Margot: Richie is cleaning out the empty falcon coop and Raleigh is talking about Margot leaving him, reinforcing the Tenenbaum roof as a significant location for the Margot-Richie relationship (and also reinforcing the metaphorical link between Mordecai and Margot, for both have left their homes). The flashback to the young Margot smoking on the roof (38) further reinforces this link between Margot and Mordecai. Finally, as mentioned already, (55) brings together in one condensed image Richie, Margot, Mordecai, and smoking.

Yet, one of the most significant scenes regarding the Margot–Richie relationship takes place on the roof of the Palace Hotel (48), not the Tenenbaum home. In scene (48) Richie tells his father that he loves Margot, and Mordecai returns to Richie a few moments later. It would seem logical that this scene form part of the Tenenbaum roof paradigm (Paradigm (c) [ii]), not least because the Tenenbaum roof is strongly coded in terms of Richie-Margot, and also because Mordecai flies into the scene (flies 'home'). Scene (48) therefore logically fits into the Tenenbaum roof paradigm, for it shares the same semantic value (scene (48) is, in any case, part of Paradigm (c) (i): Margot-Richie). The Tenenbaum roof paradigm therefore consists of separate scenes with: the young Richie, the young Margot, Richie with Raleigh (Margot's husband), Richie with Royal (Margot's symbolic father), and finally Richie and Margot together (smoking, and with Mordecai, but without Royal and Raleigh – that is, without fathers and husbands [authority male figures]). Or, more simply: Richie and Margot are presented separately on the roof; Richie then appears with Raleigh, then with Royal; and finally, Richie appears with Margot.

Scene (48), on the roof of the Palace Hotel, is also linked to scene (6), Richie informing Eli via letter that he loves Margot. Scene (6) in turn links up to (17), where Eli tells Margot about Richie's letter. In (22) Richie meets Eli and asks him why he told Margot about the letter. This series is completed with scene (46) when Richie and Margot declare their love for one another and kiss. Scenes (6), (17), (22), (46) and (48) form a paradigmatic series to the extent that they all share the same semantic value – Richie's declaration of love for Margot.

Scene (6) establishes the opposition Richie/Eli, who are both attracted to Margot, although this is not evident to the audience until scene (10) when Margot phones Eli, and he appears in her bedroom. The Richie/Eli opposition is resolved in scene (37), where Margot and Eli tell each other they do not love one another (which, incidentally, is opposite in meaning to (46), where Margot and Richie declare their love for each other).

This analysis of paradigm (c) (i), Margot–Richie, brings us back to paradigm (a): Royal–Etheline–Henry. As I pointed out at the beginning of this chapter, these two paradigms run parallel to one another: both involve declarations of love (Etheline–Henry, Richie–Margot), both involve an obstacle, in the form of Royal (husband and father, respectively, blocking the union), and both involve resolution when Royal undergoes a reversal. However, the resolutions are different: Etheline–Henry get married, while Richie–Margot enter into a deadlock of desire, although there is resolution to the extent their feelings for one another are no longer secret, thereby reducing (but not completely resolving) Margot's kinship status in the film.

Finally, Chas is in conflict with everyone in the film, due to long-term family conflicts (Royal stealing money from him, shooting him with a BB gun) and due to the trauma of his wife's death. Chas combines some of the traits of Max and Miss Cross in *Rushmore*, both of whom have lost relatives. The conflict Richie/Chas, the fourth highlighted at the beginning of this chapter (and secondary to the other three), is not evident during their childhoods (except for the resentment when Royal takes Richie on outings). The conflict becomes evident when Chas returns to his childhood room (8) and discovers a poster of Richie in there; Chas becomes annoyed and turns the picture to the wall. Later, they argue over whether Royal should be allowed back into the house. Soon afterwards (26), Chas confronts Richie in his tent:

CHAS

Looks like you and Dad are back together again, huh?

RICHIE

(pause)

He's your dad, too, Chas.

CHAS

No, he's not.

(pause)

You really hate me, don't you?

RICHIE

(puzzled)

No, I don't. I love you.

This confrontation reveals that the conflict between Richie and Chas is imagined by Chas; it also reveals that Chas rejects Royal as his father. The three Tenenbaum children therefore relate differently to Royal: Richie has no conflict with him; Chas downplays his own status as Royal's son, and Margot internalizes Royal's portrayal of her as his adopted daughter. Chas's conflict with Royal is resolved in scene (54) after Royal saves his sons from Eli's car, and for buying them a new dog, a Dalmatian;[6] and in (55) (vii), where they go on a 'reckless' outing together with Ari and Uzi.

In Wes Anderson's first three films, key characters – Dignan in *Bottle Rocket*, Max in *Rushmore*, and Eli Cash in *The Royal Tenenbaums* – are coded as relatively poor. Each character has a distinct trajectory: Dignan remains poor and ends up in jail by the end of the film. Max remains poor, but stages successful plays (even though they plagiarize films) and gains a girlfriend. And Eli becomes a successful writer who has an affair with Margot, but ends up in a drug rehab clinic.

Notes

1. We saw in Chapter 1 (in relation to Oedipus) that ambiguous kinship relations undermine social relations.
2. Margot shares this feeling with Eli, who is almost adopted by the Tenenbaums. The narrator informs us that 'He [Eli] was a regular fixture at family gatherings, holidays, mornings before school and most afternoons.'
3. In the screenplay, Eli has a wife and two children. They are introduced in scene (22), where Richie visits Eli, but Eli's wife and children have been edited out of the film.
4. In a deleted scene, Etheline talks to Margot about Henry Sherman's proposal. Margot approves, and says she is going to have a father. When Etheline reminds her she has a father, Margot replies, 'Not really. Plus, now he's dying'. This deleted scene, situated between (18), Henry talking to Etheline about his proposal, and (19), Royal meeting Ari and Uzi, appears to be the complement of scene (21), where Royal asks Richie for his opinion of Henry. In the deleted scene Margot also raises the issue of her adopted status.
5. Within this biblical narrative, Margot is aligned with Ester rather than Mordecai. Moreover, Margot is not an orphan, but is adopted (and we never find out why she was adopted).
6. Chas bred Dalmatian mice when a child. His father now gives him a gift of a Dalmatian dog.

6

Conflicts of Ambivalence: *The Life Aquatic with Steve Zissou*

The core kinship structure in *The Life Aquatic with Steve Zissou* (2004) takes place between Ned (Owen Wilson) and Steve Zissou (Bill Murray): Is or is not Ned the son of Steve Zissou? This ambivalent kinship status carries over from *The Royal Tenenbaums*, where Margot's adopted status creates conflict when Richie falls in love with her. Whereas in *The Royal Tenenbaums* the kinship ambivalence affects brother and sister, in *The Life Aquatic* the kinship ambivalence affects father and son. Moreover, neither conflict is resolved.

Plot synopsis

(1) A short presentation introducing the documentary film *The Life Aquatic*, Part 1. (2) Film screening: (i) Steve Zissou (Bill Murray) addresses the camera and introduces his film and his crew, including Klaus (Willem Dafoe), Anne-Marie (Robyn Cohen) and his wife Eleanor (Anjelica Huston); (ii) death of Steve's close friend Esteban, killed by the Jaguar shark; and (iii) Q and A with audience; Steve defines his mission (to kill the shark); Ned Plimpton (Owen Wilson) asks a question. (3) After the screening, more characters and themes are introduced: Steve's estranged wife Eleanor, Alistair Hennessey (Jeff Goldblum), formerly married to Eleanor; Klaus's young nephew Werner gives Steve a gift (a sea horse). (4) On Steve Zissou's ship, the Belafonte; discussion of money problems. (5) Ned introduces himself to Steve, mentions the death of his mother, and the possibility of Ned being his son; mention of Jane (Cate Blanchett), the reporter. (6) More exposition: Steve addresses the camera and introduces the Belafonte; (7) Explorers Club: Steve mentions giving his name to Ned;

Ned tells him how his mother died; Steve's response is to say his best friend just died. (8) On Steve's island: death of a cat; filming at night; Steve invites Ned to join his team; conflict between Claus and Ned develops; Jane turns up. (9) Ned hears Jane reading, and enters her room. He tells her about the death of his mother. (10) Jane interviews Steve; the conversion quickly disintegrates. (11) Klaus confronts Ned. (12) Steve warns Ned about Jane's line of questioning; describes Jane as a lesbian; Ned asks how long Steve has known about him ('about five years'); Steve says he never wanted to be a father; gives Ned his correspondence stock ('Kinglsey (Ned) Zissou'). (13) Jane leaves an answerphone message to her editor/father of her baby; (14) Ned donates his inheritance to the film; (15) Ned and Steve fly to the office of film producer Oseary Drakoulias (Michael Gambon); meet 'bond company stooge' Bill (Bud Cort). (16) Montage sequence: preparing for the voyage; including Ned giving Jane a sand dollar as a gift (which Steve confiscates); Ned almost drowns. (17) Team Zissou watch one of their previous documentaries. (18) Eleanor leaves the voyage after hearing about Ned's near-death drowning. (19) 'Day 1.' (20). Screening of documentary footage. (21) Steve and Jane interview continues. (22) Ned reminds Steve that he responded to Ned's fan letter seventeen years previously. (23) 'Day 5: Operation Hennessey Underwater Sea-Laboratory.' (24) Steve carries out a raid on Hennessey's underwater sea-laboratory. (25) Back on the Belafonte: the shark and a distress signal are located on the tracker. (26) In the sauna: Jane tells Ned he does not look like Steve; Ned gives Jane the sand dollar gift a second time. (27) Jane and Steve confront one another in her cabin. (28) Hennessey receives the report on the break in to his sea lab. (29) Team Zissou dive to investigate the phantom signal (a plane crash). Steve rejects Ned's idea to call him dad. (30) On deck, Ned confronts Klaus. (31) 'Day 9: In Unprotected Waters.' (32) Through the fog, Steve spots an unusual boat. Steve asks who is on watch: Klaus checks and asks 'who the hell is Kingsley Zissou?' (33) Ned in Jane's cabin; they kiss. (34) Pirates take over the Belafonte and kidnap Bill but leave their three-legged dog. One pirate is killed. The injured Ned; he looks dazed and confused. (35) 'Day 14: Mutiny on the Belafonte.' (36) Anne-Marie complains to the rest of the crew of Steve's criminal act of sailing in unprotected waters. (37) Funeral service for the dead pirate. It is interrupted by Hennessey's ship. Hennessey agrees to tow the stricken Belafonte to Port-au-Patois. (38) On deck, Anne-Marie and several interns decide to leave the Belafonte. (39) Below deck, Jane talks to her editor on the phone, then says goodbye to Ned. (40) Jane tells Steve that she is leaving. (41) Steve updates Drakoulias on the phone on the disasters he has encountered. (42) 'Day 20: Towed into Port-au-Patois Harbor.' (43) Steve visits Eleanor at Hennessey's residence. She refuses to give him money to rescue Bill and complete the film. He says that they should have had a child earlier in their marriage. (44) Conflict between Steve and Ned develops into a fist fight. The scene ends with Eleanor showing up with money to rescue Bill and complete the film. (45) Steve and Eleanor outline the plan to rescue Bill, located on the Ping Islands. (46) Eleanor informs Jane in confidence that Steve is infertile. (47) 'Day 27: Rescuing the Bond Company Stooge.' (48) Documentary footage showing Hennessey's ship stricken off the Ping Islands. (49) Team Zissou land on the Ping Islands. They rescue Bill and Hennessey. Steve reconciles with Ned. (50) Ned shows Steve the new flag he has designed. (51) Ned reconciles with Klaus. Jane writes a letter to Ned. Ned and Steve fly in the helicopter; Ned's letter to Steve from seventeen years ago is read out; Ned and Steve see signs of the Jaguar Shark's presence. But the helicopter crashes and kills Ned. (52) Ned's funeral. (53) Apparent reconciliation between Steve and Hennessey. Steve suggests to Eleanor that they could have adopted Ned. (54) The scanner reveals the location of the Jaguar shark. All the characters go down in Steve's submarine to see it. Jane mentions that in twelve years, her child will be eleven and a half. (55) Extracts from the completed documentary film are screened. Jane (with her baby) and all of Team Zissou (except Steve) are in the audience. Steve is outside the theatre with Werner. Steve gives Werner Ned's ring. The theatre doors open and all the Team Zissou members join Steve.

The film's opening credits, in the form of a documentary film, represent a condensed moment of exposition: they introduce the Team Zissou crew and the narrative disruption (Esteban's death). The documentary images are framed by curtains (cf. *Rushmore*), and the film title appears in the projected documentary film (just as the title of *The Royal Tenenbaums* appears in the storyworld, on the cover of a book). The Q and A introduces the quest (to kill the shark). The after party introduces conflict between Hennessey and Zissou, financial obstacles and introduces a second major storyline – Ned and Steve. Ned's fate is foreshadowed during the Q and A. Steve is asked: 'who you gonna kill in Part 2?' The film's answer is Ned: he almost dies in scene (16), and does die in (51).

Exchange

There are several significant moments of dyadic exchange in *The Life Aquatic*. Dyadic exchange refers to an act of giving that is reciprocated between two individuals. Klaus's young nephew Werner gives Steve a 'crayon pony-fish' (a multicoloured sea horse) in scene (3); this sets up an implicit expectation that the act will be reciprocated, which occurs in the film's final scene (55): Steve gives to Werner Ned's Zissou society ring. Werner is an underdeveloped character, for we only see him in these two scenes. But the circuit of exchange he sets up with Steve is an important aspect of the film's symbolic system. The dyadic exchange of gifts is intergenerational: from a young Werner to a 52-year-old Steve and back again. Steve's act of exchange passes his name and society onto the next generation. Steve then utters the final line of the film: 'This is an adventure.' The ring is not an isolated reply to Werner's gift; instead, it is part of a formal system that defines the symbolic place and function of its owner within a group; the owner of the ring becomes marked with the name of the father and is established as a member of his group. With the handing over of the ring and with Zissou uttering the film's final line, Werner is positioned as the next adventurer.[1]

Another significant moment of dyadic exchange takes place (or took place) between Ned and Steve: they exchanged letters seventeen years previously, and both letters are retrieved and read out. Ned's letter (51) names a bug after Steve, mentions Ned's mother, and ends by asking 'Do you ever wish you could breathe underwater?' Steve's reply (22) notes that the bug is a gnat and says he remembers Ned's mother. The contents of the Ned and Steve letters are important because the elements they manifest – the act of naming, misidentification, Ned's mother and breathing underwater – are worked through as the narrative unfolds.

The Ned–Jane relationship is also sealed via gift-giving. In scene (16), Ned gives Jane a sand dollar as a gift (which Steve confiscates), but Ned retrieves it and gives it to Jane a second time (26). When they depart (51), she in turn writes Ned a letter. And at his funeral (52), she places several letters in his coffin. These events become important from a paradigmatic perspective, explored later.

Another moment of dyadic exchange, this time unintentional, takes place when the pirates board the Belafonte: they take Bill hostage but inadvertently leave their three-legged dog (Cody). This exchange is reversed when Bill is rescued from the Ping Islands: Cody is inadvertently left behind, even though Steve insists they should go back to get him. Cody plays a role on the Ping Islands: whereas Team Zissou give up on finding the pirates, Cody locates them (and Hennessey) in a back room of the hotel.

Kinship

The kinship ambiguity and conflict in *The Life Aquatic*, Ned's ambivalent status as Steve Zissou's son, is exacerbated when both Steve and Ned develop a sexual interest in Jane. Here we see the conflict from *Rushmore* reproduced and developed in *The Life Aquatic*. In *Rushmore*, the young Max and the middle-aged Blume both develop a sexual attraction towards the 28-year-old Miss Cross. In *The Life Aquatic*, this structure is duplicated but the stakes are raised, for it could turn out to be an actual consanguine, intergenerational Oedipal rivalry between the two men if Steve and Ned are father and son ('actual' in the weak sense that biological father and son are competing for the same woman). The stakes are also raised in that Jane is pregnant, unmarried and is described (at least by Steve) as a lesbian. One of the main differences between *Rushmore* and *The Life Aquatic* in terms of this three-way relationship is that, in *The Life Aquatic*, the woman rejects the advances of the older man, whereas in *Rushmore*, the woman ends up forming a relationship with the older man.

Ned's ambivalent status draws attention to the similarity between Ned's mother and Jane. Although never stated on the film's surface, and although we never see Ned's mother in the film, several parallels exist between them: both are single women who have had various affairs; both become pregnant; and both become single mothers with little or no contact with the father (Jane leaves phone messages for the father, but we never see or hear him). The two female characters are from different generations, and Ned's mother dies of cancer before the film begins (just as Max's mother dies of cancer before *Rushmore* begins). That Ned feels attracted to Jane further reinforces the Oedipal narrative, because of her similarities to Ned's mother. The Ned–Jane relationship develops in the same way the Max–Miss Cross relationship was initiated in *Rushmore*: Ned hears Jane reading and goes to her room (9), just as Max falls for Miss Cross as she reads aloud to her class.

There is also the issue of the ambiguous identification of Ned's father, which is central to the film (Steve's infertility apparently rules him out). One of the tragedies in the film is that Ned may have misidentified and misnamed Steve as his father, and he dies in the process of trying to find out. However, it is through Ned's death that Steve publicly accepts him as his son.

Like the other fathers or father figures already discussed (in *Bottle Rocket*, *Rushmore*, and *The Royal Tenenbaums*), Steve Zissou is a post-Oedipal man in several ways: he acts in an irresponsible, selfish manner throughout the film (e.g. he takes the Belafonte through unprotected waters to save fuel; he breaks into Jane's cabin to read her notes about him); he is vindictive (especially towards Hennessey, because of his success and because he was the first husband of Steve's wife Eleanor – a fact he tries to disavowal by calling Hennessey gay); he steals from Hennessey's research lab; Steve is not financially independent, for he relies on his rich wife for financial support and for making strategic choices (on several occasions the line 'Eleanor is the brains behind Team Zissou' is uttered by different characters in the film, including Steve in scene [45]); he is also dependent on his (potential) son Ned for financial support (in the same way, Royal Tenenbaum also relies on his wife and children for financial support and acts in an irresponsible manner for most of *The Royal Tenenbaums*); finally, in scene (12) Steve says he hates fathers and never wanted to be one. He also says he cannot live up to the image of himself projected in his films and publicity.

However, Steve's character also embodies a few traits of the fable of the primal father figure outlined in chapter 4 of Freud's speculative book *Totem and Taboo*, a figure who claims total control over all women within a close community of men. When Jane first appears, Steve 'claims' her first. He says to

Klaus 'not this one', which Steve later repeats to Ned. And Klaus also repeats it to other crew members:

PELE
I like her hair-do.
KLAUS
(shrugs)
Me, too, but Steve already called her.

Steve also tells Ned that Jane is a lesbian, which perhaps is his indirect way of saying 'not this one' to Ned. But the remainder of the myth that Freud outlines does not apply; Jane simply rejects Steve's advances (twice), and Steve (unlike the primal father) is not killed. However, the mutiny on the Belafonte is a form of rejection of his authority (and is led by a woman, Anne-Marie). Interestingly, Steve's closest allay Klaus appears to be the first to mutiny, but only because he misunderstands Steve's instructions – which Steve states in a double negative:

ZISSOU
Look, if you're not against me, don't cross this line. If yes, do.
I love you all.
Klaus immediately steps across the line. He looks to Zissou. Zissou looks pained and stunned. He can barely manage to say:
ZISSOU
Are you – are you sure?
KLAUS
(confidently)
Yes, I am.
ZISSOU
I don't understand. Why?
KLAUS
(confused)
What do you mean? Wait a second. What are we doing? You said cross the line if-

ZISSOU

Cross the line if you want to quit.

Klaus quickly goes back to the other side.

KLAUS

Do it again. I misunderstood.

On the surface, Klaus's mistake creates humour, but it also points to the underlying symbolic logic where Klaus implicitly resents Steve's authority in regards to women. In addition, all the male interns join Anne-Marie in the mutiny (although one, Nico, later decides to stay behind).

Paradigms and (the lack of) mediation

Two paradigms are central to the film's symbolic structure: Steve–Ned and Ned–Jane.

Steve–Ned Paradigm

- (5) Ned introduces himself to Steve and raises the possibility of being his son
- (7) Steve mentions giving his name to Ned
- (8) Steve invites Ned to join his team
- (12) Steve says he never wanted to be a father; gives Ned his correspondence stock
- (14) Ned donates his inheritance to Steve's film
- (22) Ned reminds Steve that he responded to Ned's fan letter seventeen years previously
- (29) Steve rejects Ned's idea to call him dad
- (44) Conflict between Steve and Ned develops into a fist fight
- (49) Steve reconciles with Ned
- (51) Ned's letter to Steve from seventeen years ago is read out; the helicopter crashes and kills Ned
- (55) In the completed documentary Steve calls Ned his son

The primary semantic value within this paradigm is the attempt to secure a kinship bond between Steve and Ned. This value is largely positive, with the exceptions of scenes (29) and (44), which simply represent the inverse negative value (conflict between Steve and Ned), while the end of scene (51) brings attempts to develop a bond to an abrupt halt. Scene (12) is a pivotal, ambiguous scene, which moves from a negative polarity (when Steve says 'I never wanted to be a father') to positive, when Steve enthusiastically presents Ned with his correspondence stock, or letterheaded notepaper, which reads 'Kingsley (Ned) Zissou'. Ned Plimpton's name has been transformed: his original name is enclosed in parentheses and is surrounded by Steve's surname and the first name (Kingsley) Steve would have given to Ned. Ned's confused, ambivalent kinship status is perfectly expressed on a symbolic level via the correspondence stock.[2] Ned's death is a result of the symbolic intolerance towards ambiguity, of the irresolvable contradiction over his kinship status. Rather than resolve this contradiction via oppositions and mediation, the film resolves it by eliminating one term in the opposition (Ned).

The correspondence stock in scene (12) reveals that, although Steve does not want to be a real father, he enjoys the symbolic dimension of fatherhood. This is also evident in scene (7), when he first talks to Ned about changing his name, and in (8) when he asks Ned to join his team. Also running through the film is the reverse problem: Ned's uneasiness regarding what to call Steve. In scene (29), Steve flatly refuses to let Ned call him 'dad', although he tries to think of a nickname. However, during their fight in scene (44), Ned complains that a nickname is not the same as 'dad'. Naming also crops up in Ned's fan letter to Steve, but in this instance the naming process is reversed: the young Ned names a bug after Steve. In *The Royal Tenenbaums*, Royal has a similar issue with his grandsons about what they should call him.[3]

The correspondence stock is also important in regards to the reciprocity between the two letters between Ned and Steve in scenes (22) and (51), for the stock is to be used to write more letters. Yet, Ned never uses it. Instead, he gives some of the stock to Jane, who writes him a letter, which he reads just before boarding the fateful helicopter in scene (51), and she writes additional letters to put in his coffin in scene (52). In other words, the 'Kingsley (Ned) Zissou' correspondence stock is used by Jane to send letters *to* Ned; Ned receives letters on his own correspondence stock, but stock that is nonetheless alien to him, because it rewrites his name in terms of the name of the father, the Other that has remained absent from his life. By printing up Ned's correspondence stock, Steve facilitates the symbolic link between Ned and Jane. That link remains after his death in the helicopter crash, for Jane writes him more letters, and Steve establishes his own symbolic link with Ned by officially naming him as his son in the second part of the documentary film. In fact, it is through his death that Ned secures his symbolic role as son (reversing the *Totem and Taboo* fable, where the death of the father establishes the father's symbolic role).

The primary outcome of this paradigm is that Steve's/the father's symbolic status is upheld and in fact is increased, for he becomes a father. Ned's financial investment in the Jaguar Shark documentary ensures the second part of the film is made, and his death secures the symbolic relationship between father and son, which is officially (publicly) represented in the second part of the documentary, screened in scene (55), when Steve narrates in voice-over without equivocation that Ned was his son (and his initial 'N' is officially represented on the Zissou society flag). This is a familiar Wes Anderson trope: an important family relationship is expressed via media – in this instance in a documentary film and, within the film, on a flag (whereas Margot in *The Royal Tenenbaums* and Max in *Rushmore* expressed difficult kinship relationships via theatrical staging). Ned's money and his death also enables the Zissou society to continue, represented in the final moments of the film when Steve gives to Werner Ned's Zissou society ring.

Earlier, I defined scenes (22) and (44) as negative in terms of the kinship between Ned and Steve. This negativity is evident in other scenes as well, especially those involving Jane. A second paradigm, Ned–Jane, can be extracted from the film, a paradigm that contains many additional moments with Steve present:

Ned–Jane paradigm

(5) Ned introduces himself to Steve, and Jane is mentioned soon afterwards

(8) Steve invites Ned to join his team; Jane turns up moments later

(9) Ned hears Jane reading, and enters her room

(12) Steve warns Ned about Jane's line of questioning, and describes her as a lesbian

(16) Ned gives Jane a sand dollar as a gift (which Steve confiscates)

(26) Jane tells Ned he does not look like Steve; Ned gives Jane the sand dollar gift a second time

(33) Ned in Jane's cabin; they kiss (which Steve sees)

(51) Jane writes a letter to Ned. Ned and Steve fly in the helicopter

(52) Ned's funeral (Jane places several letters in his coffin)

(55) In the documentary film, Steve, Ned and Jane are shown together in the same shot (see Figure 6.1)

The values in this paradigm are more complex than the previous paradigm. Positive values predominate in scenes (9), (16), (26), (33) and (51), which represent the Ned–Jane relationship (Jane reading and Ned listening, the exchange of gifts (sand dollar, letter), and kissing). But this positivity is abruptly reversed at the end of (51) when the helicopter crashes. The syntagmatic juxtaposition of Ned and Jane foreshadows their successful union: in (5) Drakoulias mentions Jane the reporter soon after Steve introduces him to Ned; in (8) the bonding of Steve and Ned (Steve formally asks him to join Team Zissou) is interrupted when Jane turns up; and then the relationship

Figure 6.1 Steve, Ned and Jane (*The Life Aquatic with Steve Zissou*) © Touchstone Pictures

begins in (9). The negativity derives from Steve's attempts to intervene and break up their relationship, telling Ned that Jane is a lesbian, and confiscating Ned's gift to Jane. The younger man, Ned, wins the contest over Steve, the older man (reversing the outcome of the similar conflict in *Rushmore*), but Ned's victory is short-lived. The first paradigm has no mediation; the second paradigm is resolved (despite Steve's attempt to act as an anti-mediator), but leads to tragedy.

The surface narrative structure involves the hunt for the Jaguar shark. The underlying symbolic logic involves attempts to establish kinship links between Steve and Ned, and between Ned and Jane (a woman who resembles Ned's mother). Steve and Ned attempt to establish consanguine relationship of father and son, while Ned and Jane attempt to establish an affinal relationship (perhaps resulting in marriage). The second relationship is complicated by the first: Steve's sexual interest in Jane creates a conflict between him and Ned, a conflict that threatens both kinship relationships, with Ned at the centre of both. Ned's death means that Jane remains a single mother, and the Steve–Ned relationship is secured on a symbolic level.

Binary oppositions: Individual/collective, water/sky

Individual/collective is an important binary opposition at work in *Bottle Rocket*, *Rushmore* and *The Royal Tenenbaums*, with an emphasis on dysfunctional solitary individuals attempting to integrate into a group. *Bottle Rocket* consists of Dignan's relation to two unstable teams of petty criminals; *Rushmore* consists of Max's relation to two different schools: Rushmore Academy and Cleveland High; while *The Royal Tenenbaums* consists of Margot's problematic relation to the Tenenbaum family. The team in *The Life Aquatic* is formally named 'Team Zissou', and its dysfunctional members are visually united via a uniform. The dynamics of the group changes throughout the film: Ned, the intern Nico, the young Werner and Jane's baby join the team. Anne-Marie leaves the team, while Esteban and Ned are killed. Ned joining the team initially leads to conflict with Klaus, a symbolic sibling rivalry, but this is later resolved when Ned recognizes Klaus's status by putting him on the Team Zissou flag.

Ned is a pilot comfortable in the sky, but not in water – he cannot swim, and almost drowns in scene (16). This means that, in relation to Ned, sky is coded positively and water negatively. Even when he is introduced in scene (2) asking a question after the screening, Ned is located high up at the top of the theatre. But a reversal takes place: in (29) we see that he has mastered the art of swimming underwater, and in (51) he loses control of the helicopter, for it falls out of the sky into the water, killing him. Ned's fan letter, read out during this fateful flight, ends with the question 'Do you ever wish you could breathe underwater?' This question combines water and sky (air). When the helicopter crashes the water/air opposition collapses and Ned drowns.

Notes

1 Jane's baby is also allotted a symbolic place and function, for we see it dressed in a Zissou uniform and red cap in scene (55).
2 Klaus also experiences this confusion when he looks at the list of those on watch on the Belafonte (32): Ned's name is crossed out and replaced with 'Kingsley Zissou', to which Klaus responds 'who the hell is Kingsley Zissou?' Klaus's frustration is in part fuelled by his rivalry with Ned in regards to Steve's paternal attention.
3 Although not relevant to the Steve–Ned paradigm, fatherhood is also evident in scene (43), when Steve mentions to Eleanor that they should have had a child together (although Eleanor knows he is infertile), and in scene (53), after Ned's funeral, when he suggests to Eleanor they could have adopted Ned.

7

Fraternal Rivalry: *The Darjeeling Limited* and *Hotel Chevalier*

The main contradiction that *The Darjeeling Limited* (2007) attempts to resolve is implicit throughout the film: the absolute conflict between the mother and father, the parents of the Whitman brothers (Francis, Jack and Peter), a conflict that manifests a number of traumatic symptoms in the brothers. Early on in the film, Francis asks his brothers, 'Did I raise us?' but he only receives blank looks from Jack and Peter. Later, Peter expresses uneasiness about becoming a father. He says he expects to get divorced because of 'how we were raised'. Francis says about their mother that 'she's been disappearing all our lives'. In a flashback scene, the brothers discover that their mother has decided not to attend her husband's funeral. When questioned by her sons, she says she did not want to attend, a simple answer that hides a deeper conflict the film never directly addresses.

Jack spells out the film's secondary contradiction:

JACK
I wonder if the three of us could've been friends in real life. Not as brothers, but as people.

Jack expresses the impossible wish not to be brothers with Peter and Francis, but to be a non-consanguine friend; his comment sets up an opposition between 'kinship' and 'friendship'. The film's narrative trajectory attempts to address these contradictions and the symptoms they create via kinship relations, repetition, binary oppositions and mediation. The end result is that the brothers can only function once they have 'symbolized' their parents – that is, represented in symbolic form the absent mother and the dead father. The process of symbolization, structured around a clichéd journey of Westerners to the East, is not entirely sincere but involves elements of comedy and farce. For Nandana Bose, *The Darjeeling Limited* presents a critique of this Western cliché: 'The film takes an overtly Orientalist premise of seeking spiritual growth in India as its starting point and then subverts it through the course of the film by ridiculing such an intent through comic characterization and the farcical situations, actions and reactions of its main protagonists – three white men desperately seeking short-cuts to salvation or *nirvana*' (2008, 6). More specifically, like other Wes Anderson films, *The Darjeeling Limited* presents an oscillation between irony, comedy and farce on the one hand, and sincerity on the other; it is able to draw upon the Western cliché of the spiritual journey to India but, at the same time, it skilfully distances itself from that cliché.

Plot synopsis

(1) A taxi rushes along the street in India. The passenger (Bill Murray) is heading to the train station. (2) On the platform he runs towards the train (called The Darjeeling Limited) as it pulls out of the station. He is overtaken by Peter Whitman (Adrien Brody) who also runs towards the train, laden with bags. Peter manages to board the train, while the Bill Murray character does not. (3) On the train, Peter heads towards the compartment reserved for him and his two brothers, Jack Whitman (Jason Schwartzman) and Francis Whitman (Owen Wilson). (4) In the compartment, Peter meets up with Jack and Francis. The chief steward (Waris Ahluwalia) takes their tickets. Rita (Amara Karan) presents them with refreshments. (5) The three brothers walk to the dining car in order to talk and catch up, and share a table with an old Indian man (Kumar Pallana). Their backstories are introduced, and Francis (whose face is bandaged) continually makes formal agreements with his brothers and is identified as the brother who planned the trip. Their partners and parents are mentioned in passing, including their father's death one year previously. Jack has written a short story about their father's death, which Peter reads. (6) Back in their compartment, the brothers meet Francis's assistant Brendan (Wally Wolodarsky), and Jack has sex with Rita in the bathroom. (7) Jack checks the phone messages of his girlfriend (Natalie Portman). (8) The three brothers visit a temple (which Francis calls the

Temple of 1000 Bulls) and go shopping (for shoes, a poisonous snake and a mace). Francis asks Peter to return his belt, which Peter borrowed. Francis reads and praises Jack's story. They have to run to catch the train. (9) Brendan informs Francis that he has contacted Francis's mother, located in a convent near the Himalayas. Francis gives Peter his belt as a birthday gift. (10) The poisonous snake escapes but is caught by the chief steward, who confines the three brothers to their compartment. (11) The three brothers attend a religious service in a Sikh temple. (12) The train stops, apparently lost. The brothers attempt to perform a ceremony with feathers at the top of a hill. Francis tells Peter and Jack the reason for the journey – to visit their mother. They rush down the hill to catch the train. (13) The brothers begin to argue and fight, and Peter throws the belt at Francis, injuring him. Jack maces both brothers. All three are ejected from the train. (14) At night, the brothers build a campfire and read a letter from their mother, who says she is unable to meet them. They try to perform the feather ceremony a second time. (15) The next day, the brothers try to rescue three young boys who fall into a river. The boy that Peter tries to save drowns. (16) They take the child to the nearby village and meet the villagers. (17) The brothers catch the bus to leave, but are then invited to the funeral. (18) They get off the bus and form part of the funeral procession. (19) Flashback to the brothers (and Alice) going to their father's funeral one year previously. They stop to collect his car from a garage, but cannot get it started. (These are the events Jack wrote about in his short story.) (20) Back to the boy's funeral: his funeral pyre is lit next to a river. (21) The Whitman brothers get on the bus and head to the airport. (22) They check in and then drink tea, make telephone calls and go to the bathroom, where Francis takes off his bandages. Francis gives his belt to Peter. (23) The brothers decide not to board the plane, but instead head to the convent. (24) At the convent they meet their mother, Patricia (Anjelica Huston). (25) Late at night she asks them what they want for breakfast, and organizes it and makes agreements. (26) During this scene there is a montage sequence depicting other characters (Rita, the chief steward, the two boys saved from drowning, the pregnant Alice, the old Indian man, Brendan, Jack's girlfriend, the business man, plus the lion terrorizing the people in the convent). (27) In the morning Jack writes another short story. The brothers discover their mother has left the convent. (28) They trek up a mountain and perform the feather ceremony. (29) They travel to the train station. Jack narrates the ending of his new short story. (30) At the train

> station the brothers run for the train; they have to ditch all their luggage in order to catch it. (31) In their compartment the chief steward takes their tickets and the stewardess presents them with refreshments. The three brothers head to the dining car.

Fraternal kinship

The narrative of *The Darjeeling Limited* focuses on three generations of consanguine kin – the Whitman brothers, their mother and father, plus the future children (or child) of the brothers. More specifically, the narrative focuses on the tense relations among the three brothers. In particular, Jack and Peter share secrets but keep them from Francis – Jack tells Peter he has his own ticket and may leave early, and Peter tells Jack that his wife Alice is having a baby. The narrative also depicts the brothers' problematic relation to their dead father and to their mother, Patricia (who only appears in two scenes, [24] and [25]),[1] and to Peter's anxiety about becoming a father. Patricia is first mentioned in scene (5), and immediately afterwards the three brothers begin taking pain-relief medication, a syntagmatic juxtaposition (repeated in scene 14) that indirectly signifies their problematic relation to their mother. The three brothers have different coping mechanisms and manifest different traumatic traits in regard to their father's death. Peter appropriates various objects belonging to their father (glasses, car keys, razor). He wears his father's prescription glasses throughout the film, but they are non-functional, for he can only see when he raises them or takes them off (and they appear to give him a headache). Although never explicitly stated, Francis was unable to cope, and almost killed himself by deliberately crashing his motorcycle (an action comparable to Eli – also played by Owen Wilson – in *The Royal Tenenbaums* crashing his car into the Tenenbaum house). Jack copes by writing a short story about his father's funeral (part of which we later see in a flashback), although he initially denies his story is based on real events.

In terms of affinal kinship relations, Jack attempts to establish what others consider to be unsuitable relationships (both Francis and Peter disapprove of his relationship with the Natalie Portman character) and he has casual sex with the stewardess Rita on the train. At the end of the film, he goes through a transformation by rejecting his relationship with the Natalie Portman character – his second short story ends by saying, 'he would not be going to Italy' (to meet her). His brothers approve this move, and Jack acknowledges that his story is non-fictional.[2]

Jack is similar to Max Fischer in *Rushmore* (also played by Jason Schwartzman). We saw in Chapter 4 that Max deals with a 'broken' consanguine relationship (his mother's death) and forges affinal relationships by writing plays. In his final play Max cast his girlfriend Margaret Yang, and on stage his character asks her character to marry him. Max finally rejects an unworkable relationship with his school teacher Miss Cross and normalizes his desire by developing an interethnic relationship with Margaret. Wes Anderson revisits this scenario in *The Darjeeling Limited*, but it undergoes a series of transformations. Both Jack and Max use writing to cope with the death of a parent, whereas Max is dealing with his mother's death, Jack is dealing with his father's death:

> Max–writing–mother's death (*Rushmore*)
>
> Jack–writing–father's death (*The Darjeeling Limited*)

Both characters also resolve their relationship issues within the context of their writing. Just as the underage Max attempted to establish a socially unacceptable affinal relationship with the much older Miss Cross, in *The Darjeeling Limited* Jack establishes what his brothers consider to be an unacceptable affinal relationship with the Natalie Portman character. Whereas Max used his writing to strengthen his relation to Margaret, Jack uses his writing to break off his relationship with the Portman character. Here we see a double reversal:

> The acceptable relationship is secured in the writing (*Rushmore*)/
>
> The unacceptable relationship is ended in the writing (*The Darjeeling Limited*).

We also see Jack develop an interethnic relationship with Rita, but clearly it is negatively coded as a casual relationship, unlike the positive Max–Margaret relationship. When Jack and Rita depart, Jack says to her, 'Thanks for using me', an ironic comment that inverts the relation between them, for the comment describes the way Jack used Rita. Unlike Max in *Rushmore*, Jack ends up single (although he reconciles some of his fraternal conflicts, as we shall see later).

Peter is similar to Steve Zissou, in that he is traumatized by the thought of becoming a father. Based on the experience of his parents, Peter assumes his relationship will break up, and he does not want a child to be bought up (like he was) in a broken relationship. It is also notable that he experiences a child's death, for he was unable to save the boy who fell into the water in scene (15) – one of the significant turning points in the film, the first stage of Peter's ability to come to terms with loss and fatherhood.

Francis, the eldest brother, can only relate to his siblings by committing them to make formal binding agreements and plans with him. (In this respect, Francis is similar to Dignan in *Bottle Rocket*, also played by Owen Wilson, a manic character who makes excessive plans.) Towards the end of the film, we realize that Francis is imitating his mother, who also makes plans and agreements. In the first of many examples, in scene (5), Francis says to his brothers:

FRANCIS

How did it get to this? Why haven't we spoken in a year? Let's make an agreement.

[. . .]

A. I want us be become brothers again like we used to be and for us to find ourselves and bond with each other. Can we agree to that?

[. . .]

B. I want us to make this trip a spiritual journey where each of us seek the unknown, and we learn about it. Can we agree to that?

[. . .]

C. I want us to be completely open and say yes to everything even if it's shocking and painful. Can we agree to that?

In scene (25) in the convent, their mother Patricia says:

PATRICIA

All right. Let's make an agreement: A. We'll get an early start tomorrow morning and try to enjoy each other's company here in this beautiful place. B. We'll stop feeling sorry for ourselves. It's not very attractive. C. We'll make our plans for the future. Can we agree to that?

Francis also orders specific dishes for both Jack and Peter in the dining car in scene (5), while Patricia does the same when arranging breakfast for her sons. By imitating his mother, Francis appears to be closer to her than to his father. It is also Francis who arranged the trip to find and visit their mother. The fight between the brothers that breaks out in scene (13) is caused by Francis's revelation that the aim of the journey is to find their mother.

Francis mentions in scene (5) that he lives alone. Peter mentions that his wife Alice is fine (and tells Jack, but not Francis, that Alice is pregnant). The brothers' partners are almost entirely absent from the film: Alice appears briefly on two occasions, in the funeral flashback (scene [19]) and in the unusual montage (scene [26]). Jack's girlfriend only appears in the unusual montage scene. However, she is a central character in *Hotel Chevalier* (2007), the short film linked to *The Darjeeling Limited* (*Hotel Chevalier* is also known as *Part 1 of The Darjeeling Limited*). Jack mentions her on several occasions, and the fragment of short story he writes in scene (27) in the convent (and reads out on the way to the train station) describes the central scene in *Hotel Chevalier*. Except for the first and last shots, the thirteen-minute film is set entirely in Jack's hotel room.

Hotel Chevalier is referenced several times in *The Darjeeling Limited*: Jack's first short story is written on Hotel Chevalier notepaper; Jack wears a Hotel Chevalier bathrobe; his second short story describes a key scene in *Hotel Chevalier*; and he plays on his iPod the same song in both films, Peter Sarstedt's 'Where Do You Go To (My Lovely)?' In *Hotel Chevalier*, he plays it just before he lets his girlfriend into his hotel room (and we hear it again in the film's final moments). And in *The Darjeeling Limited*, he plays it when sharing a cigarette with Rita.

The three brothers therefore handle affinal kinship relationships and consanguine relations (especially relations to their parents) differently: Francis is single and close to his mother; Peter is married and close to his father; Jack is in between, coping with temporary, unstable relationships. In terms of his relation to his parents, Jack appears to be indifferent, whereas Peter gets upset and ends up fighting Francis when he realizes they are visiting their mother. Nonetheless, Jack is close to his father, for he dedicates his collection of short stories *Invisible*

Table 7.1 Character traits of the three Whitman brothers in *The Darjeeling Limited*

	Partner (+/−)	Close to father (F)/mother (M)?	Children?(Y/N)
Francis	−	M	N
Jack	+	F	N
Peter	+	F	Y

Ink to him (which we see in scene [19]), and he insists his mother answer the question why she did not attend her husband's funeral (in scene [25]). The brothers' character traits are represented schematically in Table 7.1.

We can also identify parallels between Jack's two lovers, the unnamed Natalie Portman character and Rita. As well as playing Sarstedt's song to both characters, we see both having a short sexual liaison with Jack, although the circumstances are different. The Portman character tracks down and invites herself to Jack's hotel room. She is the seducer actively seeking him out. In contrast, Rita is seduced by Jack. Nonetheless, according to Nandana Bose, Rita does not conform to the Western cliché of the silent, non-expressive Indian woman: 'She speaks her mind, is impatient when Jack wants to talk to her, and shows more sense than him in covering up their tryst in the toilet. [...] Thus her traditional, "authentic" Indian appearance is incompatible with her brazen, "Western" behavior, and this contrast is yet another source of comic irony' (2008, 5). Rita therefore shares some of the traits of the other non-Western women in Wes Anderson's films, especially Inez in *Bottle Rocket* and Margaret Yang in *Rushmore*, both of whom show more sense than the male characters they become romantically involved with (Anthony Adams and Max Fischer, respectively). The parallels between the Natalie Portman character and Rita explain Jack's comment to Rita ('Thanks for using me'), for the comment applies to the former but is said to the latter.

Gifts and exchange

Francis's belt (which he says cost $6,000) becomes an object of exchange throughout the film. Peter takes it from Francis without asking, and has to give it back in scene (8). But Francis gives it to him as a birthday present in scene (9). However, Peter throws the belt at Francis while they are arguing, injuring

Francis (13). Yet, Francis gives him the belt a second time in scene (22), after Peter confirms that his son will shortly be born. Peter therefore takes the belt on one occasion without asking, gives it back to Francis on two occasions, and Francis gives Peter the belt on two family occasions – as a birthday present, and when Peter confirms that his son will soon be born.³

Peter also mentions that Alice makes clay candleholders. He reminds his brothers that they received them as gifts. Peter lights one in the train compartment and the other at the convent. Francis sees it and compliments Alice, while Patricia sees it and calls it hideous, until she realizes Alice made it, and she quickly changes her opinion and praises it. The pots represent Alice in absentia, and Jack's girlfriend is also represented in absentia, via a perfume bottle (Voltaire no. 6) she put in his suitcase when she visited him at Hotel Chevalier. All three brothers agree that the bottle should be disposed of, and Jack breaks it in the compartment.

Paradigms

Running for the train paradigm

(2) Peter Whitman runs for and catches the train
(8) After shopping, the three brothers run to catch the train
(12) The three brothers run down a steep hill in order to catch the train
(30) The brothers ditch their luggage and catch the train

The film opens with a middle-aged businessman in a taxi rushing towards the train station (1). He gets out of the taxi and runs towards the train, but misses it (2). He is left behind. But Peter Whitman also runs for the same train and catches it. In the film's penultimate scene (30), the three Whitman brothers run for another train. In order to catch it, they have to ditch all of their bags – which have the initials of their father stencilled on them. In the film's final scene (31), the three brothers sit together in the train compartment, without the tension that accompanied them throughout the film. In the second scene, the middle-aged man misses the train; in the penultimate scene, the bags belonging to the father (Whitman *père*) miss the train. When comparing these scenes, which mirror each other at the beginning and end of the film (and it is notable that both are accompanied on the soundtrack by songs from The Kinks), it is easy to associate the businessman and Whitman *père*, the latter represented by his distinctive luggage. This comparison is reinforced when we realize that Whitman *père* was killed by a (presumably speeding) taxi. This gives indirect motivation for the film to open with a middle-aged man travelling in a speeding taxi: it condenses into one image the dead symbolic father. The opening scene also explains why the brothers ditch their bags at the end – the dead father dominates the lives of the Whitman brothers, and they are able to discard him by the end of the film. On a literal level, the opening scene of the businessman in a speeding taxi seems superfluous, especially since he plays no further role in the film (he only appears one more time for a few seconds in the montage sequence). But on a symbolic level, he represents the symbolic dead father who dominates the actions and thoughts of the three brothers. Although literally absent, the father is represented via his initials on the luggage of the brothers, heavy bags that weigh them down; the symbolic father still controls their lives. Discarding the heavy bags at the end of the film is an objective correlative of the brothers' ability to discard the oppressive symbolic weight of their father. After visiting the convent and performing the feather ceremony, the brothers are also able to transcend their dependency on their mother. The four terms of this 'running for the train' paradigm all manifest the same value – a positive value of success, for the train is caught on each occasion.

The brothers' transformations are signified via another repetition: in the train compartments, scenes (4) and (31). In scene (4), the brothers enter the compartment separately, at different times. In scene (31), they enter the compartment together, as a unified group; Peter even folds up his father's glasses and puts them away. In scene (2) it is significant that Peter is the brother who overtakes the businessman (the symbolic father), for Peter becomes the new father.

Feather ceremony paradigm

(8)   Francis describes the feather ceremony to his brothers

(9)   Brendan gives the feathers and the instructions to Francis

(12) The three brothers begin the feather ceremony (but interrupt it)
(14) The three brothers carry out the feather ceremony (but incorrectly)
(28) The three brothers correctly carry out the feather ceremony

In scene (8) Francis briefly mentions he wants each of the brothers to perform a ceremony involving peacock feathers. In (9) he asks Brendan if he has managed to contact Patricia Whitman, and then asks him to hand over the peacock feathers. In scene (12), Francis, Peter and Jack begin the feather ceremony, but Francis interrupts it by telling his brothers the reason for their journey – to visit their mother Patricia. In the campfire scene (14) Francis reads out a letter from their mother and they perform the feather ceremony soon afterwards (and also take pain-relief medication). However, only Francis performs the ceremony correctly. In scene (28), after realizing their mother has left the convent, the brothers successfully perform the ceremony, and then leave for the train station. Within this feather ceremony paradigm, a syntagmatic link is set up between the feather ceremony and Patricia: the ceremony functions to symbolize the brothers' relation to their absent mother. Because it is symbolized, this relation becomes stable; it takes its place in the symbolic order. The five terms of this paradigm manifest different values – neutral in (8) and (9); negative in (12) and (14), for the feather ceremony is not performed correctly; and a positive value of success in (28), where it is performed successfully.

The two paradigms – running for the train, the feather ceremony – are explicitly coded in terms of the film's primary contradiction, the unresolvable conflict between the father (running for the train) and mother (feather ceremony). The actual conflict between the parents cannot be resolved; but it is symbolically represented and resolved in the film through a variety of signs, including the discarding of the heavy baggage and the successful completion of the feather ceremony. That the brothers are able to both board the train (by discarding the father's bags) and are able to work together to perform the feather ceremony (which ends in the burial of the feather) signifies a symbolic attempt to resolve the film's primary contradiction.

The film's secondary contradiction, Jack's impossible wish not to be brothers with Peter and Francis, but to be a non-consanguine friend, is also addressed by the film's ending. Unlike affinal ties, consanguine kinship ties are not optional. But, by the end of the film, the brothers' kinship ties are strengthened, for they have overcome their dependency on their parents. That is, the synchronic relation between consanguines (the brothers) overcomes the diachronic or descent relation between consanguines (the brothers and their parents).

Binary oppositions

The paradigmatic analysis has revealed the film's basic mapping of male (the father) onto baggage and female (the mother) onto feather. This immediately invokes another binary opposition, between heavy and light – the heavy baggage and the light feather. The film also places these oppositions in particular spatial arrangements. On all three occasions, the brothers have to take the high ground in order to carry out the feather ceremony. This is exaggerated in the third and final attempt, which consists of a long-montage sequence depicting the brothers traversing various spaces in order to reach the top of a mountain. This high ground, which we can abstract to 'vertical movement', is opposed to the horizontal movement of the train in scenes (2) and (30), a movement linked to the father. This horizontal movement is exaggerated by the use of slow motion. We therefore have a series of oppositions:

Male (father)/baggage/heavy/horizontal movement, and
Female (mother)/feather/light/vertical movement

The three brothers are able to mediate between and resolve these oppositions – they eventually master both vertical and horizontal movements (they successfully catch the train, they successfully perform the feather ceremony at the top of a mountain), and they free themselves from the heavy baggage (father) and the light feather (mother). Because of this, by the end of the film, Peter accepts his role as a (future) father (he also takes off his father's glasses), and Jack rejects unsuitable relationships. Francis, who confiscated his brothers' passports, offers to return them, but Peter and Jack allow Francis to keep them. Peter and Jack now trust their older brother, regarding him as an authority figure.

Other oppositions operate in *The Darjeeling Limited*. The film sets up an opposition between fire and water. After being ejected from the train, the brothers camp outside at night and build a large fire (14). In the next scene (15), they try to save the three brothers who fall into a river, but one of the children drowns. The drowned boy's funeral (20) involves a funeral pyre, set up next to water. Fire and water are first represented separately in consecutive scenes (14) and (15), but are later represented in the same shot (20).

Finally, the opposition East/West dominates the film, and in manifest in numerous ways. The three Western brothers are paired with three Indian brothers in the film's central scenes (15–20). Whereas Jack and Francis save two of the brothers who fall into the river, Peter is unable to save his Indian 'counterpart'. Jack has two problematic and unsuccessful relationships in the film: the Natalie Portman character/Rita: one is American, the other is Indian. He goes from one to the other but without successfully mediating between them, or between East and West, and ends up single. And in scene (8) Francis has one of his expensive loafers stolen at a shoeshine stand. (Eli in *The Royal Tenenbaums* also lost a shoe after crashing into the Tenenbaum house, although Dudley returned it.) He has to put on one of the Indian shoes Peter bought. Through the rest of the film, we see Francis wearing an Indian shoe on one foot and his expensive loafer on the other: he has one foot in his Western shoe, and the other in an Indian shoe, an opposition that remains unresolved at the end of the film – and the shot of Francis wearing two different shoes becomes the film's emblematic image.

Notes

1 The shooting script (dated 22 November 2006) contains additional scenes in the convent (the laundry room, the kitchen), as well as actions and lines (Patricia gets a nose bleed, she asks about her husband's death) that did not make it into the final film.

2 These moments, in which Jack denies and then accepts an autobiographical reading of his stories, are reflexive to the extent that Wes Anderson draws upon his own biography (he is one of three brothers) and experiences (his parents divorced when he was eight). Richard Brody quotes Jason Schwartzman quoting

Wes Anderson: 'Wes said, "I think we should write a movie about three brothers in India. [...] It will be the most personal thing we could possibly make – let's try to make it even *too* personal"' (Brody 2009). But Brody also lists a series of film influences, including John Cassavetes's *Husbands* (1970), in which three men, grieving over a friend's death, leave on a trip.

3   In scene (13), just before their argument, Francis asks Peter to return the belt, but Peter refuses, saying that 'There's been too much Indian-giving' (a form of giving in which the giver wants the gift back at a later date).

8

Human versus Animal Subworld: *Fantastic Mr. Fox*

Wes Anderson and Noah Baumbach adapted *Fantastic Mr. Fox* (2009) from Roald Dahl's children's book of the same name (1970), a copy of which appears in the opening scene: unlike the books appearing in the storyworlds of Wes Anderson's other films, *Fantastic Mr. Fox* is an actual book outside the film. Both book and film are structured around an absolute irreconcilable opposition between two subworlds: the human subworld/the animal subworld. Although these subworlds share a few similar values, such as ownership of property, demarcation of boundaries and the English language, deep differences exist, including different temporalities (Fox years/Human years) and the absence of exchange. Instead of a system of linguistic, commodity or gift exchange, the relation is based on stealing: the animals steal food from the humans, and the humans steal from the animals (Mr Fox's tail and the kidnapping of Kristofferson; Mr Fox's home is also destroyed). We saw in chapter 3, when Dignan steals the earrings of Anthony's mother in *Bottle Rocket*, that theft breaks the circuit of exchange and disrupts social bonds.

Plot synopsis

(1) Title card (nursery rhyme) about the three farmers, Boggis, Bunce and Bean, followed by a book cover (Roald Dahl's *Fantastic Mr. Fox*). (2) Mr Fox stands by a tree eating an apple. Mrs. Fox joins him, after returning from a doctor's appointment. (3) They journey home to their fox hole via Berk's Squab Farm; they steal chickens but are trapped in a cage. Mrs. Fox announces she is pregnant. (4) Title card: 'Two Years Later (12 Fox-Years)'.

(5) A newspaper is delivered to a fox hole. Insert of Mr Fox's column (which includes a paragraph on his aversion to English wolves). (6) Breakfast. Mr Fox reads the paper; Mrs. Fox prepares breakfast; and their cub Ash complains of feeling ill. Mr Fox expresses his wish to live above ground, and Mrs Fox announces the imminent arrival of cousin Kristofferson. Tension is expressed between Mr Fox and Ash when Mr Fox describes Ash as 'different'. (7) Mr Fox visits a tree property for sale. He meets Kylie for the first time and sees the Boggis, Bunce and Bean farms outside the window. (8) Title card: 'Badger, Beaver & Beaver (Attorneys At Law)'. (9) Mr Fox asks his lawyer (Badger) to buy the tree property. Badger tries to dissuade him because the three farms are close. He then introduces the three farmers and the food they produce (and plays a recording of children singing the nursery rhyme). Mr Fox ignores Badger's advice. (10) The Fox family moves into the tree. (11) Title card: 'Cousin Kristofferson Arrives'. (12) Mrs. Fox paints, Mr Fox eats an apple, while the children dive into a swimming pool. Kristofferson is shown to be larger and more athletic than Ash, setting up a rivalry between them. (13) Mr Fox begins to talk to Kylie about his plan (to steal from the farmers). (14) Conflict between Ash and Kristofferson develops in the bedroom. (15) Title card: 'Mr. Fox Has a Plan'. (16) Mr Fox talks to Kylie about stealing chickens from Boggis. (17) School lab. Ash's lab partner Agnes is distracted by and attracted to Kristofferson. (18) Title Card: 'Master Plan Phase One (Boggis Chicken House 1)'. (19) Mr Fox and Kylie successfully steal chickens from Boggis. (20) Mrs Fox sees the chicken in the pantry, but becomes suspicious of its provenance. (21) Title Card: 'Bunce's Refrigerated Smokehouse (Master Plan Phase Two)'. (22) Mr Fox and Kylie successfully steal duck and geese from Bunce. (23) Mrs Fox sees the duck and geese in the pantry, and again becomes suspicious. (24) School playing field. Kristofferson takes the place of Ash on the playing field, and Ash talks to the coach about improving as an athlete, to match his father's level. Coach reminds him his father was an exceptional athlete who cannot be matched. Coach also praises Kristofferson's athleticism. (25) At dinner, Mr Fox and Kylie leave early. (26) Title card: 'Bean's Secret Cider Cellar (Master Plan Phrase Three)'. (27) Mr Fox and Kylie head towards Bean's cellar. Ash and Kristofferson join them, but Mr Fox sends Ash back, saying he is too small and uncoordinated. (28) In the cellar, Mr Fox, Kylie and Kristofferson confront Rat and steal

bottles of cider. (29) Title card: 'Emergency Meeting'. (30) Boggis, Bunce and Bean meet up and decide to kill Mr Fox. (31) Mrs. Fox questions Mr Fox about his night-time activities. (32) Title Card: 'The Shooting'. (33) Mr Fox is ambushed; he loses his tail. (34) Boggis, Bunce and Bean destroy the Fox tree; the foxes and Kylie dig underground; tension between Mr and Mrs Fox increases. (35) Title card: 'The Terrible Tractors'. (36) The farmers dig using bulldozers, and the animals dig further underground. (37) Ash and Kristofferson conflict over Agnes. (38) Boggis wears Mr Fox's tail as a necktie. (39) The farmers use dynamite, and then lay siege to the fox hole. (40) Title card: 'The Siege Begins'. (41) A news reporter narrates the events of the siege. (42) Title Card: 'Three Days Later (2 1/2 Fox Weeks)'. (43) The farmers speculate about how long a fox can survive without food or water. Underground, Badger and several other animals burrow their way to the foxes and Kylie. Several animals then burrow under the three farms to steal food and drink, accompanied by 'Petey's song'. (44) Title Card: 'Badger's Flint Mine (Refugee Camp)'. (45) The animals deliver food to the flint mine. (46) The farmers react angrily to the theft of their produce. (47) The animals underground prepare a feast, and Ash asks Kristofferson to help him steal back his father's tail. (48) Three events unfold at the same time: the farmers pour cider in the underground tunnels; the animals sit down to a feast; Ash and Kristofferson enter Bean's house to steal back Mr Fox's tail, but are distracted by newly baked nutmeg ginger apple snaps. The flint mine is flooded and Kristofferson is captured. (49) The animals end up in the sewer. Mr and Mrs Fox reconcile, and Mr Fox comforts Ash. (50) Rat attacks Ash but is killed by Mr Fox. (51) Title Card: 'A Go-For-Broke Rescue Mission'. (52) Mr Fox organizes a rescue mission and the farmers organize an ambush. (53) Mr Fox, Kyle and Ash travel to Bean's farm to rescue Kristofferson. Ash is small enough to enter the room where Kristofferson is held, and rescues him from an apple crate. (Kristofferson momentarily loses his shoe, but Ash returns it to him, just as Dudley returned Eli's shoe in *The Royal Tenenbaums*.) Ash then demonstrates his athleticism by unleashing the rabid Beagle onto Bean and his associates. Mr Fox, Kylie, Ash and Kristofferson escape. Kristofferson retrieves the remnants of Mr Fox's tail. (54) On their way back to the sewer, they encounter a wolf. (55) Mr Fox leads the other foxes and Kylie to the Boggis, Bunce and Bean supermarket. Mrs. Fox announces she is pregnant.

Due to the sharing of the English language, there are moments of indirect communication, particularly the farmers' ransom note and the animals' reply (both made of letters cut out of newspapers). There are only two direct attempts to communicate between the two subworlds: after Bean kidnaps Kristofferson, Mr Fox plans an exchange. He asks Bean if Kristofferson is present. Bean plays a bad recording of Kristofferson's voice (signifying that he is not present), and Mr Fox's response is to throw lighted pinecones, which set the street (and the farmers) on fire. After the rescue of Kristofferson, Mr Fox shouts to Bean, summarizing his grievances; Bean's response is to start shooting. In both the instances, a verbal message does not invoke a linguistic exchange but results in violence. Both attempts to communicate directly across the human/animal boundary therefore fail. Rat and the Beagles mediate between the human/animal subworlds: they are animals who work for the humans, thereby embodying the values of both, although the rabid Beagle Spitz chases the animals and humans indiscriminately.

The animal subworld is structured by a series of conflicts, all centred on Mr Fox:

(a) Mr Fox/Mrs Fox
(b) Mr Fox/Ash
(c) Mr Fox/Badger

(a) Mr Fox/Mrs Fox. The film begins by spelling out binary choices: in scene (2) Mr Fox presents Mrs Fox with two different ways to go home; Mrs Fox chooses one way, while Mr Fox recommends they take the other way. And in scene (3) when deciding how to go through Berk's farm, Mrs Fox chooses one way, while Mr Fox again overrides her choice and recommends the second way. The choices he offers her are false options, for he always follows his own preference, which are different from hers. The process of choosing therefore reveals an opposition between their ways of thinking. This is significant for comprehending the events at the end of scene (3): Mr and Mrs Fox are trapped in a cage, and Mrs Fox tells Mr Fox that, if they manage to escape, he must stop stealing from farmers and must find a new (respectable) line of work, and that she is pregnant. In other words, he needs to take on the symbolic roles of worker and father. We see the results in scenes (5) and (6): Mr Fox has conformed to Mrs Fox's demands: rather than follow his natural animal instincts, he has become a

journalist and, nominally at least, plays the role of father. In scenes (20) and (23) the conflict between Mr and Mrs Fox re-emerges when she becomes suspicious of the food that appears in the pantry, and in scene (31) she questions him. But when the farmers destroy the Fox home, she directly confronts him and scratches his face in scene (34) because his irresponsible actions have jeopardized the family. She reminds him of his symbolic kinship roles of husband and father, while he emphasizes his wild animal nature. Like many male characters in Wes Anderson's films, Mr Fox is constrained by and feels enclosed within his symbolic roles; he plots his escape via the robberies. Mr and Mrs Fox reconcile in (49), although Mrs Fox says she should not have married him.

(b) Mr Fox/Ash. The relationship between Mr Fox and Ash enacts a typical father/son conflict, based on the son's inability to live up to the (in this instance, physical and athletic) ideals the father represents. Mr Fox codes Ash as different and rejects him throughout the film – especially in scenes (6), (12) and (27). This conflict is resolved when Ash is able to rescue Kristofferson (because of Ash's small size) and because he demonstrates his athleticism when unleashing the rabid Beagle onto the humans in scene (53). The Mr Fox/Ash conflict existed before Kristofferson turned up, but it is heightened and then resolved via Kristofferson (or, more precisely, through Kristofferson's kidnapping, described later).

(c) Mr Fox/Badger. Mr Fox asks his lawyer (Badger) to help him buy the tree house (9). Badger tries to dissuade Mr Fox, because of the close proximity of the house to the three farms, but Mr Fox ignores Badger's advice and buys the house (precisely because of its proximity to the farms). In scene (48), Badger begins to toast his friends, thanking them for joining him in the flint mine, but Mr Fox interrupts Badger and delivers his own toast. Both scenes present the hierarchy between Mr Fox and Badger, with Mr Fox promoting himself as the higher authority.

Kinship

The film's storyworld is also structured around a kinship conflict between cousins Ash and Kristofferson (a conflict structured around who receives recognition from Mr Fox, the symbolic father figure) and a romantic conflict (both cousins are romantically interested in Agnes). On several occasions, Kristofferson impresses Mr Fox with his athleticism – he lives up to Mr Fox's ideal of a son. In scene (24) Coach also praises Kristofferson, and says to Ash, 'He really is your father's nephew'. But Ash replies that his father and Kristofferson are not related by blood, for Kristofferson comes from his mother's side of the family. This conflict between cross cousins is resolved via a reversal – when Ash rescues Kristofferson from the apple crate and demonstrates his athleticism by unleashing the rabid dog on to the humans. Crucial to this reversal is that the humans mistake Kristofferson for Ash (they do not recognize the animal kinship relations). It is their kidnapping of Kristofferson and mistaking him for Ash that brings about Ash's transformation: within the kidnap scenario, Kristofferson takes the symbolic position of the weak and passive son (he is tied up, blindfolded and confined in a crate) and Ash takes on the symbolic position of the active, strong athletic son. Yet, his transformation is only partial: Ash can only rescue Kristofferson because he is small (he can fit through the bars of the skylight), and he only frees Kristofferson from the apple crate by inadvertently pushing it off a ledge while trying to karate the lock (he is guided by but cannot carry out Kristofferson's karate instructions). But Ash's subsequent athleticism is genuine, and Ash finally receives praise (and a bandit mask) from his father.[1] In regard to the romance plot, Agnes rejects Ash and becomes romantically involved with Kristofferson: in the school science lab (17) Agnes compliments Kristofferson (who returns the compliment), and on the sports field (24), Agnes supports Kristofferson, to Ash's annoyance.

The film begins and ends with Mrs Fox announcing that she is pregnant. In kinship terms, this is significant because the film promotes one type of kinship relation over another: alliance between humans and animals remains impossible (it is an opposition that cannot be mediated and resolved), while descent relations within the animal subworld remain key. From (13) onwards, when Kristofferson arrives, Mr Fox neglects his symbolic roles of father, husband and worker; he ignores his family and works with Kylie to steal from the farmers. It is only from scene (34) onwards that the Fox family members spend significant time together – but only because they are trapped underground. Mr Fox continues to praise Kristofferson over his son Ash up to the moment Ash rescues Kristofferson.

Paradigms

The internal structure of *Fantastic Mr. Fox* is primarily organized around a repetitive act: animals stealing from humans:

Robberies paradigm

(3) Mr and Mrs Fox steal pigeons from Berk's Farm
(19) Mr Fox and Kylie steal chickens from Boggis's Farm
(22) Mr Fox and Kylie steal duck and geese from Bunce's Farm
(28) Mr Fox, Kylie and Kristofferson steal bottles of cider from Bean's Farm
(43) Several animals burrow under the three farms to steal food and drink
(55) Mr Fox leads the other foxes and Kylie to raid the supermarket

The film opens with an unsuccessful raid on Berk's farm (unsuccessful in that the foxes are discovered and trapped on the farmer's land); the middle part of the films is organized around consecutive successful raids on the three farms (Boggis, Bunce, Bean) over ground at night. Once confined underground, Mr Fox organizes a second round of successful raids on these three farms from underground. The film ends with a successful underground raid on the supermarket owned by Boggis, Bunce and Bean.[2] All the raids are organized and led by Mr Fox, who is accompanied by different animals. In (19) and (22), Kylie takes the place of Mrs Fox. In (28) and (43), other animals join the raids, and in (55), Mrs Fox returns to this paradigm. Her appearance in this paradigm is linked syntagmatically to another event: on the two occasions she appears in the paradigm, Mrs Fox announces that she is pregnant.

This robberies paradigm consists of several values: Mr Fox is the constant and is accompanied by different animals; all the raids are successful, except (3); and raids (3), (19), (22) and (28) take place over ground, whereas (43) and (55) take place underground (although [43] is a condensed repetition of [19],

[22] and [28]). The values in this paradigm are also structured by the following transformations:

> Reversal: from unsuccessful to successful; from over ground to underground
>
> Substitution: Mrs Fox/Kylie
>
> Addition: Kristofferson joins the raids, then other animals join in, until Mrs Fox returns (cancelling out the substitution).

The paradigmatic structure of *Fantastic Mr. Fox* resembles *Bottle Rocket*, a film that is also organized around the repetitive action of stealing (see chapter 3).

The film's answer to the conflict between Mr and Mrs Fox, especially regarding Mr Fox's propensity to steal from the farmers, is not to deny his animal instinct to steal; this option was tried but did not succeed. The solution is to steal from the farmers underground, not over ground. In Roald Dahl's book, there is no conflict between Mr and Mrs Fox (nor between father/son and between cousins, while the conflict between Mr Fox and Badger is minimal). Like the film, the book is structured primarily around the human/animal opposition, and the solution is the same – to steal from underground.

Apple paradigm

- (2) Mr Fox stands by a tree eating an apple
- (9) Badger introduces Bean and mentions the apples and cider he produces
- (12) Mr Fox eats an apple
- (28) Mr Fox, Kylie and Kristofferson steal bottles of cider
- (48) The farmers pour cider in the underground tunnels while Ash and Kristofferson are distracted by newly baked nutmeg ginger apple snaps
- (53) Ash rescues Kristofferson from an apple crate
- (55) In the supermarket the animals drink cartons of apple juice

The film's action begins (scene 2) with Mr Fox plucking an apple from a tree and eating it; the film ends (scene 55) with Mr Fox and the other animals drinking apple juice from a carton (except Ash, who drinks grape juice). In the middle (scene 28), the animals steal from Bean's farm several jars of hard cider.[3]

The significance of these apple scenes can be explained by analysing them in terms of the first three volumes of Lévi-Strauss's Mythologies (*The Raw and the Cooked, From Honey to Ashes* and *The Origin of Table Manners*). Lévi-Strauss employs the opposition between the raw and the cooked to define the transition from nature to culture, a transition marked by the cooking of food. In *From Honey to Ashes*, he distinguishes fresh honey from fermented honey (1973, 67–8): the fresh honey is raw, produced in nature, while the fermented ('cooked') honey consists of honey mixed with water and left in the sun, which transforms it into a powerful fermented drink. And in *The Origin of Table Manners* (1978, 478), he adds the distinction between unprocessed and processed food, yielding the following series of binary oppositions:

Nature/culture
Raw/cooked
Unprocessed/processed

In scene (2) Mr Fox is situated outside in the fresh air and sun picking an apple directly from the tree, which aligns him to the terms on the left: nature, raw, unprocessed (and also alludes to Christian mythology of the Garden of Eden, especially when we realize he is waiting for the pregnant Mrs Fox to return from a hospital visit). By the end of the film, Mr Fox is in an artificially lit supermarket drinking apple juice from a carton (he even comments on the artificiality of the light and the food in the supermarket). Mr Fox is now aligned with the terms on the right (culture, cooked, processed). In the middle, Mr Fox steals apple cider – fermented alcoholic drink. The raw apple, which can be freely picked from the tree, is therefore contrasted with two types of processed apple commodities, one extreme (cider, involving fermentation, in which the sugar in the apples turns into alcohol) and the other tamed (the non-fermented apple juice).

Within this paradigm we can identify a series of values and transformations linked to the apple: it is initially aligned with nature, but then it is transformed into culture, or two types of culture: to an extreme form (cider), and then to a tamed form (apple juice). As a natural object, the apple can be freely appropriated. But as a cultural object, it becomes a commodity infused with exchange value. Yet, Mr Fox behaves towards these two apple commodities the same way he behaves towards the raw natural apple – by freely appropriating them. He does not accept the farmers' private ownership rights over nature, nor does he recognize the exchange value conferred on the resulting commodities. Instead, he is guided by the need to survive.

Binary oppositions

The film's diegesis is structured around several binary oppositions. The most fundamental is the opposition above/below, especially above ground/below ground. This is mapped onto another fundamental opposition, human/animal:

Above/below
Human/animal

But these are not static oppositions, for the animals take on attributes of the opposed terms. First, the animals are of course anthropomorphic, and in scene (52) Mr Fox draws attention to the animals' dual identity: he defines them collectively as wild animals, but then defines each in terms of their professional roles (lawyer, estate agent, tailor, painter). Mr Fox also remembers the Latin names of each animal (unlike Steve Zissou in *The Life Aquatic*). Second, although the default value for the animals is to live underground, they can transition from one level to the other, whereas the humans cannot. The animals can move downwards (diving into a swimming pool; digging; Mr Fox, Kylie and Kristofferson sliding down into the cider storeroom; Ash climbing down to save Kristofferson; the apple crate falling) and upwards (the animals enter the farms of Boggis, Bunce and Bean and the supermarket from underground). Even though the farmers are unable to go underground, they are able to flood the underground tunnels with cider. This leads to additional oppositions:

Open/closed (space)
Fire/water (or cider)

'Open' is mapped onto 'above' and 'human', and 'closed' is mapped onto 'below' and 'animal'. The animals' primary advantage – living and digging underground – is also their weakness, for the underground spaces are closed spaces.

This mapping is not completely static, for Mr and Mrs Fox are enclosed in a cage above ground, while Kristofferson is enclosed in an apple crate above ground. In other words, in scenes (3) and (53), the film's default values 'above/human/open (space)' are transformed into 'above/animal/closed (space)'. In (3) it is the act of digging and in (53) it is the rescue mission that restores the default values 'above/human/open' and 'below/animal/closed'.

The closed underground space the animals occupy is flooded with cider – the animals are momentarily engulfed in the liquid. The animals' response is to use fire: pinecones are lit underground and are thrown at the farmers over ground, leading to the burning of several buildings, as well as the farmers themselves, who are momentarily engulfed in smoke and fire. The closed underground space is flooded, while the open over ground space is set on fire.

Finally, the farmers themselves are characterized in two ways in the film: they consume their own produce, and the nursery rhyme defines them in terms of body type. Boggis eats 12 chickens a day; Bunce eats donuts filled with chopped up goose liver; and Bean drinks his own cider. The nursery rhyme about Boggis, Bunce and Bean define them as (respectively) fat/short/lean. Boggis and Bunce's body shapes are defined in terms of oppositions (the absent terms are in parentheses):

Boggis
+Fat[/thin]
Bunce
+Short[/tall].

Bean is defined as lean, a term that embodies both the absent terms used to describe Boggis and Bunce:

Bean
+Thin, +tall.

Bean is therefore defined in opposition to both Boggis and Bunce. He also sets himself up as the leader who organizes the revenge attacks on the animals. But the animals' command of the underground subworld, and their ability to transition from below to above ground, give them the advantage over the humans.

Notes

1. The reversal between Ash and Kristofferson that takes place in scene (53) is a response to a substitution in scene (24) on the playing field, when Coach takes off Ash and replaces him with Kristofferson.
2. Although the humans also steal from the animals as an act of revenge (scenes 33–36; 48), this constitutes a much weaker paradigm.
3. In the UK, 'cider' refers to a fermented alcoholic drink, whereas 'apple juice' refers to a non-alcoholic drink, usually made from apple concentrate mixed with water and preservatives. In the United States, 'cider' refers to clear (filtered) apple juice, while the term 'hard cider' is used to refer to the a fermented alcoholic drink. Mr Fox has to explain this to Kylie when they break into Bean's farm to steal cider.

9

The Orphan and the Bachelor:
Moonrise Kingdom

In indigenous or primitive societies, Lévi-Strauss argues, marriage is necessary for a man in order 'to prevent those two calamities of primitive society from occurring in his group, namely, the bachelor and the orphan' (1969, 39). The stigma attached to the bachelor and especially the orphan is also prevalent in Western societies, although to a lesser degree. The identity of the orphan, the child whose biological parents are dead, is defined by its lack of a place in the symbolic order, while the identity of the bachelor is defined as a failure to enter into the symbolic circuit of exchange. Commenting on the work of James Frazer, Lévi-Strauss notes that 'the "poor and desperate" bachelor who cannot obtain a wife in the normal manner by exchange is forced to lead the life of an outlaw, for his only chance lies in carrying off one of the women of his group, or in capturing a woman from another group' (1969, 135). Both character types dominate *Moonrise Kingdom* (2012).

Plot synopsis

(1) Credit sequence: In the Bishop home. Suzy Bishop (Kara Hayward) looks off screen while her family become engrossed in their own activities; Suzy's three brothers listen to a record, of Benjamin Britten's *Young Person's Guide to the Orchestra*; Suzy reads fiction, and collects a letter from the mailbox. (2) The narrator (Bob Balaban) addresses the camera to introduce the Island of New Penzance, and warns of an incoming storm. (3) Camp Ivanhoe. Scout Master Ward (Edward Norton) inspects various activities of his Khaki Scouts Troop 55 before sitting down to breakfast. One scout – Sam Shakusky (Jared Gilman) – is missing. (4) Scout Master Ward contacts

Captain Sharp (Bruce Willis) about the lost boy and the supplies he stole. (5) Captain Sharp (a bachelor) telephones Sam's (foster) parents about his disappearance. They say they are unable to accept him back into their foster home. (6) Scout Master Ward organizes his scouts into a search party. (7) The search begins: the scouts spread out, and Captain Sharp distributes Sam's photograph on the island; he ends up visiting the home of the lawyers Mr and Mrs Bishop (Bill Murray and Frances McDormand). (8) Mrs Bishop and Captain Sharp secretly meet up soon afterwards, but are seen by Suzy. (9) Sam travels along New Penzance Island and stops when he sees Suzy. (10) Flashback (one year earlier): at a performance of Britten's *Noye's Fludde*, Sam meets Suzy (dressed as a raven). They decide to write to each other. End of flashback. (11) Sam and Suzy meet in a meadow. They plan their journey. (12) Montage sequence: moments in Sam and Suzy's journey, including Sam's preparation of a hotdog meal. (13) Sam makes a fish lunch and then writes an inventory, including the 'impractical' items Suzy brings (tins of cat food, stolen library books, record player). Suzy reads from one of her books. (14) The Bishops discover that Suzy is missing and ask Captain Sharp to find her. (15) Mr Bishop and Captain Sharp drive around in the dark. (16) Mrs Bishop discovers Suzy's stash of letters from Sam. Several are read out. (17) The Bishops join the search for Sam and Suzy. (18) The scouts catch up with Sam and Suzy. A fight ensues. (19) One scout (Redford) is injured and the others escape. The scout's dog Snoopy is killed. (20) Redford is loaded onto the seaplane. A fight ensues between the Bishops and Scout Master Ward, with Captain Sharp in the middle. The narrator points out where Sam and Suzy might be headed (mile 3.25 tidal inlet). (21) Sam and Suzy camped at mile 3.25 tidal inlet; they jump into the water. (22) Sam and Suzy on the beach (painting, making earrings, dancing, kissing, camping, reading). (23) The Bishops and Scout Master Ward discover the camp; Sam and Suzy are separated. Scout Master Ward delivers a letter to Sam and discusses with him his status as an orphan. (24) Captain Sharp telephones Social Services (Tilda Swinton) about Sam's care. (25) Suzy and Mrs Bishop discuss Suzy's situation. (26) Sam and Captain Sharp discuss Sam's situation. (27) The scouts decide to rescue Sam and Suzy and help them on their journey. (28) Suzy is rescued, Mrs Bishop and Captain Sharp break up, Sam is rescued. (29) Mr and Mrs Bishop discuss their problems. (30) Suzy reads to the scouts. (31) Scout Master Ward realizes he has lost all of his troop. (32) Sam, Suzy and the scouts end up at Fort Lebanon.

(33) Cousin Ben (Jason Schwartzman) 'marries' Sam and Suzy. (34) The Fort Lebanon scouts chase Sam, but he is struck by lightning. He escapes with his own scout troops. (35) Head of the Lebanon scouts, Commander Pierce (Harvey Keitel), phones Captain Sharp. (36) The storm mentioned by the narrator arrives, and all the characters (including Sam and Suzy, disguised as animals) meet up at St Jack's church. (37) Redford identifies Sam and Suzy, who then head to the church tower. (38) Captain Sharp attempts to rescue them, and prevents them from jumping by agreeing to be Sam's foster parent. But lighting strikes the tower and the three characters (Captain Sharp, Sam, Suzy) hang by a thread. (39) The narrator addresses the camera to narrate the storm's aftermath (including the erasure of mile 3.25 tidal inlet). (40) In the Bishop house. Suzy reads while Sam paints. The Bishop children are called down to dinner. Sam leaves via the window and is driven home by Captain Sharp. Sam's painting shows mile 3.25 tidal inlet, renamed Moonrise Kingdom.

Sam's orphan status is the irreconcilable lack that drives the narrative forward, and the bachelor Captain Sharp resolves this lack on a symbolic level by presenting himself as a foster parent. Although Captain Sharp is the opposite of 'the outlaw', his bachelorhood still works against him. He is portrayed as impoverished (he lives in a small caravan), is described as sad, lonely and dumb (the opposite of his name), and he does try to 'carry off' one of the women of his group, Mrs Bishop, but without success. His application to be a foster parent is at first denied precisely because he is a bachelor. It is only when the lawyers (Mr and Mrs Bishop) quote the law on discrimination that his application is granted.

Interweaved into *Moonrise Kingdom* is the myth of the flood, a myth popular throughout world religions, which is partly recounted in the film via one particular version – Benjamin Britten's children's opera *Noye's Fludde* (1958), itself based on the medieval Chester Miracle Play that recounts the Old Testament story of Noah's Ark. Fragments of this myth are integrated into *Moonrise Kingdom*, especially the role of the raven, the symbolic cleansing of the flood, plus the basic semantic cluster Sky/Water/Earth. An actual flood takes place towards the end of the film.

Moonrise Kingdom establishes multiple relations with *The Royal Tenenbaums* (and, to a lesser extent, *Bottle Rocket*). One narrative strand of *The Royal Tenenbaums* – the problematic childhood relationship between Richie and Margot – is expanded and transformed into its own narrative in *Moonrise Kingdom*. When 11, Richie and Margot ran away from home and camped out in the African Wing of the natural history museum. The young Richie obsessively paints portraits of Margot and, as an adult, Richie returns to the family home and camps out in the ballroom in his yellow tent, a space where he reads Margot's plays, listens to music on a record player and eventually resolves his emotional conflict with Margot. The similarities between the two narratives are evident: both involve the successful escape from the parental homes to an isolated but improbable hiding space (the beach on the small island of New Penzance/the African wing of the Natural History museum at night); Richie and Sam are amateur painters; both narratives involve a yellow tent, reading and a record player; Suzy has many affinities with the young Margot, and Sam has many affinities with the young Richie. Other similarities are also evident: Margot's first play, performed at her eleventh birthday party, is played by children dressed as animals, similar to the Noah's Ark play performed in *Moonrise Kingdom*; and a dog is killed in both films. The differences are equally significant: whereas Sam and Suzy live apart, Richie and Margot already live in the same house; Margot is adopted, whereas Suzy is alienated from her family (there is no kinship conflict); Sam is an orphan whereas Richie is a brother. Semantically, there is more affinity between Margot and Sam, for both share a similar kinship status: adopted/orphan respectively.

Kinship

Moonrise Kingdom begins with a series of tracking, panning and crane shots describing the interior and exterior of the Bishop home (in much the same way that the opening of *The Royal Tenenbaums* describes the Tenenbaum home). The parents are shown on their own carrying out various activities (reading, washing hair), while the three young Bishop brothers are usually together, listening to music or playing games. Suzy is alone, either with a cat, a book and/or binoculars. She is several years older than her three brothers, a significant age difference that partly accounts for her isolation. (However, the age difference is not as great as that between brother and sister Anthony and Grace in *Bottle Rocket*.)

The lack of interaction in the Bishop home between the adults, the adults and children and between Suzy and her brothers, hints at a dysfunctional nuclear family. This is confirmed in the flashback (10), where Suzy's troublesome childhood is depicted, together with her association with the troubled orphan Sam. Mrs Bishop's liaison with Captain Sharp (8) is further conformation, as is Mr Bishop's erratic behaviour when he discovers his daughter has eloped (throwing a shoe at scout master Ward, going into the garden at night with an axe and bottle of wine to find a tree to chop down). This is despite both being lawyers upholding the law.

Sam's orphan status was first raised in scene (5). Sam's status can be organized into a paradigm:

Orphan paradigm

(5) Captain Sharp telephones Sam's (foster) parents about his disappearance. They say they are unable to accept him back into their foster home

(16) Mrs Bishop discovers Suzy's stash of letters from Sam. Several are read out. (22) Sam and Suzy camped at mile 3.25 tidal inlet. Suzy says she prefers to read stories about orphans

(23) Scout Master Ward discusses with Sam his status as an orphan

(24) Captain Sharp telephones Social Services about Sam's care

(26) Sam and Captain Sharp discuss Sam's situation

(27) Due to his orphaned status, the scouts decide to help Sam

(38) Captain Sharp agrees to be Sam's foster parent

The narrative role of 'orphan' is coded negatively as a disadvantage in this paradigm, although it works to Sam's advantage in (22), (27) and (38). In (22), Suzy says she prefers orphans in the fictional works she reads (implying she also likes Sam), while in (27) the scouts (once Redford is out of action) decide to help Sam because he is a disadvantaged orphan. Scene (38) is the response to (5) and (24): in (5), both Captain Sharp and Scout Master Ward express surprise when they discover on the phone that Sam is an orphan. (24), an almost identical setup (another phone call), paints a negative image of Sam's fate as an orphan. In (38) Captain Sharp responds to Sam's lack of place in the symbolic order by offering to be his foster parent.

Joining a non-family community (the scouts) is not enough for Sam. To establish a place and identity in the symbolic order, he decides (at aged 12) to enter into a marriage with Suzy. Cousin Ben performs the ceremony in a church tent while acknowledging it has no basis in law – it does not register in the symbolic order.

Paradigms

Kinship categories, particularly the outliers 'orphan' and 'bachelor', represent a dominant paradigm informing the underlying symbolic system of *Moonrise Kingdom*. Other material open to paradigmatic analysis include the preparation and sharing of food:

Preparation and sharing of food

(3) Camp Ivanhoe. Scout Master Ward sits down to breakfast with his scouts

(5) Captain Sharp telephones Sam's (foster) parents about his disappearance The switchboard phone operator (Becky) eats a sandwich

(12) Montage sequence: moments in Sam and Suzy's journey, including Sam's preparation of a hotdog meal

(13) Sam makes a fish lunch

(14) At dinner the Bishops discover that Suzy is missing

(24) Captain Sharp telephones Social Services about Sam's care. Becky passes around some food for Captain Sharp and Scout Master Ward. Only the latter accepts

(26) Sam and Captain Sharp discuss Sam's situation. Sharp cooks a sausage and gives Sam some beer in his milk glass

(31) At breakfast, Scout Master Ward realizes he has lost all of his troop

(39) The narrator addresses the camera to narrate the storm's aftermath (including high yield of crops the following year)

(40) The Bishop children are called down to dinner

All the scenes in this paradigm focus on the preparation of food: very little eating actually takes place (Becky takes one bite from her sandwich, and Suzy takes one bite of the cooked fish). Scene (13) is key because we see the transformation of the fish from raw to cooked, which is then eaten by Suzy – who is coded as 'the raven' in the flashback (scene 10). In 'The Structural Study of Myth' (see Chapter 1), Lévi-Strauss defined the raven and the coyote as carrion-eating animals that mediate between hunting and farming because they combine elements from both: they are 'like beasts of prey (they eat animal food), but they are also like food-plant producers (they do not kill what they eat)' (1972, 224). Suzy catches and eats the fish but Sam prepares it for consumption. Of course, the raven does not have one fixed meaning. Suzy, coded as a raven, combines several meanings from different sources: in addition to eating but not killing animals, she also embodies some of the meanings from the story of Noah's Ark as well as from Ovid's *Metamorphoses*, to be discussed later.

Scene (3) of the food paradigm develops multiple relationships with other scenes in the paradigm. First, scene (31) is a near repetition of (3), but with a major difference: whereas in (3) one member of the scout troop is missing (Sam), in (31) the entire troop is missing. Scene (3) also establishes a double parallel with (14): in (3) Sam's absence is discovered at breakfast, while in (14) Suzy's absence is discovered at dinner time. Scene (26) is the inverse of (3): whereas Sam is absent from the meal in (3) he is the only scout present for the supper in (26). The relation between (3) and (26) also signifies a transfer of parental authority over Sam: Scout Master Ward in (3), Captain Sharp in (26).

The dinner ritual in the Bishop family home is the same in scenes (14) and (40), but Suzy is absent in (14) and present in (40). Sam is also present in (40) but is not invited to dinner. Like Captain Sharp, Sam is coded as a potential threat to the fragile unity of the Bishop family. The film begins and ends in the Bishop home, which is markedly different to Captain Sharp's home (26), a small caravan. Scene (26) is important because it condenses three of the film's key values: 'food (preparation)', 'orphan', and 'bachelor'. This is the only scene where Sam is the recipient of the food rather than its provider. Sam initially drinks milk, but is offered some beer. Sam pours most of the milk out of his glass, and Captain Sharp pours some beer into it. The glass contains a mix of milk and beer. Whereas milk is traditionally coded as nourishment for children, beer (like tobacco) is defined as an 'anti-food', for it does not have any nourishing qualities, but is intoxicating. Sam's glass is structured around at least three oppositions:

Child/adult
Milk/beer
Food (nourishment)/anti-food (intoxicant)

The mixing of both in the same glass blurs the boundary between the three oppositions, signifying a transitional moment in Sam's journey. This moment can be defined as the child's orphan status coming up against the adult's bachelor status – two negatives, or lacks, that partly cancel out one another when Captain Sharp adopts Sam. (Captain Sharp does define Sam as a bachelor, but the category does not apply to children, just as marriage between children in Western societies is not recognized. Sam therefore experiences two illegitimate identities – bachelor/married – before Captain Sharp adopts him.) Once he is adopted by Captain Sharp and once he renames mile 3.25 tidal inlet as 'moonrise kingdom' does Sam find his symbolic identity.

A third paradigm is also important:

Reading fiction paradigm

(1) Suzy reads by herself for a few moments
(13) Suzy reads to Sam from one of her books (although Sam is asleep)
(22) Sam and Suzy on the beach. Suzy reads to Sam from one of her books (and he is awake)
(30) Suzy reads to all the scouts
(40) Suzy reads by herself

The paradigm begins and ends on the same value – Suzy as a solitary reader reading silently in (1) and (40). But between these moments she reads aloud – to Sam (asleep [13], then awake [22]), and then to the whole troop of scouts (30). Suzy is the consumer but also the provider of stories. Reading aloud creates a sense of community.

The film is structured by further repetitions, although not sufficiently strong to organize into paradigms. Suzy and Sam escape twice: the first time by themselves, the second time with the help of the scouts. Images of bloody penetration punctuate the film: the arrow that kills snoopy the dog (19); the left-handed scissors Suzy uses to stab Redford (19); and the earrings that Sam makes using fish hooks, which he pushes into Suzy's unpierced earlobes (22).

Exchange (gift/theft)

The early part of the film's storyworld is dominated by the exchange of letters between Sam and Suzy. The first indication of this exchange is at the end of scene (1) when Suzy collects a letter from the mailbox. In scene (2), the narrator points to the seaplane flying overhead, which brings mail to the island. In the flashback (10), Suzy initiates the letter writing by sending a note to Sam, asking him to write to her. The resulting exchange of letters is dramatized in (16), when several are read out.

The Sam–Suzy letters function to overcome loss, absence and isolation. They establish a conventional narrative pattern. Other letters create more interesting patterns. For example, in scene (3), Scout Master Ward receives Sam's letter of resignation from the scouts. In scene (23), Scout Master Ward delivers a letter to Sam from his foster parents, explaining that they cannot invite him back. These two letters mirror each other: Sam's letter separates himself from the scouts, and the foster parents' letter separates themselves from Sam. Scout Master Ward receives the first letter and delivers the second letter. Sam leaves his letter in his scout tent, where Ward finds it, and Ward delivers the letter to Sam soon after he is discovered in the tent with Suzy. But crucially, the tent is overturned and discarded (by Mr Bishop) before Ward delivers the letter. In other words, in (3) Sam is absent from his tent (Figure 9.1); in (23) Sam is present but the tent is absent (Figure 9.2). In (3) Ward receives a letter from Sam; in (23) Ward delivers a letter to Sam.

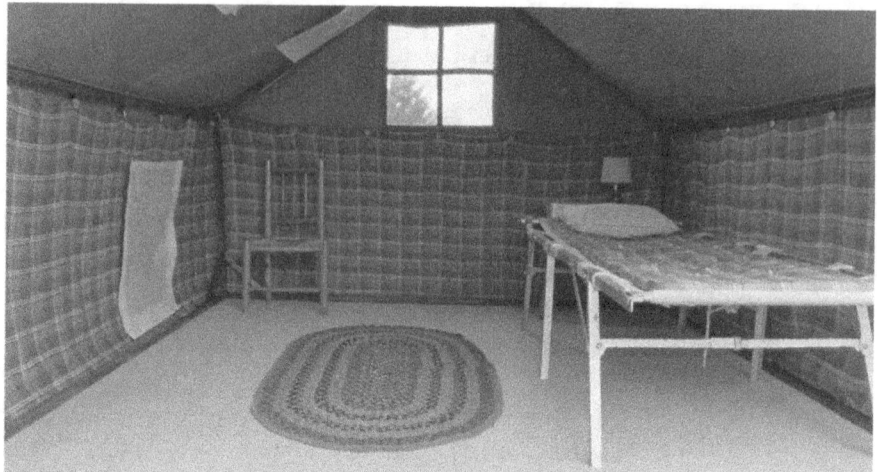

Figure 9.1 Sam is absent from his tent (*Moonrise Kingdom*) © Focus Features

Figure 9.2 Sam is present (with Suzy), but the tent is absent (*Moonrise Kingdom*) © Focus Features

The letter Ward delivers to Sam in (23) also establishes a link to the letter Suzy receives in (1):

(1) Suzy receives a letter from Sam finalizing their plan to be together

(23) Sam receives a letter from his foster parents finalizing their separation

The letter from the foster parents motivates Sam's desire to marry Suzy.

Phone calls are also an important form of exchange and communication. With the assistance of Scout Master Ward and Becky, Captain Sharp phones Sam's foster parents (5) and social services (24). The head of the Lebanon scouts, Commander Pierce (Harvey Keitel), phones Captain Sharp (35) about the sighting of Sam and Suzy at Fort Lebanon. Scout Master Ward also sends a Morse code message to the Fort Lebanon scouts (31), saying he has lost all of his scouts.

The ultimate symbol of exchange, money – in the form of a tennis ball tube full of nickels – is paid to Cousin Ben to perform the wedding ceremony (compare to the envelope of money Anthony gives to Inez in *Bottle Rocket*). Cousin Ben gladly accepts the payment (even though the ceremony he performs has no legal status), but the scouts persuade him to return the money to the newly married couple.

Gifts: Sam presents Suzy with some flowers when they meet up in the meadow (11) and, in (22), he makes her a pair of earrings from beetles and fish hooks. Earrings also function as a gift in *Bottle Rocket* – a gift from Anthony to his mother (which become stolen property that Dignan steals during the practice burglary). Because Sam is an orphan, he is unable to give the earrings to his mother, but gives them to his girlfriend instead.

Stealing is also prevalent in *Moonrise Kingdom*. Captain Sharp tries to steal one of the women in the small community (Mrs Bishop) but settles in the end for foster parenthood without a wife. Sam steals a canoe and supplies in order to escape, while Suzy steals the portable record player from her brother (twice, although she leaves a note the first time), and she admits to stealing the library books (in order to have a secret). But, by the end of the film, Suzy has another secret, which she inherited from her mother. The relationship between Mrs Bishop and Captain Sharp, their secret liaisons (which Suzy discovers), is transferred to Suzy and Sam, who continue to meet up secretly on the top floor of the Bishop home. The top floor is never occupied by the adults, although the children can and do occupy the other floors. Similarly in *The Royal Tenenbaums*, we never see the Tenenbaum parents on the roof, although we do see Royal on the roof of the Lindbergh Palace Hotel.

Water: The flood

Benjamin Britten's children's opera *Noye's Fludde* is integrated into *Moonrise Kingdom*. Britten's version of the flood myth fits in with Wes Anderson's worldview. In a review of Britten's opera, Joe Law wrote: 'Like many other plays of this sort, [*Noye's Fludde*] mixes naiveté with sophistication, serious purpose with low comedy' (Joe Law 1990, 181) – an evaluation that can easily apply to *Moonrise Kingdom* itself.

The Noah's ark flood myth is the opposite of the creation myth: the destruction of life/the creation of life. Noah sends the raven and dove from the ark to find land but only the dove succeeds. Suzy is first seen dressed as a raven in scene (10). The raven is argumentative, and quarrels with Noah, qualities that are transferred to Suzy. She also inherits some of the values of the raven from Ovid's *Metamorphoses*, where Apollo uses fire to turn the raven black for bringing a message of his beloved's unfaithfulness. Suzy discovers that her mother is unfaithful, although she only conveys her knowledge back to her mother. Furthermore, it is Sam, not Suzy, who is blackened by lightning (celestial fire) in scene (34). Sam, Suzy and Captain Sharp are struck by lightning in scene (38) while standing at the top of the church tower in the rainstorm. After the lightning strike, all three occupy a transitional space: they are literally suspended in a void between sky and (flooded) earth. (Unlike Anthony in the opening of *Bottle Rocket*, they are unable to climb down from sky to earth.)

The film's title has a variety of semantic values. 'Moonrise' – the moon that has risen above the horizon – refers to the moon existing between sky and earth. The three characters suspended from the church tower temporarily occupy the same space as the rising moon. 'Kingdom' has both religious and secular meanings: it refers to the kingdom of God, and the rising moon represents Christ, but it also refers to the territory (dominion) ruled over by a king. Sam and Suzy temporarily live in and rule over mile 3.25 tide inlet (which they rename Moonrise Kingdom), although the flood permanently obliterates it. At the end of the film (40), the tide inlet only exists as a painting – although the film's final image returns to the inlet before it was flooded.

10

Rules of Descent and Laws of Inheritance: *The Grand Budapest Hotel*

Western conventions governing the inheritance of wealth were traditionally based on kinship rules of descent, on intergenerational relationships between parents and children. This chapter argues that the narrative of *The Grand Budapest Hotel* (2014) initially follows a primogeniture rule of descent – where the (elder) son inherits the wealth of the parents – before switching to a juridical law of inheritance. The film is also structured around a matriarchal family system but with matricide at its centre.

Plot synopsis

(1) Title card: 'The Former Republic of Zubrowka'. (2) Old Lutz cemetery: a student places a key on the tomb of an author (known as 'the author' throughout the film). The student holds a book 'the author' wrote: *The Grand Budapest Hotel*. (3) 1985. 'The author' (Tom Wilkinson) addresses the camera, talks about the process of storytelling. He ends by introducing the story of *The Grand Budapest Hotel*. (4) 'The author' narrates his visit to the hotel in 1968, illustrated with a montage sequence of the guests in the hotel. His voice changes to his younger self (Jude Law). (5) 'The author' talks to the concierge, M. Jean (Jason Schwartzman) about Zero Moustafa (F. Murray Abraham). (6) 'The author' and Zero introduce themselves to one another. (7) At dinner, Zero tells 'the author' his story. (8) Title card: 'Part 1: M. Gustave'. (9) 1932. Gustave (Ralph Fiennes) and Madame D. (Tilda Swinton). Madame D. departs from the hotel. (10) Gustave notices the new lobby boy, Zero (Tony Revolori). He interviews Zero and discovers he is an orphan. (11) One month later. Zero (in 1968) narrates the events in The Grand Budapest hotel circa. 1932. (12) Deputy Kovacs (Jeff Goldblum)

inspects the hotel's accounts. (13) Agatha (Saoirse Ronan) is introduced working in Mendl's bakery. (14) Title card: 'Part 2: Madame C.V.D.u.T'. (15) Zero and Gustave discover that Madame D. has died. (16) They take a train to visit her but are almost arrested because Zero's identity papers are not in order. (17) Zero and Gustave arrive at Madame D.'s mansion. (18) Deputy Kovacs reads out parts of the will. Gustave inherits the painting *Boy with Apple*. Madame D.'s son Dmitri (Adrien Brody) and Jopling (Willem Dafoe) confront Gustave. (19) Zero and Gustave steal the painting. The butler Serge (Mathieu Amalric) helps them. (20) Return journey on the train. Gustave draws up a will, to bequeath all his possessions to Zero. (21) Zero and Gustave place the painting in the hotel's safe. (22) Gustave is arrested for the murder of Madame D. (23) Title card: 'Part 3: Check-point 19. Criminal Internment Camp'. (24) One week later. Zero visits Gustave in prison. He informs Gustave that Serge accuses him of murdering Madame D. (25) Jopling visits Serge's sister. (26) Gustave becomes involved in an escape plan masterminded by Ludwig (Harvey Keitel). (27) Montage sequence: 1 month earlier. Zero gets engaged to Agatha. Agatha makes Mendl's cakes with tools in them, to aid the escape. (28) Deputy Kovacs angers Dmitri over discrepancies in Madame D.'s will. Jopling kills Kovacs' cat. (28) Gustave, Ludwig and other inmates begin their escape from prison. (29) Zero gives Agatha the code to the safe to retrieve the painting in the event of an emergency. (30) Jopling follows and kills Kovacs. (31) Gustave, Ludwig and other inmates escape from prison. (32) Zero meets up with Gustave. Zero explains how his parents died. (33) The police discover the breakout, and Jopling discovers that Agatha assisted. (34) Gustave phones the society of crossed keys to help him escape. Montage sequence of hotel concierges. (35) Zero and Gustave travel to meet Serge. (36) Serge's sister is found dead. (37) Serge informs Gustave of Madame D.'s second will. But Jopling murders him soon afterwards. (38) Zero and Gustave chase Jopling, who is eventually killed. (39) Title card: 'Part 5: The Second Copy of the second Will'. (40) Twenty-four hours later. Agatha, Zero and Gustave take the 'Boy with Apple' painting from the Grand Budapest Hotel and discover the new will, which leaves all of Madame D.'s wealth to Gustave. (41) Zero and Agatha get married, but Agatha died two years later. (42) On the train, Gustave is arrested and eventually killed. Zero inherits all of Gustave's wealth. (43) The dinner between Zero and 'the author' ends. Voiceover narration switches back to 'the author'. (44) 'The author' in 1985, followed by the student at the cemetery.

The film's title appears within the diegesis, on the cover of a book held by a student standing in the Old Lutz cemetery, rather than on the filmophanic (surface) level of the image. The narration then shifts to 'the author' of the book (in 1985), who talks directly to camera about the process of writing. He narrates his visit to the Grand Budapest Hotel in 1968, where he met its owner, Zero Moustafa, who invited 'the author' to dinner and narrated to him his life story, beginning in 1932. The book we see at the start of the film – and the greater part of the film itself – is the outcome of this dinner engagement.

The Grand Budapest Hotel resembles *The Royal Tenenbaums* in several respects: the film title appears on the cover of a book; both films are narrated in voice-over (but whereas the narrator of *The Royal Tenenbaums* is never seen in the diegesis, the narrators – 'the author', Zero Moustafa – in *The Grand Budapest Hotel* do appear in the diegesis); both films are divided into sections, signified by title cards; the voice-over narration is accompanied by images from the past (the childhood of the Tenenbaum children, the writer's visit to the hotel, Zero Mustafa's childhood); and both films are based on matrilineal family systems.

Kinship, gifts and theft

The aristocratic family at the centre of *The Grand Budapest Hotel* is dominated by a benign matriarch, Madame D., whose husband died forty-six years ago. She has one son (Dmitri) and three daughters. Madame D.'s first will follows the conventions of the aristocratic rule of descent: to maintain the unity of the family estate, she passes on all her wealth to her son (but also makes special allowances to her three daughters) – with the exception of the painting *Boy with Apple*, which she bequeaths to Gustave (scene 18). The painting is therefore a gift from Madame D. to Gustave, bequeathed to him for his companionship. Dmitri argues the gift is illegitimate and questions Gustave's intentions. To circumvent the son's cancelling of the gift to the non-family member (the mother's lover), Gustave and Zero decide to steal the painting. The theft is not, however, a simple act of stealing, for the object stolen is a gift bequeathed to the 'thief'. The painting causes disruption and eventually leads to the final state of affairs, to Dmitri's disinheritance – although the ultimate cause of his changing fortunes is the second will (a copy) hidden in the back of the painting, which comes into effect due to the matricide committed by Dmitri. This second will disinherits the children and leaves all the wealth to Gustave. The film promotes laws of inheritance and downplays rules of descent. Laws of inheritance also govern Gustave's own will (written on the train in [20]), in which he bequeaths all of his wealth to Zero.

The film's main characters are associated with the *Boy with Apple* painting: Madame D. bequeaths it to Gustave; Serge hides the second copy of the second will in the back panel when he wraps it up; Gustave and Zero steal the painting and hide it in a safe; Agatha retrieves it from the safe; Dmitri tries to retrieve it from Agatha. In other words, like all of Madame D.'s wealth, the painting travels from Madame D. to Zero via Gustave and Dmitri (with Agatha assisting with the painting). The painting ends up in the lobby of the Grand Budapest Hotel, where 'the author' sees it on his stay in 1968.

Madame D.'s second will (bequeathing all her wealth to Gustave) and Gustave's will (bequeathing all his wealth to Zero) form a chain of inheritance:

Madame D.–(Dmitri)–Gustave–Zero

This chain decisively rejects kinship rules of descent, for the immigrant orphan Zero ends up inheriting all the wealth. More specifically, Dmitri becomes the 'zero' and Zero becomes rich by inheriting his wealth via Gustave. Dmitri is disinherited because he is charged with matricide.

Zero's ethnic identity and immigrant status become an issue on several occasions: on the first train journey, to visit Madame D. (16), Zero is almost arrested, but Gustave steps in to defend him; this scenario is repeated in (42), which leads to Gustave's death as he tries to defend Zero a second time. Between these two pivotal moments, Gustave expresses his own suspicions of Zero's immigrant status. After escaping from prison, Gustave and Zero meet up (32), but Zero's lack of preparation leads Gustave to criticize him for leaving his own country. Zero's explanation (his parents were murdered) leads Gustave to retract his criticisms. Zero calls Gustave his brother, and they briefly hug. But Gustave's momentary criticism of and suspicions towards Zero's immigrant status demonstrate that the symbolic order is structured around a self/other opposition, in which the other is coded negatively, as non-self or outsider, due to the anxiety the self (whether individuals or entire societies) experiences in regards to the other.

On a symbolic level, Gustave is positioned as a son to Madame D. for he is treated as a descendent like Dmitri who inherits some (and later, all) of her wealth. This sets up an immediate opposition between the two characters:

Dmitri/Gustave

Gustave the subject struggles with Dmitri the opponent over the possession of an object (painting) and, more generally, over their relation to Madame D. But their relationship to Madame D. is coded in significantly different ways: Gustave is having a sexual relationship with her (moreover, an intergenerational relationship) whereas Dmitri is the son who ends up committing matricide:

Death (matricide)/sex (intergenerational)

Yet, both are transgressive, and Gustave is also accused of killing Madame D. In other words, Gustave inherits both transgressions. He freely admits the sexual relationship (Dmitri accuses Gustave of being homosexual but also his mother's lover) but is driven to clear his name of the murder charge. The conflict between Gustave and Dmitri is not mediated but is resolved via Dmitri's sudden disappearance, as reported in a newspaper story in scene (40). In regard to T. K. Seung's reworking of the concept of symbolic resolution (1982, 203–9), the conflict between Gustave and Dimitri is resolved via the suppression of one of the terms (Dmitri) in dispute. Gustave lives long enough to inherit Madame D.'s wealth, but after he is arrested and later killed for defending Zero (42), he in turn passes on the wealth he inherited. Gustave is therefore like Dmitri in that he is suppressed/ eliminated from the narrative, which facilitates the flow of wealth. Zero initially becomes very rich, but later he made a deal with the new Government by handing over most of his wealth to keep his freedom, although he also keeps the Grand Budapest Hotel. Zero therefore ends up with one of Madame D.'s assets, the Grand Budapest Hotel, which he keeps because it reminds him of his short relationship with Agatha. Structurally, Zero takes the place of Madame D. and Agatha takes the place of Gustave: Madame D. was the secretive owner of the Grand Budapest Hotel, while Zero is its new secretive owner; Madame D. was in an intergenerational relationship with Gustave, while Zero was in an interethnic relationship with Agatha:

Madame D. –Grand Budapest Hotel–Gustave →
Zero–Grand Budapest Hotel–Agatha

The Grand Budapest Hotel contains but transforms some of the kinship and narrative elements from *Rushmore*. In *Rushmore*, the intergenerational conflict Blume–Miss Cross–Max is resolved by pairing off Blume–Miss Cross in an intergenerational relationship and Max–Margaret Yang in an interethnic relationship. *The Grand Budapest Hotel* begins with the intergenerational relationship between Madame D. and Gustave, and achieves an interethnic relationship between Zero and Agatha. But *Rushmore* ends by achieving these relationships, whereas by the end of *The Grand Budapest Hotel* both these relationships are dissolved, leaving Zero as the sole and lonely survivor.

Madame D. dies early in the film, in scene (15). The deaths of Agatha and Gustave are announced in sequential scenes: (41), (42). Zero loses Agatha but inherits the Grand Budapest Hotel. Although the film's kinship logic enables the interethnic marriage between Zero and Agatha to take place, it does not allow the union to survive and propagate, for we learn that Agatha and their young son died. Zero lives up to his name by beginning with nothing (when Gustave interviews him, he lists Zero's previous experience and family background as 'zero'). The film charts Zero's gains, including all of Madame D.'s wealth, but this is cancelled out with his loss of Agatha and their child.

Binary oppositions

In addition to the oppositions mentioned above – Dmitri/Gustave, Death (matricide)/Sex (intergenerational) – the film is dominated by three additions oppositions:

Individual/collective
Rich/poor
Commensality/solitary eating

Wes Anderson's films are structured around the individual/collective opposition, with the individual usually coded as a solitary outsider. The movement of each of the film's narratives is from the individual to the collective. *The Grand Budapest Hotel* reverses this movement: from collective to individual. Zero initially becomes part of the Grand Budapest Hotel team but ends up as a lonely individual – a sentiment 'the author' expresses in his initial impression in scene (5):

AUTHOR (V.O.)
In any case, one evening, as I stood conferring elbow-to-elbow with M. Jean, as had become my habit, I noticed a new presence in our company. A small, elderly man, smartly dressed, with an exceptionally lively, intelligent face – and an immediately perceptible air of sadness. He was, like the rest of us, alone – but also, I must say, he was the first that struck one as being, deeply and truly, lonely.

An oppositional value found in *Rushmore* reappears in *The Grand Budapest Hotel*: rich/poor, but it is mapped onto locations rather than individuals. That is, the Grand Budapest Hotel and Madame D.'s mansion are rich and opulent, whereas the prison and monastery are poor and sparse, although the hotel contains two rooms coded as poor – the living quarters of both Zero and Gustave are sparse and narrow.

Gustave eats alone in his room (an anti-social behaviour) in contrast to the rest of the hotel staff, who eat together (setting up the opposition: solitary eating/commensality), and in contrast to 'the author' and Zero in the framing story, who participate in two rituals at the same time: sharing a meal and stories in the hotel restaurant. Gustave also prepares and delivers the food while in prison, although only one solitary prisoner decides to eat it.

The film is renowned for its emphasis on the luxurious Mendl cakes Agatha makes. Gustave delivers a Mendl cake to his friends in prison (who consume it within seconds) and, later, tools to escape from prison are hidden in Mendl cakes. To retrieve the *Boy with Apple* painting from the Grand Budapest Hotel's safe after the military take it over, Agatha uses a Mendl cake as a gift to bribe the guard in order to gain entry. This scenario is repeated moments later when

Gustave and Zero realize that Agatha may be in danger: they offer the guard another cake while he is still consuming the first.

Water continues to play a significant role in Wes Anderson's films. 'The author' and Zero introduce themselves in the hotel baths in scene (6) – or, more accurately, Zero's disembodied voice complements 'the author' before he emerges from one of the baths and introduces himself to 'the author'. This meeting is a weak version of the meeting between Inez and Anthony in *Bottle Rocket*, containing many transformations: Anthony emerges from the swimming pool and sees Inez and greets her with a wave; Zero emerges from the bath and sees 'the author', whom he has already greeted vocally; Anthony is in the water and Inez is on dry land, while both Zero and 'the author' are in the water, in separate baths; Inez and Anthony develop a sexual relationship, while Zero and 'the author' form a creative alliance, of author and subject; they are linked via storytelling and the sharing of a meal.

Gustave asks for ice-cold water when he arrives at Madame D.'s mansion, while Zero drinks milk (17). Gustave ends up pouring the water onto a cactus plant, and Zero leaves his milk in the room where the *Boy with Apple* painting is located. These events echo the central scene in *Moonrise Kingdom*, in which Sam drinks milk and Captain Sharp drinks beer (and pours some of it into Sam's glass of milk). In *The Grand Budapest Hotel*, there is no crossover or contamination between the cold water and the milk, but there is a structural relation between the orphans (Sam, Zero) drinking milk in opposition to the adults (Captain Sharp, Gustave) caring for them.

Verticality paradigm

Topography plays a significant role in *The Grand Budapest Hotel*. Four of the main locations are positioned on high ground: the Grand Budapest Hotel, Madame D.'s mansion, the Criminal Internment Camp and the observatory-monastery where Gustave meets Serge. Travelling towards these high locations is a key feature in the film (as it is in *The Darjeeling Limited*, when the brothers successfully perform the feather ceremony): the funicular leading up to the

Table 10.1 High locations in *The Grand Budapest Hotel*

Building	Movement (up/down)	Value (rich/poor)
Grand Budapest Hotel	up	rich
Madame D.'s mansion	up	rich
The Criminal Internment Camp	down	poor
The observatory-monastery	up/down	poor

hotel; the drive towards Madame D.'s mansion; and the cable cars leading to the observatory-monastery. The internment camp is shown to be high up on a mountain, and the key movement is downwards, as prisoners dig a tunnel and escape (echoing scenes from *Fantastic Mr. Fox* – although the foxes naturally use their claws to burrow underground, whereas the prisoners must rely on technology – tools – to burrow and escape). Jopling and Gustave-Zero also take the long journey down from the monastery, in a chase scene that ends in Jopling's death (see Table 10.1).

As with *Bottle Rocket*, *Rushmore* and *The Royal Tenenbaums*, the lift/elevator in *The Grand Budapest Hotel* becomes the privileged object of vertical movement.

Lift paradigm

(5) 'The author' enters the lift to go up

(9) Gustave-Madame D.-Zero go down in the lift

(10) Gustave interviews Zero, in part in the lift

(40) Agatha (carrying the *Boy with Apple* painting)-Dmitri follows her; Gustave and Zero go to the top of the hotel in the service lift

(43) Zero enters the lift to go up

Scenes (5) and (43) take place in 1968; they are almost identical in their depiction of solitary characters standing in the lift. In (43), Zero invites 'the author' to take the lift with him, but 'the author' declines; he remains in the lobby and writes notes. The lasting image of Zero is of a solitary figure standing in the lift by himself (Figure 10.1). Scenes (9) and (10) repeat each other, with variation: in (9) *three* characters travel *down* in the lift (Gustave, Madame D., Zero); in (10) *two* characters travel up in the lift (Gustave, Zero).

Figure 10.1 Zero standing in the lift by himself (*The Grand Budapest Hotel*) © Fox Searchlight

Similarly, in (40), Agatha travels up in the lift with Dmitri (and the *Boy with Apple* painting).

Scene (9) is central in terms of the chain of inheritance, for the three main characters in that chain are present in the lift. Scene (10) eliminates the first character in that chain (Madame D.), leaving the second and third characters, Gustave and Zero, while (43) focuses on the sole survivor, Zero. Scene (40) develops a complex relation with (9): (a) Zero is paired with Agatha; (b) Gustave is paired with Dmitri; and (c) Madame D. is paired with the painting (that she bequeathed to Gustave). The values in these pairing are also of interest: (a) and (c) are based on love, and (b) is based on hate.

In the 1968 segment of the film, only Zero and *Boy with Apple* remain, together with the hotel and 'the author'. But, as the film winds its way back to the cemetery, all that remains of the past events depicted in the film is The Grand Budapest Hotel book written by 'the author'.

Part Three

Finale

11

The Symbolic Storyworld of Wes Anderson

Beneath the level of [...] simple narrative meaning, we get a more elementary level of forms themselves, communicating with each other, interacting, reverberating, echoing, morphing, transforming one into the other. And it is this background, this background of proto-reality, a real which is more dense, more fundamental than the narrative reality, the story that we observe. It is this that provides the proper density of the cinematic experience.

Slavoj Žižek, *The Pervert's Guide to Cinema*

My semiotic analysis of Wes Anderson began with the individual films and abstracted from them core themes and hidden structures, including paradigms, kinship systems and binary oppositions, supplemented with other symbolic codes such as mediators, systems of exchange and rules of transformation. Although these structures are still defined in terms of content, the structural relations between those units of content within individual films as well as across films constitute my primary interest and focus. In this final chapter, I consider the relation between content and structure, before presenting a model of the overall structural organization of Wes Anderson's storyworld which, I argue, is dominated by: three types of kinship structures ('death/ absence of parents or spouses', 'intergenerational relationships', 'interethnic relationships'); 'death/life (funerals and pregnancies)'; 'exchange and gifts'; 'mediation'; 'relative worlds'; 'water and drowning'; plus 'verticality, movement, and water'.

Form versus structure

In *The Pervert's Guide to Cinema* (Fiennes 2006) Žižek contrasts simple narrative meaning, generated from the syntagmatic concatenation of signs, to the symbolic density of forms – what I have called throughout this book paradigmatic codes, structures and transformational variations – that resonate with each other beyond the actual film. In the foreword to his edited book on Hitchcock, Žižek states that the book aims 'to subtract from Hitchcock's films all their narrative content and to isolate the intensity of their formal patterns' (2010a, vii). And in his short essay in the same volume, 'Hitchcockian *sinthoms*' (2010b), he identifies two types of interpretation of paradigms across Hitchcock's films (repeated motifs such as the glass of milk, or one person suspended from another's hand). The first type of interpretation identifies a fixed, universal meaning across the repeated motifs, while the second type describes formal similarities and patterns. Žižek insists that the first (universal) type of interpretation says too much, for it applies pre-existing ready-made meanings to the films, whereas the second type of interpretation does not say enough, because it is too formal, focusing on empty signifiers (2010b, 126). 'The right balance', he concludes, 'is attained when we conceive them as *sinthoms* in the Lacanian sense: as a signifier's constellation (formula) which fixes a certain core of enjoyment, like mannerisms in painting – characteristic details which persist and repeat themselves without implying a common meaning' (2010b, 126). The sinthom/sinthome is the symptom that resists interpretation: it is not a pathological disturbance of the symbolic exchange of meaning that needs to be explained, but is a structure governed by enjoyment that lies outside the symbolic.

But, do we need to go beyond the symbolic to develop the 'right balance' between the two forms of interpretation? To understand the place of the structural semiotic analyses carried out in this book in relation to the two forms of interpretation Žižek identifies, we need to consider Lévi-Strauss's distinction between 'structure' and 'form' in his review of Vladimir Propp's *Morphology of the Folktale* (1968), and the debate between Emilio Garroni and Christian Metz on medium specificity. 'Contrary to formalism', wrote Lévi-Strauss, 'structuralism refuses to set the concrete against the abstract and to ascribe greater significance to the latter. *Form* is defined by opposition to content, an entity in its own right, but *structure* has no distinct content: it is content itself' (Lévi-Strauss 1976, 155). Whereas Propp studied abstract formal constants (functions), for Lévi-Strauss structuralism remains grounded in concrete content. Moreover, with its emphasis on transformations (addition, subtraction, inversion, substitution, transposition), structuralism is also a dynamic model. Garroni (1968, 1974) followed the formalist agenda by arguing that the attempt to define filmic specificity is a spurious activity. Following Hjelmslev (1961), he divorced codes from material of expression, claiming that codes should be defined in purely formal, abstract terms. This, in effect, implies that codes are not tied to or manifest in the material of expression of any particular language and are not, therefore, specific to any language; a code is pure form and can therefore be manifest in the material of expression of multiple languages. Metz (1974b) followed the structural semiotic agenda; he agreed with Garroni that a language consists of multiple codes, but disagreed that all codes are formal, not related to material of expression. For Metz, some codes are specific – are tied to film's material of expression – and some are non-specific. But Garroni rejected the attachment to the immediate material qualities of media, and instead defined a shared system of codes. Metz defined film in terms of a specific combination of formal and manifest codes, whereas Garroni argued that all codes are formal, non-manifest and abstract.

In terms of Žižek's two types of interpretation, the formalism of Propp and Garroni does not say enough, while the structural semiotics of Lévi-Strauss and Metz maintain the right balance (and both formalism and structuralism reject the universalizing tendency to ascribe predetermined, fixed meanings to texts). The film analyses carried out in this book follow the structural semiotic approach advocated by Lévi-Strauss and Metz.

Archi-film revisited: Storyworld as World 3

In Chapter 1 we saw that, just as the anthropologist collects and studies variations of the same invariant archi-myth, for Peter Wollen each film an auteur makes is a variation of his or her archi-film, and the ultimate goal of auteur structuralism was to construct a model of an auteur's underlying archi-film, the totality of their storyworld. An auteur's storyworld can be defined as a meaningful whole only insofar as its underlying structure can be delineated across several films. Yet, this archi-film or storyworld only exists retrospectively in the sense that it comes into being from all the variants; this invariant kernel can only be grasped as it emerges from specific films. Nonetheless, it is understood to pre-exist those variants: 'Once it is here', writes Žižek (discussing retrospective logic), 'it was always already here' (2010a, xii). The cause (the kernel) comes after the effects (the variants), but the effects retrospectively create their cause.

This retrospective logic also applies to the creation of storyworlds and to Popper's World 3. In Chapter 1 we saw that Popper's World 1 refers to physical objects, World 2 refers to psychological phenomena and mental states and World 3 refers to the ideas and systems that transcend human minds (i.e. the realm of the symbolic). Popper rejected a purely psychological understanding of World 3 while avoiding conceptualizing it as a metaphysical Platonic form. He achieved this by arguing that, although World 3 is a creation or invention of the human mind, it nonetheless takes on a life of its own. Popper gives the example of the invention of numbers: once invented, they take on an autonomous existence and create emergent qualities – unintended and unexpected consequences (such as prime numbers) – that were not part of the original invention of the number system (Popper 1972, 118; 159–60). These unintended consequences exceed human consciousness (that is, transcend World 2), and become part of World 3. One advantage of conceptualizing storyworld in terms of Popper's World 3 is that it directs attention towards the abstract structures that constitute the storyworld's symbolic dimension and away from an exclusive focus on the mimetic, manifest, represented parts of a director's storyworld.

The analysis of paradigms, binary oppositions and kinship in particular has yielded a number of key structures at the core of Wes Anderson's storyworld. The following pages represent an overview of these structures as embedded in the films.

Kinship (1): Death/absence of parents or spouses

The key invariant kinship issue in Wes Anderson's storyworld is the death or absence of parents or spouses (and/or close friends). This issue yields a double structure of paradigmatic oppositions:

Death/absence
Parent(s)/spouse(s)

One term from each opposition can be combined with one or both terms from the other opposition: the death of a parent and/or a spouse; the absence of a parent and/or a spouse. The parent can therefore be either dead or absent, and the spouse can either be dead or absent.[1]

These two oppositions define the matrix of possibilities of this kinship issue in Wes Anderson's storyworld, only some of which are manifest in his films. In *Bottle Rocket* the parents of the three main characters are absent; in *Rushmore* Max Fischer's mother is dead (cancer), as is Miss Cross's husband (drowning), a parallelism that fuels their relationship; in *The Royal Tenenbaums* Chas's wife died in a plane crash, Henry Sherman's wife died of cancer, Royal Tenenbaum dies of a heart attack at the end of the film and Margot's blood relatives give her up for adoption (they are absent, except in one flashback); in *The Life Aquatic with Steve Zissou* Ned Plimpton's mother dies of cancer, which leads him to search for his father (but which results in his own death) and Esteban (although not officially related to anyone in the film) dies from a shark attack; in *The Darjeeling Limited* three brothers travel in search of their mother one year after their father dies in a car accident; in *Fantastic Mr. Fox* Kristofferson lives with his relatives due to his uncle's illness; in *Moonrise Kingdom* Sam Shakusky is an orphan (the film does not explain how his parents died) and a solitary outsider, and the film is focused around his juvenile attempts to establish a relation with fellow outsider Suzy Bishop; and in *The Grand Budapest Hotel* Zero is an orphan (his parents were shot) but becomes part of the hotel's community and marries Agatha, before losing her, their child, and the hotel community (including Gustave, who was also shot), while maintaining ownership of the hotel. The film begins and ends with a visit to the grave of 'the author'. Royal, Ned, Madame D., Gustave and 'the author' form a subgroup to the extent that they are major characters who die during the narrative unfolding of the films they appear in, and from this subgroup only Royal and 'the author' die a natural death.

From this matrix of possibilities emerges the dominance of the solitary character, epitomized in the orphan (the death of both parents turn children into orphans). The typical Wes Anderson character is a dysfunctional solitary male who tries to overcome isolation via the establishment of a community of like-minded individuals. Although we can express this issue as an opposition (solitary hero/community, self/other), the trajectory of the narrative aims to dissolve this opposition via the solitary hero joining a community or by creating his/her own. This most extreme form of isolation (the orphan) is manifest in Wes Anderson's later films, *Moonrise Kingdom* (Sam) and *The Grand Budapest Hotel* (Zero^2), although Eli (who lives with his aunt) in *The Royal Tenenbaums* is presumably an orphan, as is Kristofferson (*Fantastic Mr. Fox*), who lives with his uncle (who in turn becomes ill). Dignan in *Bottle Rocket*, Max Fischer in *Rushmore* and the three grown up Whitman brothers in *The Darjeeling Limited* suffer less to the extent that they lose one parent (it is indeterminate whether Dignan's biological father is absent or dead). In *The Life Aquatic* Ned's mother dies and he attempts to find his father, which he narrows down to the solitary male hero Steve Zissou (who has formed a community of misfits). Ned joins Zissou's community, but Zissou in turn loses Ned, who dies in a helicopter crash at sea. Miss Cross's husband drowns, while Chas and Henry lose their wives. And Royal Tenenbaum dies at the end of the film.

In her study of modal structures in narrative universes, Marie Laure-Ryan organizes different narrative possibilities into a ranked hierarchy (1985, 727). We shall follow Ryan's suggestion by organizing Wes Anderson's storyworld into a hierarchy in regard to the death of parents, spouses and friends, beginning with the highest (most serious) value at the top:[3]

Death of both parents: Sam, Zero, (Eli), (Kristofferson)

Death of one parent: Max, Tenenbaum family, Ned, (Dignan)

Death of spouse: Miss Cross, Chas, Henry, Zero

Death of descendants: Zissou's 'son' Ned, Zero and Agatha's son

Death of close friend: Zissou's friend Esteban

Sam and Zero occupy the top of the hierarchy, although Zero is the representative figure in this hierarchy because he is alone at the end of *The Grand Budapest Hotel*, and he also appears on two other occasions in the hierarchy (death of spouse, death of descendant).

Kinship (2): Intergenerational relationships

After *Bottle Rocket*, intergenerational relationships (either non-sibling or complex, quasi-consanguine) recur throughout Wes Anderson's films. They function as a possible solution to death/absence of parents or spouses. In *Rushmore* the 28-year-old Miss Cross is pursued by the 15-year-old Max Fischer and by the middle-aged Herman Blume. This is resolved at the end of the film, with Miss Cross pairing off with Blume, while Max apparently resolves his Oedipal complex by pairing off with Margaret Yang. In *The Royal Tenenbaums* Raleigh St Clair is unhappily married to the much younger Margot Tenenbaum, while Richie Tenenbaum is in love with Margot, his adopted sister. The same woman (Margot) is therefore caught up in a quasi-incestuous (quasi-consanguine) relation with her brother her own age and an intergenerational marriage to a much older man (and she had many brief affairs). In *The Life Aquatic* Jane Winslett-Richardson is pursued by Ned Plimpton (roughly the same age) and by the older Steve Zissou. This three-way relationship is complicated by Jane's pregnancy (and being labelled a lesbian), and especially by Ned's attempt to establish if Steve Zissou is his biological father, creating a potentially consanguine, intergenerational Oedipal rivalry between the two men. It is only resolved via Ned's death. In *The Grand Budapest Hotel* this kinship structure in presented in an exaggerated form via Madame D.'s intergenerational relationship with Gustave.

These variations can be represented schematically:[4]

Rushmore:
Blume–Miss Cross–Max → Blume–Miss Cross and Max–Margaret Yang (resolution via equilibrium).

The Royal Tenenbaums:
Raleigh St. Clair–Margot Tenenbaum → Margot–Richie–Eli (unresolved)

The Life Aquatic with Steve Zissou:

Zissou–Jane–Ned → Jane–Ned, until Ned dies (resolution via suppression). Ned–Zissou are potentially blood relatives (father-son conflict)

The Grand Budapest Hotel

Madame D. –Gustave–Dmitri → Gustave → Zero. The conflicts are resolved via extreme suppression: by the death of Madame D. (matricide), the disappearance of Dmitri, arrest and shooting of Gustave. Gustave and Dmitri are symbolically positioned as rival sons (the latter is actual, the former symbolic).

Kinship (3): Interethnic relationships

The whiteness of Wes Anderson's world has been raised frequently (Dean-Ruzicka, 2013; Weiner 2007). Nonetheless, in Wes Anderson's storyworld, interethnic relationships attempt to offer a solution to the death/absence of parents or spouses, or solutions to the conflicts generated by intergenerational relationships: Anthony and Inez; Max and Margaret; Jack and Rita (a casual relationship); Zero and Agatha.

The Max and Margaret interethnic relationship takes the place of the Max-Miss Cross intergenerational (non) relationship – a (non) relationship that in turn supplements the two deaths (Max's mother, Miss Cross's husband Appleby). Another (non) relationship takes place in *The Royal Tenenbaums*: the Margot–Raleigh intergenerational relationship is dissolved and replaced with the Margot–Richie (non) relationship (via Eli and several other brief relationships). In Wes Anderson's storyworld the death or absence of parents or spouses therefore activates the kinship conventions of Western society, which nonetheless are rarely adhered to, and which seldom lead to resolution. Intergenerational relationships lead to conflict, and interethnic relations offer partial or temporary solutions.

Death/life (funerals and pregnancies)

The death of parents and/or spouses is so prominent in Wes Anderson's storyworld that visits to a cemetery constitute an invariant element after

Bottle Rocket. In *Rushmore* Max visits his mother's grave on two occasions (to meet Blume, and to take Margaret's potted plant to his mother's grave). In *The Royal Tenenbaums* there are a total of three visits to the cemetery: to the grave of Royal's mother and of Chas' wife, Rachel; Royal visits Rachel's grave alone; and Royal's funeral. In *The Life Aquatic* Ned is buried at sea, as is a pirate, and Hennesey's crew is buried on the Ping Islands. In *The Darjeeling Limited* the funeral of the Indian boy is combined with a flashback to the three Whitman brothers driving to their father's funeral. In *Fantastic Mr. Fox* Rat dies and is unceremoniously dumped into the sewer. In *Moonrise Kingdom* Sam and Suzy plan to jump into the flooded church graveyard. And *The Grand Budapest Hotel* begins and ends in the Lutz cemetery where 'the author' is buried. Madame D. is shown in an open coffin. Other characters die (Agatha and her son, Gustave, Jopling, Serge's sister), although their funerals are not shown.

Pregnancies and births begin to appear in the storyworld from *The Life Aquatic* onwards. All are presented problematically, although in different ways: Jane's pregnancy in *The Life Aquatic* creates conflict (for the baby's father is already married), although in terms of the film's symbolic logic, the successful birth of Jane's child structurally balances out Ned's death. The opening and closing scenes of *Fantastic Mr. Fox* are punctuated by Mrs Fox's announcements that she is pregnant (the first announcement forces Mr Fox to change his career). Alice's pregnancy in *The Darjeeling Limited* is the main cause of Peter's anxiety, and in *The Grand Budapest Hotel* Zero reports that Agatha gave birth (but both mother and young child later died). This smattering of births does not balance out the dominance of death in Wes Anderson's storyworld and, as the last example shows, birth is overshadowed by death.

Exchange and gifts

In Wes Anderson's storyworld, and his early films in particular, exchange and gift-giving play a role in establishing a range of possible relations between solitary individuals. In *Bottle Rocket* the dyadic exchange of gifts dominate the developing relationship between Anthony and Inez, while

Dignan disrupts the circuit of exchange between Anthony and his mother (by stealing the earrings Anthony gave to his mother); Dignan gives to Inez the envelope of money from Anthony. In *Rushmore* Dirk and Max reconcile via an exchange of gifts (penknife, haircut), and Margaret gives Max a potted plant. Several significant moments of dyadic exchange take place in *The Life Aquatic*: between Steve and Werner (crayon ponyfish; Zissou ring). The Ned–Jane relationship is also sealed via dyadic exchange: Ned gives Jane a sand dollar, and when they depart, she in turn writes Ned a letter. Pirates take Bill hostage but inadvertently leave their three-legged dog. This dyadic exchange is reversed when Bill is rescued from the Ping Islands and the dog is left behind. Throughout *The Darjeeling Limited* Francis's belt becomes a gift to Peter several times. In *Moonrise Kingdom* Sam presents Suzy with flowers and he makes her a pair of earrings from beetles and fish hooks. And Madame D. bequeaths a painting to Gustave, who nonetheless has to steal it in order to take ownership of it.

One option that facilitates exchange, letter writing, is a privileged choice manifest throughout Wes Anderson's storyworld. Like gifts, the letter is a material object, one that is more permanent than (non-recorded) speech.[5] The exchange of words is therefore fixed and can be retrieved from the past or read by others. In *Bottle Rocket* Anthony writes a letter to his younger sister Grace, offering advice on the future; in *Rushmore* Max writes to Miss Cross to apologize for his behaviour at dinner (a letter that Blume delivers, initiating his relationship with Miss Cross); Dirk writes to Max about Miss Cross and Blume; in the script (but not in the film), Dirk pretends to be Max and writes to Margaret, to encourage them to meet up; and Miss Cross receives a card inviting her to the ground-breaking event. In *The Royal Tenenbaums* Richie writes a confessional letter to Eli, revealing that he is in love with Margot. In *The Life Aquatic* Ned and Steve exchanged letters in the past, and both letters are retrieved and read out; Jane writes a letter to Ned. In *Fantastic Mr. Fox* the animals try to communicate with the humans by exchanging notes (made up of letters cut out of newspapers). Sam and Suzy's relationship in *Moonrise Kingdom* is built up through an exchange of a series of letters (which the adults discover and read), while the adults exchange phone calls with each other. On one occasion, a letter is sent from a child to an adult: Scout Master Ward receives Sam's letter of resignation; and on another occasion a letter is sent from adults to a child: Sam receives a letter (delivered by Scout Master Ward) from his foster parents finalizing their separation. And in *The Grand Budapest Hotel* Madame D. sends a missive to her lawyers bequeathing the *Boy with Apple* painting to Gustave, which sets up the conflict between Gustave and Dmitri. Other pieces of writing are also linked to the painting: the second will is hidden in the back, and the instructions to retrieve it from the hotel's safe are written on a small piece of paper exchanged between Zero and Agatha.

An absence of exchange also plays a role in Wes Anderson's storyworld: stealing (*Bottle Rocket, Fantastic Mr. Fox*, ambiguously in *The Grand Budapest Hotel*). Stealing is also prevalent in *Moonrise Kingdom*: Captain Sharp tries to steal one of the women in the small community (Mrs Bishop), Sam steals a canoe and supplies in order to escape, while Suzy steals the portable record player from her brother and she admits to stealing the library books. Captain Sharp tries to 'steal' Mrs Bishop because he is a solitary bachelor (for bachelorhood is one of the 'calamities' of society according to Lévi-Strauss, as pointed out in Chapter 9); Sam steals for pragmatic reasons, to escape from the scouts. Suzy's stealing is more ambiguous – she borrows the library books and the portable record player, but fails to return them (she even writes a note to her brother seeking permission to borrow the record player). Her act of stealing is not a form of criminal theft (prevalent in *Bottle Rocket* and *Fantastic Mr. Fox*) but a compulsion fuelled by her isolation and emotional turmoil.

Mediation

Dignan unintentionally acts as the mediator between Anthony and Anthony's mother, his sister and his new girlfriend Inez; that is, he assists Anthony's Oedipal transition from mother to mother substitute, Inez. In the intergenerational conflict in *Rushmore*, Miss Cross remains the constant, while Max and Blume swap roles as mediator, swap roles as Miss Cross's love interest and also transform in relation to each other: from friends to rivals and back again. Richie Tenenbaum is not dissimilar to Dignan's unintentional mediator, for he indirectly functions as mediator between his father and Henry-Etheline.

Relative worlds

Marie Laure-Ryan notes that fictional characters can create their own fictional worlds, called relative worlds: 'the actual world of narrative systems is inhabited by individuals who build their own modal systems by engaging in such world-creating and/or world-representing acts as forming beliefs, wishing, dreaming, making forecasts, and inventing stories' (1985, 722). Some of Wes Anderson's most troubled solitary characters go much further than simply forming beliefs, wishes and stories: they manifest their ideas in plays, films and fiction (short stories and novels): Max Fischer and Margot Tenenbaum write plays (see Joseph 2014); Eli Cash and 'the author' (*The Grand Budapest Hotel*) write novels; Steve Zissou makes documentary films; Jack Whitman writes short stories, and both Richie Tenenbaum and Sam Shakusky are (failed) painters. With the possible exception of Eli Cash (who writes a counterfactual historical novel, *Old Custer*[6]), the creative efforts of Wes Anderson's characters are autobiographical: Max and Margot's plays, Zissou's documentary films, Jack's short story, 'the author's' novel, and Richie and Sam's paintings (they both attempt to paint the women they fall in love with) are infused with autobiographical (sub)plots. Wes Anderson's model for the artist is therefore the disturbed solitary Romantic dealing with troubled feelings via self-expression. The self-expressive autobiographical artist can in turn become a trope with which to interpret Wes Anderson's films (see endnote 2 in Chapter 7).

Water and drowning

We have discovered through the film analyses that water is a fundamental element in Wes Anderson's storyworld. In *Bottle Rocket* Anthony is associated with water: he ended a relationship with his former girlfriend Elizabeth during an argument over water sports, and he initiated a new relationship with Inez after emerging from a hotel swimming pool (in which we see Anthony in the first of several underwater shots in Wes Anderson's world). But Mr Henry also pours water on Dignan's head, and Dignan is arrested in an ice storage room. In *Rushmore* Blume dives from a great height into a pool when he realizes his relationship to his wife is in crisis (Blume is filmed in an underwater shot). The Max–Miss Cross relationship is initiated via the book *Diving for Sunken Treasure*; Max tries to please Miss Cross by building an aquarium; and her husband Appleby drowned. Royal Tenenbaum and Chas's two young sons Ari and Uzi dive into a swimming pool, and they are filmed in an underwater shot; and Royal's headstone says (fictitiously) that he died (presumably he drowned) trying to save his family from a sinking battleship. In *The Life Aquatic with Steve Zissou* water becomes of course a central theme, in which Zissou's best friend Esteban dies at sea and his 'son' Ned almost drowns while learning to swim. The quotation from Ned's letter ('Do you wish you could breathe under water?') expresses at the same time the attraction of water and the danger of drowning. In *The Darjeeling Limited* the drowning of the Indian boy becomes a turning point for the three Whitman brothers. In *Fantastic Mr. Fox* Kristofferson is an expert swimmer who dives from a great height into a small swimming pool. However, all the animals almost drown when the farmers pour cider down the foxholes. *Moonrise Kingdom* is dominated by water – Benjamin Britten's opera *Noye's Fludde* and a real flood. In addition, after Sam goes missing, Scout Master Ward dictates into his tape recorder: 'Please, don't let him [Sam] fall off a cliff or drown in the goddamn lake or something'. Sam tries to address the lack of drinking water by suggesting that he and Suzy should put pebbles in their mouths, although he realizes the plan does not work, and declares that he brought some water with him. Towards the end of the film, Suzy and Sam look down at the flooded graveyard. Suzy says they should jump and swim away, although Sam expresses his fear of drowning, for he did not bring his life jacket (he declared that he is not a good swimmer just before both he and Suzy jump into the water near the mile 3.25 tidal inlet). And in *The Grand Budapest Hotel* 'the author' and Zero meet in the hotel's baths.

Drowning combines two separate elements: water + death, in that water becomes the agent of a character's death. In Wes Anderson's storyworld, water, death, and drowning are qualified with a series of oppositions:

Young/old
Actual/fictitious

Appleby, Ned and the Indian boy are young, and therefore suffer a premature death by drowning. Royal Tenenbaum's drowning is fictitious but his death is not premature. Esteban's death is actual, is not premature, and is not technically a drowning, for the agent of his death is not water, but a shark living in the water.

Verticality

In Wes Anderson's storyworld, verticality is correlated with movement (along the vertical axis) and is opposed either to movement along the horizontal axis, or to stillness:

Vertical axis/horizontal axis
Movement/stillness

Verticality is rarely paired with stillness but is instead paired with movement. From this matrix of possibilities emerges the dominance of movement along the vertical axis: Anthony climbs down from his hospital room using knotted sheets and moves up through the water in the motel swimming pool; Max Fischer climbs up to (and then down from) Miss Cross's window after pretending to be hit by a car; Margot escapes from school (age 14) by climbing out of the window using knotted sheets; Chas's wife dies in a plane crash; Richie and Margot meet on the roof of the Tenenbaum house (movement up or down is not shown), and Royal and Richie meet on the roof of the Lindbergh Palace Hotel (movement up and down the lift is shown); Ned dies when his helicopter plunges into the sea; the three Whitman brothers move up to higher ground to perform the feather ceremony; the foxes and other animals dig downwards to safety; the scouts build a hut in an incredibly high location in a tree; Sam and Suzy move up to the church tower, and Sam climbs through the high window to see Suzy; movement upwards to the four main locations is key to *The Grand Budapest Hotel* (plus the rapid icy descent from the monastery), and Jopling dies after being pushed off a cliff. The window becomes the privileged site of the vertical movements, as do lifts, which are prominent in the Hinckley robbery in *Bottle Rocket*, in the hotel and hospital in *Rushmore*, in the Lindbergh Palace Hotel in *The Royal Tenenbaums*, and is central to *The Grand Budapest Hotel*.

Verticality, movement, water

Wes Anderson's storyworld combines verticality, elevation and water. Mr Henry pours water from a great height onto Dignan's head; Blume jumps from a great height into a swimming pool; Ned dies after the helicopter falls from a great height into the sea; Kristofferson dives from a great height into a small swimming pool; as we have already seen, Scout Master Ward combines height and water when he dictates into his tape recorder, 'Please, don't let him [Sam] fall off a cliff or drown in the goddamn lake or something'; yet, Suzy and Sam almost enact Scout Master Ward's fears when they look down from a great height at the flooded graveyard and prepare to jump; Jopling, Gustave, and Zero travel at great speed down a snow-covered slope.

**

This preliminary study of the overall structural organization of Wes Anderson's storyworld parallels in some respects A. J. Greimas's analysis in *Structural Semantics* of the micro universe created by the novels of Georges Bernanos (Greimas 1983, chapter 12), an analysis that condenses concepts Greimas derives from Hjelmslev, Lévi-Strauss, Propp and Jakobson. Greimas begins with life/death as the dominant elementary semantic structure in Bernanos, the same structure Lévi-Strauss (in 'The Structural Study of Myth') analysed in Zuni and Pueblo myths, where it is identified as an irresolvable contradiction. Whereas Zuni and Pueblo myths translate this contradiction into the analogous binary opposition agriculture (life)/warfare (death), in Bernanos's micro universe this contradiction, Greimas argues, is translated into the following series of analogous binary oppositions:

Life/death
Fire/water
Mobile/immobile
Joy/boredom
Truth/lie
Health/disease
Assertion/denial
Pain/disgust

The final opposition (which Greimas does not introduce in any detail) initially looks jarring, but in fact it characterizes the specific modal value of Bernanos's micro universe. Greimas concludes that, in Bernanos's universe, a true life combines pain and joy: to experience one is to experience the other. To avoid pain, one must give up joy, and resign oneself to boredom and disgust, a denial of life that in Bernanos's universe is a type of death.

The first two oppositions (life/death, fire/water) also dominate Wes Anderson's storyworld, with death and water the dominant terms, life subordinate to death, and fire hardly present at all. In place of mobile/immobile, Wes Anderson's storyworld is dominated by the opposition vertical/horizontal, with horizontal subordinate to the dominant term vertical, which is linked to movement and elevation. The storyworld attempts to address death (of parents and/or spouses) with intergenerational relationships, interethnic relationships and relative worlds. The success or failure of these strategies varies from film to film (see Table 11.1).

Reading each column of Table 11.1 separately, we can immediately see that intergenerational relationships dominated three early films plus *The Grand Budapest Hotel* and was only successful in two; that interethnic relationships also dominated three early films and were successful in all three. But when interethnic relationships reappear, they are either negative (Jack's treatment of Rita in *The Darjeeling Limited*) or equivocal (Zero's ultimately tragic relation to Agatha in *The Grand Budapest Hotel*). Relative worlds were also successful in coming to terms with mourning the death of spouses and/or relatives in three films: Max's plays in *Rushmore* (he dedicates his final play to two dead people – his mother and Appleby); part 2 of Steve Zissou's prize-winning

Table 11.1 Strategies for handling death in Wes Anderson's storyworld

Film	Intergenerational Relationships	Interethnic Relationships	Relative Worlds
Bottle Rocket	N/A	+	N/A
Rushmore	+	+	+
Royal Tenenbaums	–	+	+/–
The Life Aquatic	–	N/A	+
The Darjeeling Limited	N/A	–	+
Fantastic Mr. Fox	N/A	N/A	N/A
Moonrise Kingdom	N/A	N/A	+/–
The Grand Budapest Hotel	+	+/–	+

documentary film (which sets out to avenge the death of Esteban, but leads to the death of Ned, who is officially named in the documentary's voiceover as Zissou's son); and Jack's story in *The Darjeeling Limited* about his dead father and absent girlfriend. In *The Royal Tenenbaums* Richie's paintings are unsuccessful, Eli Cash's novels are commercially successful, and Margot Tenenbaum's autobiographical play performed at the end of the film is described as only partly successful. Sam's paintings and drawings are only partly successful (his final painting skilfully represents the now vanished mile 3.25 tidal inlet where he and Suzy camped out). And 'the author's' novel *The Grand Budapest Hotel* is very popular and successful. Reading the table horizontally, we see that *Rushmore* is the most positive and consistent film in terms of these three strategies, while the other films are mixed.

The structural semiotic analysis of key paradigmatic, kinship, and binary structures in Wes Anderson's storyworld leaves out a number of minor events that do not fit into a system, but which draw attention to themselves simply by being repeated – including characters punched in the face (usually resulting in a black eye) and characters losing their shoes. In *Bottle Rocket* Dignan punches Anthony and, later, Bob punches Dignan (and Dignan is punched in the face in a bar). In *Rushmore* Max is punched twice – during the first performance of his Serpico play, and by Angus; and Blume is seen with a black eye (apparently from his twin sons). In *The Royal Tenenbaums* Chas hits Richie in the eye while fighting Eli; Richie takes off his shoe when playing tennis, and Eli loses his shoe when he crashes his car. In *The Life Aquatic* Steve and Ned punch each other; in *The Darjeeling Limited*, the brothers fight and Francis is hit in the face with his belt buckle; the shoeshine boy steals one of Francis's shoes. Mrs Fox scratches Mr Fox's face; Kristofferson loses one of his shoes while escaping from Bean's farm (and Ash retrieves it and returns it to Kristofferson, just as Dudley returns the shoe to Eli in *The Royal Tenenbaums*). In *Moonrise Kingdom* Sam discards his shoes when they catch fire, after being struck by lightning; Mr Bishop takes off a shoe and throws it at Scout Master Ward. Mr Bishop also has two black eyes, as does Gustave while in prison in *The Grand Budapest Hotel*. In the latter film, during the ritual reading of Madame D.'s will, the 'punching ritual' in Wes Anderson's storyworld moves up a notch, involving three people in quick succession: Dmitri punches Gustave,

Zero punches Dmitri, and Jopling punches Zero. Yet, the sheer repetition of these minor events (punches, black eyes, loss of a shoe, plus others such as the use of binoculars) suggests that they are akin to the repeated motifs such as the glass of milk or one person suspended from another's hand that Žižek identifies in Hitchcock's films. These repeated motifs obliquely address the key invariant kinship issue in Wes Anderson's storyworld – the death or absence of parents or spouses, and the character's subsequent sense of loss and isolation.

Coda: Wes Anderson's film style

The structural semiotic analysis also leaves out the study of film style. In *Signs and Meaning in the Cinema* Peter Wollen ended his chapter on auteur structuralism by re-introducing the need to return to the surface of individual films and to study film style (1972, 104–15). He developed the distinction between the digital (the coded) and the graded (the analogue), or what he preferred to call 'composition' (the musical score, the painter's reliance on an iconographic programmer, the film's screenplay) and 'performance' (the process of producing an individual artwork): 'We need to develop much further a theory of performance, of the stylistic, of [the] graded rather than [the] coded' (1972, 113). To end this chapter (and book), I shall briefly survey the numerous analyses of Wes Anderson's visual and aural style (as presented in Piechota 2006; McDowell 2010, 2012; Boschi and McNelis 2012; Lee 2016, among others),[7] from which we can identify seven characteristic components:

1. Tableau shots: 'a static, flat-looking, medium-long or long "planimetric" shot [...] that appears nearly geometrically even, depicting carefully arranged characters, often facing directly forward, who are made to look faintly ridiculous by virtue of a composition's rigidity (seen particularly plainly in Anderson's character introductions). Partly because of their presentational neatness, there is a degree of "self-consciousness" to such shots [...]' (MacDowell 2012, 9; see also Lee 2016, 414–17). Via this tableau shot, Wes Anderson's camera develops a specific strategy – what

Figure 11.1 Tableau shot (*The Darjeeling Limited*) © Fox Searchlight

Figure 11.2 Close up (*Bottle Rocket*) © Columbia Pictures

Jeffrey Sconce calls the 'clinical observation' of eccentric characters (2002). See Figure 11.1.

2. Close-ups of characters (still facing forward) (Peberdy 2012, 48; 50; Lee 2016, 431–7). Especially in the case of Bill Murray, the close up shows a deadpan expression. Sometimes these frontal close up shots are linked together as shot/reverse shot since the camera is placed *between* the characters, not beside them filming over their shoulders. See Figure 11.2.

3. Overhead shots in which the direction of the camera's look is perpendicular to the horizon, which is achieved when the camera points straight down – either at objects (usually on a table), or characters lying down (MacDowell 2010, 5; Lee 2016, 417–20; 431–7). These shots

function narratively to give spectators maximum information, but the angle and composition are stylistically marked. Francesco Casetti calls this the 'unreal objective shot' (1998, 50) – 'unreal' because it refers to unusual camera angles and 'objective' or omniscient because it take a God's eye viewpoint and cannot be attributed to any character in the diegesis (the spectator identifies with the camera's look). See Figures 11.3–11.4. Casetti gives an example similar to Wes Anderson's overhead shots – those shots found in Busby Berkeley musicals where the camera is pointing downwards on a group of dancers who form an abstract pattern.

4. Within the tableau shots, there is a general lack of camera movement, which helps to convey a precise, static quality to the film (although this applies more to his earlier films – later films use more camera movement). When movement is introduced into a shot, it becomes noticeable: either in

Figures 11.3–11.4 Overhead shots (*Rushmore*) © Columbia Pictures

Figure 11.5 Centred framing (*Rushmore*) © Columbia Pictures

the form of a 90 degree whip pan, or extensive tracking shots (numerous examples exist in his later films, especially the credit sequence of *Moonrise Kingdom*).

5. Wes Anderson's early films contain at least one montage sequence. In the montage the images are unified by an abstract theme and are accompanied by a song (Piechota 2006; Boschi and McNelis 2012). In *Rushmore* Max's membership to many clubs is conveyed in a montage sequence accompanied by the song 'Making Time' by The Creation; in *The Royal Tenenbaums* a montage sequence of Margot's affairs is accompanied by 'Judy is a Punk' by the Ramones and so on.
6. Brief slow motion shot (in all films, except *Fantastic Mr. Fox* and *The Grand Budapest Hotel*). In *Bottle Rocket*, *Rushmore*, *The Royal Tenenbaums*, and *The Life Aquatic*, a slow motion shot appears in the final scene.
7. Centred framing, or a proclivity towards symmetrical composition, which has been explored in Kogonada's exemplary video essay 'Wes Anderson // Centered' (Kogonada 2014). See Figure 11.5.

Wes Anderson's film style is noticeable, but it still broadly serves the themes of the story. In Adrian Martin's terms, this type of film style falls into the category of expressionist (rather than classical or mannerist) mise en scène (Martin 1992; 2014). Although a popular activity among critics, fans and film scholars, simply listing the elements of Wes Anderson's film style is insufficient. The next step involves analysing specific sequences, to: (a) determine how filmic techniques manifest themes and structures; (b) identify how frequent these techniques are (preferably using the methods of statistical style analysis; see Barry Salt 1974; 2006; Buckland 2007); (c) determine the evolution of Wes Anderson's style; and (d) define the affects these stylistic traits create in spectators, which can be subsumed under the term 'new sincerity'. New sincerity is generated from the dynamic relation between sincerity and irony, in which sincerity undermines the detached cynicism and nihilism of irony, but irony in turn undermines the simple, earnest directness of sincerity. The study of Wes Anderson's new sincerity, his distinctive mix of sincerity and irony, can be carried out after one has analysed his storyworld.

Notes

1. We can also consider the near deaths that take place in Wes Anderson's storyworld: Applejack's heart attack in *Bottle Rocket*; Guggenheim's illness in *Rushmore*; in *The Royal Tenenbaums* the plane crash that almost killed Chas, his sons, and their dog (and which did kill Chas's wife Rachel); Eli's near fatal car crash; Ned's near fatal drowning in an early scene in *The Life Aquatic*; Francis's near fatal motorcycle crash in *The Darjeeling Limited*; in *Moonrise Kingdom*, Sam is struck by lightning but survives, and Suzy stabs Redford with scissors (although his injuries are not life-threatening).
2. Gustave is also a solitary hero whose identity is linked almost exclusively to the hotel.
3. Parentheses around a name indicate that the death or absence of a parent or spouse is implicit or indeterminate.
4. The arrow represents a transformation (a transformational relationship between what comes before and what comes after the arrow).
5. Speech is occasionally recorded in Wes Anderson's storyworld: by Raleigh St. Clair in *The Royal Tenenbaums* (he dictates a summary of Dudley's case); in *Fantastic Mr. Fox* the humans record the voice of Kristofferson; and in *Moonrise Kingdom* Scout Master Ward records his thoughts into a Dictaphone.
6. His novel *Old Custer* poses a counterfactual historical argument: suppose that Custer did not die at little big horn. There are too few clues in the film to

determine the content of his first novel, *Wildcat*, except that it was written in an 'obscure vernacular', as he says to the (real) Charlie Rose when interviewed on the *Charlie Rose* Show that the Tenenbaum family watch.

7 Kunze also points out that 'Robert Yeoman's cinematography has immeasurably impacted the visual style we too often credit to Wes Anderson alone' (2014, 4).

Works Cited

Abel, Richard. 1978. 'Paradigmatic Structures in *Young Mr. Lincoln*'. *Wide Angle* 2 (4): 20–26.

Altman, Rick. 1984. 'A Semantic/Syntactic Approach to Film Genre'. *Cinema Journal* 23 (3): 6–18.

Barthes, Roland. 1972. 'The Structuralist Activity'. In *Critical Essays*, translated by Richard Howard, 213–20. Evanston, IL: Northwestern University Press.

Barthes, Roland. 1984. *Writing Degree Zero and Elements of Semiology*. Translated by Annette Lavers and Colin Smith. London: Jonathan Cape.

Barthes, Roland. 1992. *On Racine*. Translated by Richard Howard. Berkeley: University of California Press.

Bellour, Raymond. 2000. *The Analysis of Film*. Edited by Constance Penley. Bloomington: Indiana University Press.

Boschi, Elena and Tim Mcnelis. 2012. '"Same Old Song:" On Audio-Visual Style in the films of Wes Anderson'. *New Review of Film and Television Studies* 10 (1): 28–45.

Bose, Nandana. 2008. '*The Darjeeling Limited*: Critiquing Orientalism on the Train to Nowhere.' *Mediascape: UCLA's Journal of Cinema and Media Studies*: 1–8.

Brody, Richard. 2009. 'Wild, Wild Wes. A Master of High Style Goes Looking for Adventure'. *New Yorker*, November 2, http://www.newyorker.com/magazine/2009/11/02/wild-wild-wes.

Bruner, Jerome. 2010. *Going Beyond the Information Given: Studies in the Psychology of Knowing*. New York: Routledge.

Buckland, Warren. 2007. 'What Does the Statistical Style Analysis of Film Involve?' *Literary and Linguistic Computing* 23 (2): 219–30.

Buckland, Warren, ed. 2012. 'Special Issue: Wes Anderson'. *New Review of Film and Television Studies* 10 (1): 1–5.

Butler, Judith. 1990. *Gender Trouble: Feminism and the Subversion of Identity*. New York: Routledge.

Caws, Peter. 1988. *Structuralism: The Art of the Intelligible*. Atlantic Highlands, NJ: Humanities Press.

Chabon, Michael. 2013. 'Introduction'. In *The Wes Anderson Collection* by Matt Zoller Seitz, 21–23. New York: Abrams.

Chomsky, Noam. 1964. *Current Issues in Linguistic Theory*. The Hague: Mouton.

Clarke, Simon. 1981. *The Foundations of Structuralism: A Critique of Lévi-Strauss and the Structuralist Movement*. Brighton: Harvester Press.

Cowie, Elizabeth. 1997. *Representing the Woman: Cinema and Psychoanalysis*. Basingstoke: Macmillan.

Dean-Ruzicka, Rachel. 2013. 'Themes of Privilege and Whiteness in the Films of Wes Anderson'. *Quarterly Review of Film and Video* 30 (1): 25–40.

Deleuze, Gilles. 2004. *Desert Islands and Other Texts, 1953–1974*. Edited by David Lapoujade and translated by Michael Taormina. New York: Columbia.

Descombes, Vincent. 1980. *Modern French Philosophy*. Translated by Lorna Scott Fox. Cambridge: Cambridge University Press.

Doležel, Lubomír. 1998. *Heterocosmica: Fiction and Possible Worlds*. Baltimore: The Johns Hopkins University Press.

Doubrovsky, Serge. 1973. *The New Criticism in France*. Translated by Derek Coltman. Chicago: The University of Chicago Press.

Dubuisson, Daniel. 2006. *Twentieth Century Mythologies*. 2nd edn. Translated by Martha Cunningham. New York: Routledge.

Eco, Umberto. 1976. *A Theory of Semiotics*. Bloomington: Indiana University Press.

Eco, Umberto. 1979. *The Role of the Reader*. Bloomington: Indiana University Press.

Editors of *Cahiers du cinéma*. 1972. 'John Ford's *Young Mr. Lincoln*'. *Screen* 13 (3): 5–44.

Fiennes, Sophie, dir. 2006. *The Pervert's Guide to Cinema*. P. Guide Ltd. DVD.

Garroni, Emilio. 1968. *Semiotica ed estetica. L'eterogeneità del linguaggio e il linguaggio cinematografico*. Bari: Laterza.

Garroni, Emilio. 1974. 'The Heterogeneity of the Aesthetic Object and Problems of Art Criticism'. *Afterimage* 5: 68–78.

Glucksmann, Miriam. 1974. *Structuralist Analysis in Contemporary Social Thought*. London: Routledge.

Godelier, Maurice. 2011. *The Metamorphoses of Kinship*. Translated by Nora Scott. London: Verso.

Gray, J. Patrick. 1978. 'Structural Analysis of Folktales: Techniques and Methodology'. *Asian Folklore Studies* 37 (1): 77–95.

Greimas, A. J. 1983. *Structural Semantics: An Attempt at a Method*. Translated by Daniele McDowell, Ronald Schleifer and Alan Velie. Lincoln: University of Nebraska Press.

Greimas, A. J. 1987. *On Meaning: Selected Writings in Semiotic Theory*. Translated by Paul J. Perron and Frank H. Collins. London: Pinter Press.

Hawkes, Terence. 1977. *Structuralism and Semiotics*. London: Methuen.
Herman, David. 2002. *Story Logic: Problems and Possibilities of Narrative*. Lincoln: University of Nebraska Press.
Herman, David. 2009. *Basic Elements of Narrative*. Malden, MA: Wiley-Blackwell.
Hjelmslev, Louis. 1961. *Prolegomena to a Theory of Language*. Translated by Francis J. Whitfield, rev. edn. Madison: University of Wisconsin Press.
Houston, Beverle and Marsha Kinder. 1980. *Self and Cinema: A Transformalist Perspective*. Pleasantville, New York: Redgrave.
Jakobson, Roman. 1971. 'Pattern in Linguistics (Contribution to Debates with Anthropologists)'. In *Selected Writings, Volume II: Word and Language*, 223–28. The Hague: Mouton.
Jakobson, Roman. 1981. 'Linguistics and Poetics'. In *Selected Writings, Volume III: Poetry of Grammar and Grammar of Poetry*, 18–51, edited, with a preface, by Stephen Rudy. The Hague: Mouton.
Jakobson, Roman and Morris Halle. 1971. *Fundamentals of Language*, 2nd rev. edn. The Hague: Mouton.
Jameson, Fredric. 1981. *The Political Unconscious. Narrative as a Socially Symbolic Act*. Ithaca: Cornell University Press.
Jenkins, Henry. 2006. *Convergence Culture: Where Old and New Media Collide*. New York: New York University Press.
Jonnes, Denis. 1990. *The Matrix of Narrative: Family Systems and the Semiotics of Story*. Berlin: Mouton de Gruyter.
Joseph, Rachel. 2014. '"Max Fischer Presents:" Wes Anderson and the Theatricality of Mourning'. In *The Films of Wes Anderson: Critical Essays on an Indiewood Icon*. Edited by Peter C. Kunze, 51–64. New York: Palgrave Macmillan.
Kaufman, Eleanor. 2013. 'Do Dual Structures Exist? Deleuze and Lacan in the Wake of Lévi-Strauss'. *Yale French Studies* 123: 83–99.
Kitses, Jim. 1969. *Horizons West*. London: Thames and Hudson/ British Film Institute.
Kogonada. 2014. 'Wes Anderson // Centered'. http://vimeo.com/89302848.
Kunze, Peter C. 2014. 'Introduction: The Wonderful Worlds of Wes Anderson'. In *The Films of Wes Anderson: Critical Essays on an Indiewood Icon*. Edited by Peter C. Kunze, 1–9. New York: Palgrave Macmillan.
Law, Joe. 1990. '*Noye's Fludde*. Benjamin Britten'. *The Opera Quarterly* 7 (3): 181–82.
Lee, Sunhee. 2016. 'Wes Anderson's Ambivalent Film Style: The Relation Between *Mise-en-Scène* and Emotion'. *New Review of Film and Television Studies* 14 (4): 409–39.

Lévi-Strauss, Claude. 1967. 'The Story of Asdiwal'. In *The Structural Study of Myth and Totemism*. Edited by Edmund Leach, 1–47. London: Tavistock.

Lévi-Strauss, Claude. 1969. *The Elementary Structures of Kinship*. Translated by J. H. Bell and J. R. V. Sturmer. Edited by R. Needham. Boston: Beacon Press.

Lévi-Strauss, Claude. 1970. *The Raw and the Cooked*. Translated by John and Doreen Weightman. London: Jonathan Cape.

Lévi-Strauss, Claude. 1972. *Structural Anthropology*. Translated by C. Jacobson and B. G. Schoepf. London: Allen Lane.

Lévi-Strauss, Claude. 1973. *From Honey to Ashes*. Translated by John and Doreen Weightman. London: Jonathan Cape.

Lévi-Strauss, Claude. 1976. 'Structure and Form: Reflections on a Work by Vladimir Propp'. In *Structural Anthropology II*, 115–45. New York: Basic Books.

Lévi-Strauss, Claude. 1978. *The Origin of Table Manners*. Translated by John and Doreen Weightman. London: Jonathan Cape.

Lévi-Strauss, Claude. 1981. *The Naked Man*. Translated by John and Doreen Weightman. London: Jonathan Cape.

Lotman, Jurij. 1979. 'The Origin of Plot in the Light of Typology'. *Poetics Today* 1 (1/2): 161–84.

Lovell, Alan. 1975. *Don Siegel: American Cinema*. Rev. edn. London: British Film Institute.

Lyons, John. 1977. *Semantics, Volume 1*. Cambridge: Cambridge University Press.

MacDowell, James. 2010. 'Notes on Quirky'. *Movie: A Journal of Film Criticism* 1: 1–16.

MacDowell, James. 2012. 'Wes Anderson, Tone and the Quirky Sensibility'. *New Review of Film and Television Studies* 10 (1): 6–27.

McNulty, Tracy. 2014. *Wrestling with the Angel: Experiments in Symbolic Life*. New York: Columbia University Press.

Martin, Adrian. 1992. '*Mise en Scène* is Dead, or the Expressive, the Excessive, the Technical and the Stylish'. *Continuum* 5 (2): 87–140.

Martin, Adrian. 2014. *Mise en Scène and Film Style: From Classical Hollywood to New Media Art*. Basingstoke: Palgrave Macmillan.

Martinet, André. 1964. *Elements of General Linguistics*. Translated by Elisabeth Palmer. London: Faber.

Meletinsky, Eleazar. 1998. *The Poetics of Myth*. Translated by Guy Lanoue and Alexandre Sadetsky. New York: Routledge.

Metz, Christian. 1974a. *Film Language: A Semiotics of the Cinema*. Translated by Michael Taylor. New York: Oxford University Press.

Metz, Christian. 1974b. *Language and Cinema*. Translated by Donna Jean Umiker-Sebeok. The Hague: Mouton.

Mulvey, Laura. 1989. *Visual and Other Pleasures*. Basingstoke: Macmillan.

Nichols, Bill. 1975. 'Style, Grammar, and the Movies'. *Film Quarterly* 28 (3): 33–49.

Nowell-Smith, Geoffrey. 1967. *Visconti*. London: Secker and Warburg/British Film Institute.

Olsen, Mark. 2014. 'Wes Anderson Is off in a New World with "Grand Budapest Hotel"'. *LA Times,* March 6, http://articles.latimes.com/2014/mar/06/entertainment/la-et-mn-wes-anderson-grand-budapest-hotel.

Parret, Herman. 1983. *Semiotics and Pragmatics. An Evaluative Comparison of Conceptual Frameworks*. Amsterdam: John Benjamins.

Pavel, Thomas. 1986. *Fictional Worlds*. Cambridge, Mass.: Harvard University Press.

Peberdy, Donna. 2012. '"I'm Just a Character in Your Film:" Acting and Performance from Autism to Zissou'. *New Review of Film and Television Studies* 10 (1): 46–67.

Piechota, Carole Lyn. 2006. 'Give Me a Second Grace: Music as Absolution in *The Royal Tenenbaums*'. *Senses of Cinema*, 38: http://sensesofcinema.com/2006/on-movies-musicians-and-soundtracks/music_tenenbaums/.

Pomorska, Krystyna. 1992. *Jakobsonian Poetics and Slavic Narrative: From Pushkin to Solzhenitsyn*. Durham: Duke University Press.

Popper, Karl. 1972. *Objective Knowledge: An Evolutionary Approach*. Oxford: Clarendon Press.

Propp, Vladimir. 1968. *Morphology of the Folktale*, 2nd edn. Translated by Laurence Scott. Austin: University of Texas Press.

Rich, Jamie S. 2010. 'Criterion Confessions: *The Darjeeling Limited* – #540'. http://www.criterionconfessions.com/2010/10/darjeeling-limited-540.html.

Robé, Chris. 2013. '"Because I Hate Fathers, and I Never Wanted to Be One:" Wes Anderson, Entitled Masculinity, and the "Crisis" of the Patriarch'. In *Millennial Masculinity: Men in Contemporary American Cinema*. Edited by Timothy Shary, 101–21. Detroit: Wayne State University Press.

Rohdie, Sam. 1969. '[Review of] *Signs and Meaning in the Cinema*'. *New Left Review* 55: 66–70.

Ronen, Ruth. 1994. *Possible Worlds in Literary Theory*. Cambridge: Cambridge University Press.

Ryan, Marie Laure. 1985. 'The Modal Structure of Narrative Universes'. *Poetics Today* 6 (4): 717–55.

Ryan, Marie-Laure and Jan-Noël Thon, eds. 2014. *Storyworlds Across Media: Toward a Media-Conscious Narratology*. Lincoln: University of Nebraska Press.

Salt, Barry. 1974. 'Statistical Style Analysis of Motion Pictures'. *Film Quarterly* 28 (1): 13–22.

Salt, Barry. 2006. *Moving Into Pictures: More on Film History, Style, and Analysis*. London: Starword.

Saussure, Ferdinand de. 2011. *Course in General Linguistics*. Translated by Wade Baskin and edited by Perry Meisel and Haun Saussy. New York: Columbia University Press.

Scholes, Robert. 1974. *Structuralism in Literature: An Introduction*. London: Yale University Press.

Sconce, Jeffrey. 2002. 'Irony, Nihilism, and the New American "Smart Film"'. *Screen* 43 (4): 349–69.

Seitz, Matt Zoller. 2013. *The Wes Anderson Collection*. New York: Abrams.

Seung, T. K. 1982. *Semiotics and Thematics in Hermeneutics*. New York: Columbia University Press.

Souriau, Étienne. 1951. 'La structure de l'univers filmique et la vocabulaire de la filmologie'. *Revue International de Filmologie* 2 (7–8): 231–40.

Stam, Robert. 1986. 'Film and Language: From Metz to Bakhtin'. *Studies in the Literary Imagination* 19 (1): 109–30.

Thanouli, Eleftheria. 2014. 'Diegesis'. *The Routledge Encyclopedia of Film Theory*. Edited by Edward Branigan and Warren Buckland, 133–37. Abingdon: Routledge.

Todorov, Tzvetan. 1969. 'Structural Analysis of Narrative'. *NOVEL: A Forum on Fiction* 3 (1): 70–76.

Verhaeghe, Paul. 2000. 'The Collapse of the Function of the Father and its Effects on Gender Roles'. In *Sexuation*. Edited by Renata Salecl, 131–54. Durham: Duke University Press.

Weiner, Jonah. 2007. 'Unbearable Whiteness: That Queasy Feeling You Get When Watching a Wes Anderson Movie'. *Slate*, September 27, http://www.slate.com/articles/arts/culturebox/2007/09/unbearable_whiteness.html.

Wigley, Samuel. 2014. 'Looking for Signs and Meaning in the Cinema'. http://www.bfi.org.uk/news-opinion/news-bfi/interviews/looking-signs-meaning-cinema.

Wilden, Anthony. 1980. *System and Structure: Essays in Communication and Exchange*. 2nd edn. London: Tavistock.

Wilden, Anthony. 1981. 'Lacan and Discourse of the Other'. In Jacques Lacan and Anthony Wilden, *Speech and Language in Psychoanalysis*, 159–311. Baltimore: The Johns Hopkins University Press.

Willemen, Paul. 1980. 'Presentation'. In Steve Neale, *Genre*. London: British Film Institute.

Wolf, Mark. 2012. *Building Imaginary Worlds: The Theory and History of Subcreation*. New York: Routledge.

Wollen, Peter. 1969. 1972 (rev. edn). *Signs and Meaning in the Cinema*. London: Secker and Warburg/British Film Institute.

Wright, Will. 1975. *Six Guns and Society: A Structural Study of the Western*. Berkeley: University of California Press.

Yacavone, Dan. 2015. *Film Worlds: A Philosophical Aesthetics of Cinema*. New York: Columbia University Press.

Žižek, Slavoj. 1999. *The Ticklish Subject: The Absent Centre of Political Ontology*. London: Verso.

Žižek, Slavoj. 2010a. 'Foreword to the Second Edition'. In Slavoj Žižek, ed., *Everything You Always Wanted to Know About Lacan (But Were Afraid to Ask Hitchcock)*, vii–xviii. London: Verso.

Žižek, Slavoj. 2010b. 'Hitchcockian *Sinthoms*'. In Slavoj Žižek, ed., *Everything You Always Wanted to Know About Lacan (But Were Afraid to Ask Hitchcock)*, 125–28. London: Verso.

Index

Abel, Richard 38–9
Altman, Rick 40–1
Anderson, Wes (individual films):
  Bottle Rocket (1992) (short) 67–9
  Bottle Rocket (1996) 28, 49–69, 74, 80, 83, 84, 85, 91, 102, 110, 116, 124, 126, 133, 140, 148, 149, 155, 156, 164, 165, 173–80, 182, 184, 185, 189, 190
    binary oppositions 53–5, 58–65
    exchange 55–6
    kinship 55–6, 65–7, 69 n.1
    mediation 56–8
    paradigms 51–5
    transformations 58, 63, 65, 69
  Darjeeling Limited, The (2007) 119–32, 164, 173–4, 177–8, 181, 184–5, 187, 190 n.1
    binary oppositions 130–1
    exchange 126–7
    kinship 119–20, 122–8, 130
    mediation 130–1
    paradigms 127–30
    transformations 123
  Fantastic Mr. Fox (2009) 133–44, 165, 173, 174, 177, 178, 179, 181, 184, 189, 190 n.5
    binary oppositions 133, 136–7, 140–4
    exchange 133, 136
    kinship 136–9
    mediation 136
    paradigms 139–42
    transformations 138, 140, 143
  Grand Budapest Hotel, The (2014) 157–66, 173–7, 179–82, 184, 185, 189
    binary oppositions 160–1, 162–4
    exchange 159
    kinship 157, 159–62
    mediation 161
    paradigms 164–6
    transformations 162
  Hotel Chevalier (2007) (short) 125, 127
  Life Aquatic with Steve Zissou, The (2004) 22, 105–17, 142, 173–8, 181, 184, 185, 189, 190 n.1
    binary oppositions 116–17
    exchange 108–9
    kinship 105, 109–16
    mediation 112, 116
    paradigms 112–16
    transformations 176
  Moonrise Kingdom (2012) 145–56, 164, 173, 174, 177–9, 181, 184, 185, 189, 190 n.1, 190 n.5
    binary oppositions 151, 152, 155–6
    exchange 153–5
    kinship 145, 147, 148–50
    mediation 145, 151
    paradigms 149–53
    transformations 148, 151
  Royal Tenenbaums, The (2001) 28, 87–103, 105, 107, 110, 113, 114, 116, 122, 131, 135, 148, 155, 159, 165, 173–8, 182, 184, 185, 189, 190 n.1, 190 n.5
    binary oppositions 90–2, 96, 101
    kinship 87, 90–102
    mediation 94–6
    paradigms 94–102
    transformations 175
  Rushmore (1998) 22, 71–85, 87, 91, 97, 101, 102, 107, 109, 110, 114, 116, 123, 126, 162, 163, 165, 173, 174, 175, 177–80, 182, 184, 185, 189, 190 n.1
    binary oppositions 74–6, 78
    exchange 83
    kinship 84–5, 85 n.2
    mediation 75, 79–84

paradigms 76
transformations 81, 175
Apocalypse Now (Coppola, 1979) 79
auteur structuralism viii–ix, xi–xii, 3, 26–7, 33–40, 172, 186

Barthes, Roland ix, 4, 7, 8–9, 10, 27, 29 n.3
Baumbach, Noah 133
Bellour, Raymond 42
Bose, Nandana 120, 126
Britten, Benjamin 145, 146, 147, 156, 181
Brody, Richard 131–2 n.2
Bruner, Jerome 29 n.7
Butler, Judith 20–1, 66

Casetti, Francesco 188
Caws, Peter x
Chabon, Michael 23–4
Clarke, Simon 3
Cowie, Elizabeth 43

Deleuze, Gilles xi
Descombes, Vincent 5, 8, 29 n.4
diegesis 44–5, 87, 159
Doubrovsky, Serge 9
Dubuisson, Daniel xi, 7

Eco, Umberto 3, 5, 30 n.12
ethnic identity 91, 123, 160, 162, 176, 184
  see also whiteness

film semiotics *see* Metz, Christian; structural semiotics
Ford, John 37–9
form 18, 30 n.10, 45, 169–71

Garroni, Emilio 170, 171
genre theory 40–1
Godelier, Maurice 20–1, 30 n.11
Gray, J. Patrick 16–18, 34–5
Greimas, A. J. 4, 7, 26, 183–4

Hawkes, Terence 33
Hawks, Howard 37
Herman, David ix, 12, 25
Hjelmslev, Louis 4, 29 n.1, 171, 183
Houston, Beverle 39–40

Jakobson, Roman 4, 29 n.4, 29 n.5, 29 n.6, 99–100, 183
Jameson, Fredric 18, 30 n.9, 30 n.10, 31–2
Jenkins, Henry 23
Jonnes, Denis 8, 22–3

Kaufman, Eleanor xi
Kinder, Marsha 39–40
Kitses, Jim 36–7
Kristeva, Julia 4
Kunze, Peter 5, 191 n.7

Lacan, Jacques ix, 4, 170
Last Frontier, The (Mann 1955) 36
Lévi-Strauss, Claude ix, xi, 3, 4, 7, 8, 9–21, 24, 25, 28, 30 n.9, 30 n.10, 31, 34, 41, 58, 61, 62, 67, 92, 141, 145, 151, 170–1, 179, 183
Lotman, Jurij 15, 33
Lovell, Alan 35–6

Man of the West (Mann 1958) 36
Man Who Shot Liberty Valence, The (Ford 1962) 38
Mann, Anthony 36–7
Martin, Adrian 189
Metz, Christian 17, 27, 29 n.4, 31, 34, 42, 46, 170, 171
mise en scène (and film style) ix, 45–6, 186–90
Mulvey, Laura 42–4
My Darling Clementine (Ford 1946) 38
myth analysis 9–18 *see also* structural semiotics (paradigmatic analysis)
mythemes 11, 16, 17

Naked Spur, The (Mann 1952) 36
new sincerity 190
Nowell-Smith, Geoffrey 35, 45

Oedipal 8, 9, 11, 13, 22, 56, 58, 75, 92, 103 n.1, 109, 110, 175, 179
  Post-Oedipal 84, 91, 110
  Pre-Oedipal 56, 67
Olsen, Mark 24

Parret, Herman 4
Peirce, C. S. 37
Picard, Raymond 9
Pomorska, Krystyna 61
Popper, Karl ix, 26–7, 171–2
Propp, Vladimir 10, 30 n.10, 41, 170–1, 183

Queneau, Raymond x

Rich, Jamie S. viii
Robé, Chris 91
Roddick, Nick viii
Roeg, Nicholas 39–40
Rohdie, Sam 45–6
Ryan, Marie-Laure ix, 174, 180

Salt, Barry 190
Saussure, Ferdinand de ix, 4, 6, 10, 29 n.3
Scholes, Robert 32–3
Sconce, Jeffrey 187
Searchers, The (Ford 1956) 38
Seitz, Matt Zoller 23
semiotics *See* structural semiotics
Serpico (Lumet 1973) 79
Seung, T. K. 14, 78, 161
Siegel, Don 35–6
Souriau, Anne 45, 46 n.1
Souriau, Étienne 26, 44–5, 87
Stam, Robert viii
storyworld ix–x, xii, 5, 12, 23–7, 169–91
structural semiotics
    binary opposition xii, 7, 9–10, 16–18, 35–42, 173, 174, 176–7, 181, 182, 183–4 *see also* Anderson, Wes (individual films)
    code ix, xii, 3–9, 24, 26, 29 n.4, 30 n.12, 32, 34, 43–4, 169–71, 182
    exchange xii, 19–20, 177–9 *see also* Anderson, Wes (individual films)
    film semiotics viii–ix, 17, 27, 31–44
    kinship systems xii, 7–8, 15–16, 18–27, 169, 173–6 *see also* Anderson, Wes (individual films)
    mediation xii, 9–18, 169, 179 *see also* Anderson, Wes (individual films)
    paradigm x, 5–18, 32, 39–40, 41, 170 *see also* Anderson, Wes (individual films)
    paradigmatic analysis x, 9–12, 15, 16–18, 34–5, 38–9, 83
    sign 5–7, 29 n.3
    signification (definition) 5
    syntagm 5–9, 11, 15, 17, 32, 41, 82, 98, 115, 122, 139, 170
    transformation xii, 5, 9, 12–13, 15, 16, 17, 23, 33, 39, 40, 170, 171 *see also* Anderson, Wes (individual films)
    see also auteur structuralism; Barthes, Roland; Greimas, A. J.; Lévi-Strauss, Claude; Metz, Christian; Saussure, Ferdinand de
structuralism viii–xi, 33, 170–1 *see also* Lévi-Strauss, Claude; structural semiotics
style *see* mise en scène
symbolic order ix, 3–8, 16, 18, 25–6, 30 n.8, 33–4, 84, 145, 160

Terra Trema, La (Visconti 1948) 35
Thanouli, Eleftheria 45, 46 n.1
Todorov, Tzvetan 4, 10
Totem and Taboo (Freud) 110, 114

Verhaeghe, Paul 21

Weiner, Jonah 66
whiteness 66, 120, 176 *see also* ethnic identity
Wigley, Samuel viii
Wolf, Mark ix, 23, 25
Wollen, Peter viii, 3, 37–8, 45–6, 171, 186
Wright, Will 41

Yacavone, Dan 45
Young Mr Lincoln (Ford 1939) 38–9

Žižek, Slavoj 4, 84, 169, 170, 171, 172, 186

www.ingramcontent.com/pod-product-compliance
Lightning Source LLC
Chambersburg PA
CBHW052041300426
44117CB00012B/1914